California Spas & Urban Retreats

by
Laurel Cook

ISBN 0-935701-71-0

51495>

Foghorn Press
BOOKS BUILDING COMMUNITY™

Foghorn Press, Inc.
555 DeHaro Street
The Boiler Room #220
San Francisco, CA 94107
(415) 241-9550

Foghorn Press titles are distributed to the book trade by
Publishers Group West, Emeryville, California. To contact
your local representative, call 1-800-788-3123.

To order individual books, please call Foghorn Press at
1-800-FOGHORN (364-4676).

Library of Congress
Cataloging-in-Publication Data:

Cook, Laurel

California Spas & Urban Retreats / by Laurel Cook
p. cm.
"A pack-along leisure guide"—Cover.
Includes index.
ISBN 0-935701-71-0: $14.95

1. Health resorts—California. 2. Hot springs—
California—Guidebooks. 3. Mineral waters—
California—Guidebooks. I. Title.

RA807.C2C65   1993
613'.122' 09794—dc20
91-36922 CIP

Printed in the United States of America.

California Spas & Urban Retreats

by
Laurel Cook

Foghorn Press

BOOKS BUILDING COMMUNITY.

Credits

Managing Editor:	Ann-Marie Brown
Copy Editors:	Samantha Trautman
	Howard Rabinowitz
Layout/Maps:	Michele Thomas
Illustration:	Kirk McInroy
Cover Design:	Ann-Marie Brown

Photographs

Front cover: Sharpshooters/Randy Miller
Back cover: The Oaks/The Palms (yoga)
Color Section: (in order of pages)
1) Skylonda Fitness Center
2) Spa de Jour (pedicure)
    Kabuki Hot Spring (communal tub)
    Marriott's Desert Springs Resort (massage at sunset)
3) The Palms (group walking)
    Skylonda Fitness Center (water exercise class)
4) Roman Spa
5) Two Bunch Palms (two getting massaged)
    Mr. Lee's Beauty, Hair and Health Spa (bath)
    Two Bunch Palms (outdoor pool)
6) Vichy Springs (girls in outdoor tub)
    Sonoma Mission Inn (pool and inn building)
    Norma Jean's The Beauty Studio (manicure)
7) Cal-a-Vie (man's thalassotherapy treatment)
    Osmosis (enzyme bath)
    Osmosis (drinking tea)
    Claremont Resort and Spa (pool)
8) Pocket Ranch Institute (spa food)
    Norma Jean's The Beauty Studio (combo treatment)

Acknowledgements

As in past years, I am indebted to the spa owners, directors, publicists and hotel/resort staff who provided me with the updated information I needed for this 1994 edition, *California Spas and Urban Retreats*. I also want to thank the staff at all of the newcomer facilities I included this time around. I am very pleased to have discovered the classy Skylonda in Woodside as well as so many wonderful local urban retreats from San Francisco to Palm Springs. Other new spa "finds" took me to such diverse places as Santa Cruz, Weed and Del Mar. For the spas in Santa Cruz, I have my readers to thank. Please continue to write about places you like and don't like.

I appreciate the assistance, also, of the two Chambers of Commerce I consulted, one in Calistoga and the other in Desert Hot Springs.

Beyond that, my deep appreciation goes to my family—daughters who sometimes accompanied me and offered their perspectives (and who staunchly stand by their mom in whatever she does) and to my "big sister" Barbara and her husband J.D., who have been there for me through thick and a lot of thin.

I am also thankful, in equal measure, for having such good friends in Sonja, Vivian and Deanne. They occasionally accompanied me on a spa jaunt, occasionally put me up and always put up with me, and generally shored up my spirits this past year.

—*Laurel Cook, Sausalito, 1993*

About the Author

Laurel Olson Cook entered the publishing world and the spa world at the same time, when Pat Cooper invited her to co-author *Hot Springs and Spas of California* in 1978. Since then, as a member of the Kensington Ladies' Erotica Society, she has contributed several stories to *Ladies' Own Erotica* and *Look Homeward Erotica*, both published by Ten Speed Press. She sold option rights to one of her stories to a local screenwriter, produced a first novel (unpublished), and is still, yes still, at work on a fictionalized autobiography.

In the seventies, the renaissance of the health and fitness movement, Laurel worked at the innovative U.C. Berkeley-U.C. San Francisco Joint Medical Program. She also has edited a textbook in physiology and numerous articles related to health in general and women's health in particular.

Laurel now operates her own professional writing and editing business ("A Way with Words") out of her houseboat in Sausalito.

This book is dedicated to
Nikki, Kylie, Eva and Lucas

Table of Contents

Northern California 59

Central California 279

Southern California 293

Desert Hot Springs 363

Appendices 401

How to Use This Book

This book is divided into six chapters—each covering a particular geographical area of the California spa world. Those areas are: Northern California, Calistoga, San Francisco Bay Area, Central California, Southern California and Desert Hot Springs.

Look at the maps at the front of each chapter. You can find every spa in that chapter on the map—just look for its number, which is noted on the first page of each spa listing.

Each spa listing also has a chart on its first page that highlights some of the general features of the spa. The chart provides the following information:

Cost - see pages 26-27 for explanation of $$ symbols

Overnight - has overnight accommodations

Program - has structured programs

Day Use - open for day-use

Hot Springs - has natural mineral water springs

Hot Tubs - has public or private hot tubs

Sauna - has sauna facilities

Massage - has massage available

Skin Care/Salon - offers skin-care and other beauty services

Exercise - has structured exercise classes

Meals - food is provided or can be purchased

Spa Products - health and beauty products are sold

Workshops - educational classes are offered

Children - children are welcome (check for age restrictions)

Pets - pets are allowed

Weddings - wedding site rentals/weddings performed

Introduction

As those who write know, when an introduction is called for it is the last piece of writing an author tackles. You can't introduce what you haven't yet written—or, as Lionel Trilling wrote: "How do I know what I think till I see what I've said?"

So now that I see what I've said, let me first lament that I was not able to include all of the spas and urban retreats I came across; some popped up too late and others are about to but had not yet opened their doors by my publisher's deadline. (Look for Rosemarie's in Guerneville, for one, and also check the appendix section "Too Late to Visit" on pages 402 to 408 where I have listed Paraiso in Soledad, Post Ranch Inn in Big Sur and some new places in Southern California that you should try.)

Let me introduce this expanded edition, *California Spas and Urban Retreats*, by first letting you know what I mean by the different types of facilities covered here, including the *urban retreat* that has been added to the title of the book. (For that name, I thank Essentials, a lovely new spa in Santa Rosa.)

A **spa** is a facility devoted to spa services and spa services only; it must offer water therapy (hot mineral water, cold mineral water or heated city water), massage and sauna. Most spas in this category now include body treatments (wraps, scrubs and such) and, in some facilities, skin-care services. (According to literature from Harbin Hot Springs, the word *spa* came from the town of Spa in the Belgian Ardennes and was used to refer to any natural hot or cold mineral spring and/or the town, resort or location surrounding the watering place. European spas usually have a medical staff on site, not surprising given that a high percentage of their visitors flock to these sites for a "cure." I also read that "bracing air and beautiful scenery" have always been prerequisites for the European spas traditionally used by royals and aristocrats.)

A **massage therapy center** is, as you might have guessed, a facility devoted to massage. In some cases, it might encompass other health services. F. Joseph Smith's (page 227) and Body, Mind and Spirit (page 207) are two that are featured in this book. Massage therapy centers usually provide a tub or a sauna as a preliminary (complimentary) service, not as a service in itself.

A **retreat** is a place, usually secluded, sometimes remote, where you are expected to relax, reflect, meditate, spend time with yourself and on yourself. For my purposes, no retreats are included that don't offer at least massage, and often more, as part of your time out.

A **hotel/resort spa** is self-explanatory. A fairly recent add-on to major, full-service hotels and resorts that offer many amenities and recreations for their guests, these spas provide yet another inducement to travelers and their partners to stay at the hotel. In most cases, the spa is also open to the public for day use.

An **urban retreat,** the new category included in this edition is a hybrid. Although the many day spas located in urban areas can well be regarded as urban retreats, (Spa Nordstrom, Cheek t' Cheek, etc.), for my purposes an urban retreat is a facility that started out as a salon—beauty salon, hair- and nail-care salon, and the like, to which massage and/or spa services have been added as a way of expanding and elaborating the original salon services. (My criterion for inclusion here was that these facilities also offer massage therapy services.)

A **fitness facility** is a spa (not a public or private health club, for example) where fitness programs constitute the spa's *raison d'être.* They invariably offer packaged programs ranging from three days to a week or more, and many, if not most, also offer a packaged day program as an appetite whetter. (Fitness programs offered as perks to guests staying at one of the large hotel/resort complexes listed are excellent and often as dedicated, but they are not the focal point of the resort.)

As for trends in the spa world, they go beyond the increased attention being given to aromatherapy and couple's (side-by-side) treatments. What has been gradually occurring reflects a more substantive shift in our general thinking about massage, about skin care, about exercise—indeed, about the whole concept of fitness. We are now well past the "fat farm" notion of the '50s where ladies, almost exclusively, made yo-yo treks to places that worked them over until the scale showed a number they could take home to the husbands, who invariably paid for the trip, and to the girlfriends who "oohed" and "aahed," until they saw the flesh pile on again.

And I hope we are well beyond the macho notion of "no pain, no gain" that sprung up in the '80s and is now denigrated by most *au courant* fitness experts. The best thinking today recognizes that health and fitness cannot be measured by body weight alone or even by the appearances of thinness or muscularity. More and more, fitness instructors and spa owners are seeing the need for integrated services and are developing programs that address well-being at the level of the body, mind and spirit. (And there is a great deal of latitude in the way "spirit" is regarded, so those who resist that word need not.)

The buzzword in the '80s was "stress" and the response from spas was "stress reduction." Still among us and still a valid concept, it is the word "wellness" that you will see more and more and a move toward health centers that offer integrated (alternative health) services.

In terms of exercise, the latest thinking is that when done on a regular basis, even moderate exercise—walking at a decent pace three times a week, for example—is clearly of benefit. Another exciting development that comes from increasing research done with older and elderly populations is the finding that fitness can be significantly improved by exercise in all age groups, and that working with free weights can strengthen muscles in men and women well into their 70s and 80s.

All exercise programs should be worked out with the advice and guidance of professionals if they are to address your individual needs, satisfy your personal intentions, conform to your fitness level, and be balanced in terms of the three prime goals of all fitness programs: cardiovascular health, joint flexibility and maximum strength and endurance.

And that leads me to a question many, the fit and the less fit, have asked me. (In a very real sense, too, it has to do with the role the mind has to play in all this.) What value can I expect to get from a program that lasts only one week? Without pretending to be an expert in exercise physiology, I am perfectly comfortable agreeing that one week is not going to turn you from a couch potato to a triathlete. What it does do, I am convinced, is set you on a path. If you are serious about extracting the most benefit from your one-week excursion, and if you pick a spa that offers you take-home information (and most do), and if you don't try to do it all at fever pitch, and if you are serious about following through once back in your home environment, then one week, I believe, can give you the boost you need.

Still, that turnaround occurs at the physical level of well-being. The body, however, as you might have discovered, is a bit of a slug. Enlightenments of other kinds can transform your thinking and your outlook in a New York minute. We may be a bit slower in California, for, as you will see when you read about Pocket Ranch Institute, the workshop coordinator turned his whole life around after a 17-day intensive at this country retreat. For many, that level of in-depth work is not necessary to awaken body, mind and spirit to the possibility of living life every day with a sense of renewed well-being.

Another trend I welcome in the spa world is its increasing usage and staffing by a multicultural, multiracial population. At one time, whether you went to your neighborhood spa or a major hotel/resort complex, you could be pretty certain that you would see mostly Caucasians and mostly Caucasian women, at that. Now, the integration that is occurring in spa services may be seen as a metaphor for the integration gradually occurring in the populations using and working in California's spas.

Closely related to this trend is the increasing attention spas are giving to skin care—no wonder when you learn that skin is the largest organ in the body. More and more spas have hired estheticians and tout European skin care and European skin-care products in their literature. As mentioned in my write-up of Espirit in Mill Valley, estheticians no longer need to be trained in Europe. "We have caught up," Espirit's owner Genna Lewis told me.

Along with growing awareness of the importance of skin as a reflection of inner health and as a vital organ deserving of (and responsive to) preventive care, spa and urban retreat owners, in the northern part of the state and even more so in the southland, are like the owner of Norma Jean's in Larkspur Landing: women of color who, while offering all women and men extensive skin-care services, are particularly knowledgeable about the skin care (and makeup) needs of Asian, Hispanic and African-Americans. It's been a long time coming.

Other features about this guidebook that I would like you to know are that, as before, I continue to speak throughout as if I am talking to someone new to the spa world. Sixteen years since my friend and I co-authored *Hot Springs and Spas of California*, I still find many people, women and men, who remain timid about this whole spa experience—or set of experiences—from massage right down to the more esoteric offerings you'll find at the pricey spas.

You will also find that I am frequently irreverent. When you read brochures and spa treatment menus as much as I do, and you have a mildly cynical world view anyway, you can, and I do, occasionally get the giggles to see yet another flowery name for some body-soothing ministration. The word-scholar in me winces at the overused "glo" for the already perfumed word "glow" but, on the other hand, I use words like "splendiferous" that make my computer spell-check stop dead in its tracks.

Having said that, I feel the need to confess that even I, from time to time, start writing as if I am on the spa's marketing staff. Usually that happens when I am particularly fond of the place, but every once in awhile I feel the need to return to the detached, objective eye that you, the reader, expect and deserve from a book written as a *guide*. And, as I have said elsewhere in this book, one person's "yuk" is another person's "yum." Everything, you know, is in the eye of the beholder.

I also need to repeat that I do not make health claims about any of the treatments offered—from mud baths to aromatherapy. My own disposition is a conservative one, in the sense that I would approach all heat therapies with care and knowledge about your state of health, caution you that drinking alcohol should never be a part of a hot water or sauna experience, and remind you to pay strict attention to any signals of distress your body gives you in the course of a treatment.

The decision about how much is enough and how much is too much is one only you can make. In some spas, the personnel are very competent and will spend time educating you about exercise physiology and general rules of fitness, and, in fact, on the more strenuous week-long and longer programs, they know exactly when your spirits are likely to flag or your withdrawal from a fat-, caffeine-, or sugar-laden diet will get to you. In other facilities, however, you are left on your own entirely. In general, unless you're out for a complete do-it-to-me pampering vacation, you need to be responsible for yourself.

As in previous editions, I did not include natural hot springs out in the wilds without any commercial development.

As you browse through the pages that follow, you will see that a broad range of facilities is included—those rooted in a spiritual philosophy, those devoted primarily to pampering and beautification, those claiming to heal the body of its ills, those offering maximum physical challenge, those connected to major, posh hotels, those sitting on historically rich sites, those providing simple one-hour vacations, those offering hair- and nail-care in addition to spa services, those whose programs and services seek to integrate the needs of body, mind and spirit, and those sitting in the country with no pretensions of any kind.

If there was something about a spa that gave me pause, and/or if I got negative feedback from my readers, I checked it out and, in some cases, removed it from the book. On the other hand, as I mentioned before, it is very difficult to second-guess everyone's tastes and tolerances. The matter of nudity is a simple example of what might bother some, whereas the presence of a Pepsi machine, a spiritual community or children might deter others. For that reason, and because ownership and programs change over the years, I must file a disclaimer if you find the services or the atmosphere other than what I have described.

Some places have been around for years under the same ownership, some have been around for years under many different ownerships, some started up relatively recently, and some were hardly developed at the time of writing and may be altogether different by the time you are reading these words. (I am still hoping that Murrieta Hot Springs will reopen.)

Spa fees and services as of this writing range in price from a $10 tub to a $4,000 fitness week, but cost is not what makes a spa "the best." In fact, there is simply no best spa. The one for you depends not only on who you are and what you're comfortable with, but also on what your mood, your intentions and your expectations are at the time you go.

Besides deciding on whether you want to get fit, have fun, throw in a "do" and a manicure, or play golf along with a spa program, a significant criterion in choosing a spa is the people you'll be with. If you move with money and designer fashions, you might feel comfortable only at spas where others use it pretty much as you do. If you are older rather than younger, you might feel comfortable knowing you'll find some people in your age group. If you are a "New Ager" wanting a retreat with like-minded spiritual seekers, a stressed-out nine-to-fiver or a restless executive, there are spas listed here where you'll find your "tribe."

Whether or not you ever talk to your spa cohorts, these subtleties related to how you live, or at least to shared intentions in going to a given spa, play a major role in making your stay satisfying. I know there are also people who are adventuresome and want to try something entirely out of their experience, and others who can be dropped into any social setting and have a good time. For them, this book should be an introduction to new worlds. Lastly, I trust that night-table travelers will enjoy using this guidebook to go from one spa to another without ever leaving home.

Although from time to time I mentioned some of the side trips and recreations in a given area, I barely touched on what is available in the vicinity of each spa. Because they are not the focus of this book, I made no attempt to religiously seek them out. In fact, there are many places to go and things to do in almost every geographical area included here, and, if you want to plan a vacation with the assurance that you can find other sights and sounds and activities nearby, then check with the spas of your choice or contact the local Chamber of Commerce or Visitors' Bureau in the area that attracts you.

The "basic bag"—those items you'll want to pack or keep in the trunk of the car, at the ready—has not changed much since last itemized in *California Spas*. Of course, what you carry with you depends on where you are going, whether you'll be in the city or in the country, and whether you're off for a one-hour vacation, an overnight, or a week-long or longer program. Unless you're going to one of the posh hotel spas where you'll be stepping out in the evening, you'll be dressing very informally. I leave that to you as well as all of the special personal articles you know you'll want.

The Basic Bag
- A thin nylon swimsuit, pretty or not, that will dry quickly, and definitely another that

can take a beating.

- A lightweight kimono for moving in and out of spa areas where such clothing is not provided.
- A thin, nylon windbreaker.
- Unbreakable bottles of moisturizers, hand lotion, shampoo, rinse and other personal articles you depend on.
- Footwear that can get damp or wet and not fall apart or cause you to slip.
- A flashlight.
- A thermometer in an unbreakable case so that you can test the temperature of the water yourself.
- A pocket mirror.
- A towel or two for the rare places that don't supply them.
- A hairdryer for the same reason.

Trip Checklist
- A loose, lightweight, cotton sweatsuit that holds up and feels endlessly comfortable (with or without underwear).
- A brimmed hat or visor for sun/eye protection.
- A camera and film.
- Sunscreen (but observe rules general to all spas about rinsing it off before stepping into the tubs and pools).
- Medicated sunburn lotion if you goof (when will we ever learn?)
- Good sunglasses—100% UVA and UVB protection is now advised.
- A Swiss Army knife.
- A first-aid kit, including one for snakebite.
- Poison oak medication and insect repellant.

- Manicure supplies including tweezers.
- Binoculars.
- A thermos bottle.
- Books, magazines, a sketch pad, easily portable crafts and games for evenings in relatively isolated places.
- Letter-writing materials.
- A fanny pack.

When Traveling by Car or Van
- Bottled drinking water (for desert areas where you drink as well as sit in mineral water, and generally for the desert in case of car breakdown).
- Candles and matches (for emergencies, not romance; be extremely careful in dense wooded areas where fire hazards are high.)
- Tins of durable snack foods and a can opener.
- A plastic "spritz" bottle you can fill with water and use to cool yourself off in hot areas.
- A lightweight fold-up mat for stretching out on hard surfaces.

I'm sure you'll come up with more things. Feel free to write and let me know if I have omitted something you found vital to your spa trip. Write to me anyway to tell me about your experiences in the spas and urban retreats of California.

Laurel Cook
c/o Foghorn Press, Inc.
555 DeHaro Street, Suite 220
San Francisco, CA 94107

About Prices

In this book, I have avoided all reference to specific prices, whether of accommodations or spa services, for three reasons:

• Prices change far too frequently.

• Spas are constantly playing with their package offers and introducing newly priced programs.

• You will definitely want to send for a brochure and/or discuss your individual needs and goals with the personnel at the spa you are considering.

At most spas where overnight accommodations are available, basic spa services—hot tub and sauna—are included in the price. Massage and other special treatments are always additional, usually in the $20 to $100 range. In many of the spas where you design your own program, you might be asked at the time of reservation what spa services you will want so that advance appointments can be made to suit your schedule. Massage appointments, for example, not only go quickly but in many places massage practitioners are not in-house; they are brought in on an on-call basis.

The $$$$ symbols are designated on the first page of each spa write-up. The ratings are as follows:

$-$$ indicates a day-use facility where a hot tub or sauna is typically in the $10 range and massage and treatments are more than $20 and less than $100.

$$ applies to the $20-$99 menu of *à la carte* services typical to all urban retreats; it is also used for spas where room rates and *à la carte* services are typically under $100.

$$$ indicates a nightly room rate minimum (or spa package) that is over $100.

$$$$ All spas in this category feature special fitness programs lasting from four days to one week, where the price usually covers everything, with the exception of extras such as tennis lessons or other recreational or instructional fees that classify more as resort features than spa services.

A Look Into the World of Massage and Bodywork

Why this section on massage and bodywork? As I mentioned in the Introduction, my vantage point throughout this guidebook, as in the last edition, is still one of a novice with the *soupçon* of savvy that comes from the (delicious) research necessary to put together such a book.

What I discovered early on as I went from spa to spa was that I did not know Swedish from Esalen, shiatsu from Amma, or deep tissue from Trager. I was glad to get rid of the words "masseur" and "masseuse" (although you will still hear them used, alas) in favor of massage *therapist*, massage *practitioner* and massage *technician*, terms that are discussed in more detail in the section to follow. (When you look in the Yellow Pages for a massage therapy center or an urban retreat, however, you still have to sift your way through the "masseuse" set to locate dedicated professionals who offer legitimate massage and bodywork. Some are obvious: Avoid names like "Paula's Pleasure Palace," for example.)

Being massaged in the course of doing this book, I frequently found that I wanted to ask my massage practitioner to talk me through what she was doing (I always ask for a "she"). What was my body telling her, was one of my questions, but I was also curious to know the differences between one form of massage and another, why she had gone into this work and a host of other questions. But these investigative impulses are not exactly appropriate when you're lying on the table and being kneaded into turning down the mind's beta waves. You can wait until afterwards, of course, but by then you are so mellow you can hardly recall the questions you came in with. Anyway, most likely your massage practitioner has quietly slipped out of the room, leaving you to come back slowly to the reality of your surroundings.

Because of my increasing curiosity about what the experience is like from the practitioner's side of the table, I did take advantage of my position as an author to initiate tentative conversations with the few I could find who had the inclination to talk about their work. I started out with what seemed to me simple, straightforward, information-seeking questions, such as why Swedish and Esalen types of massage are so often hyphenated throughout the spas I had visited in California. What was Swedish on its own and Esalen on its own?

I got various answers, all vague and all inadequate from my point of view. Only one person gave me an explanation of Swedish that I could get hold of (maybe because she included the mental picture of Spencer Tracy and Katherine Hepburn in *Pat and Mike*) and no one was very articulate about Esalen massage.

By the end of my spa tour, I concluded that most people who do massage and bodywork as a living are more intuitive than analytical in their thinking.

My final decision, then, given that the availability of massage is my criterion for including a facility in this guidebook, was to provide you with a glossary that would explain the different types of massage you can expect to encounter in the land of spas. To that end, I used reference books and checked what they had to say against my own knowledge, I talked with people who do bodywork, and, in some trademarked systems like Trager and Hellerwork, I reprinted their own text.

For example, in tracking down what shiatsu is—the word means simply "finger pressure"—I was led to The Amma Institute in San Francisco. There I finally got a considerable amount of information delivered in a way that satisfied my craving for clarity. (Incidentally, The Amma Institute trains most of the practitioners who work at the nearby Kabuki Hot Spring in San Francisco.)

David Palmer, former director of The Amma Institute, is one of those unusual individuals who is able to bring together two philosophic dispositions, as Alan Watts calls them: the "prickly" (logical, rational, analytic) and the "gooey" (chaotic, irrational, mystical). According to Watts, most of us will find we are predominantly one or the other. In David Palmer I found a satisfying integration of the prickly and the gooey personality; that is, he manages to write lucidly and intelligently about massage in general and Amma in particular, without losing his passion for the subject.

Palmer also has authored a pamphlet on *How to Choose a Massage School;* publishes a newsletter for professional bodyworkers; has developed a portable "High Touch Massage Chair"™ which allows a practitioner to do 90% of a full-body massage in 25% of the space occupied by a massage table and, more important, which makes massage safe, convenient and affordable; and, finally, in 1983, founded Pacific Health Systems to provide 15-minute hands-on stress reduction treatments to corporate employees.

He and the present director of the institute, Gary Bernard, are not only articulate and sophisticated about this subject, but the way they regard the work they do—what Palmer calls his "world view" about the massage profession—suits my own disposition. David's contribution on "How to Evaluate a Massage Practitioner" is included here, along with two informative pieces Sheila Cluff developed for her guests at The Oaks (Ojai) and The Palms (Palm Springs): "Tips for Receiving a Massage" and "Beneficial Effects of Massage."

In this new edition, I am also delighted to have Dietrich Miesler's informative piece, "Massage for Seniors." Miesler is the director of the Day-Break Geriatric Massage Project in the Northern California town of Guerneville, and lectures at various spas. I have also come across local massage practitioners who serve elderly clients. Wholistic Alternatives for Better Health, for example, is run by a Mill Valley massage therapist who told me that one of her elderly clients takes public transportation from San Francisco to keep her weekly appointment.

I hope that the glossary and reprinted material from others is useful to you and, better yet, that all of this information induces you to explore further the experiential benefits to be had from regular massage and bodywork.

How to Evaluate a Massage Practitioner

(Which Practitioner is Right for Me?)

by David Palmer,
The Amma Institute, San Francisco ©1987

(NOTE: These comments are directed to individuals who want to select someone to give them regular massage over a period of time, more than to those who drop in for an occasional massage—although the same assessment can be made in those circumstances as well.—Laurel Cook)

Whether or not they are aware of it, the work of every massage practitioner has three components: intention, training and experience. By knowing how a practitioner deals with these three elements, individually and in relationship to each other, you can better assess her or his qualifications.

The level of intention in massage also falls into three categories of objectives the practitioner might hold—again, singly or in combination. They can be referred to as seeking wellness, correction and/or transformation. Let me describe each of those in turn.

With a *wellness* intention, massage is regarded essentially as a personal care service, much like getting your hair or nails done—or like taking your car in for a tune-up to maintain it in peak condition.

With a *correction* intention, the practitioner, in consultation with the client, identifies problems or problem areas, and tries to correct them during the course of the massage. If a client comes to a practitioner and says, "Can you make my headache go away?" the corrective practitioner would probably say, "I'll see what I can do." In contrast, the wellness practitioner is more likely to say, "No, I don't fix headaches, I do massage. But sometimes in the course of a massage, the headache goes away."

With a *transformation* intention, massage is seen as a personal growth experience—an opportunity for the client (and often the practitioner as well) to explore the body and the mind as inextricably linked entities. Here, the goal is to move you to ever-increasing levels of awareness, particularly of self-imposed limitations that obstruct your realizing your full potentials. To accomplish this intention, practitioners are usually verbally directive, instructing you when and how to release tension in your body and in your breath patterns, and to become aware of holding patterns in the musculature—all of which are seen as having their counterparts in the mind as expressed (or not expressed) in your actions and behaviors.

All three of these intentions are valid approaches to massage and bodywork. Unfortunately, all too frequently, the level of training and experience does not match the level of intention. A wellness intention, for example, requires the least training; practitioners who have had 200 to 300 hours of schooling would generally be considered to qualify. A corrective intention, on the other hand, begins to tread on the realm of medical diagnosis and treatment, and you should be attentive and perhaps cautious when encountering practitioners who speak in corrective and curative terms about the work they do.

Transformational massage also requires a great deal of training and experience because here the practitioner is part bodyworker, part teacher and part therapist. Check carefully the credentials of any practitioner operating with this intention. It also should be said under the heading of training that few massage schools in the country train potential practitioners for more than 500 hours—startling when contrasted with the 1,200 or more hours of schooling demanded of cosmetologists and barbers.

The third element, experience, is key. You don't learn massage in school—you learn massage technique and some relevant anatomy and physiology of the human body. The only way a person truly learns the art and craft of massage—or carpentry, or computer programming—is by doing it. Someone who has been working on bodies for ten years will invariably know more than someone fresh out of school. To a degree, schooling can be offset by experience, so it is important to find out from the practitioner how long he or she has been practicing massage.

How to Evaluate a
Massage
Practitioner

Know also that there is currently a lot of confusion among bodyworkers about their profession—partly because they were never taught to be clear about the level of intention at which they are working. In fact, if you are interested in helping the field mature, try asking practitioners to articulate what they see as the intention of their work. Most of them never will have considered the question before, and you will be doing them, yourself and the profession a favor by asking the question.

In summary, the best way to choose a massage practitioner is to find out the intention with which the practitioner works and then try to determine whether the person's training and experience are up to that level of intention. (And you also need to be aware of what your intention is if you are to hook up with the right practitioner for you.) Remember also that massage involves a relationship, and relationships are built on trust. Honest practitioners who are willing to discuss the limits of their skills and who are not afraid to say "I don't know" are preferable, to me, over those who claim to have healing hands that can solve all your problems. Finally, of course, your own experience on the table is the deciding factor in your evaluation of the person's competence. It should feel good to your body (a massage really shouldn't hurt—even shiatsu) and right to your mind.

What's Behind the Words—A Glossary of Massage Terms

Before presenting a formalized glossary defining the types of massage, I would like to comment on the definitions of massage, bodywork and the three commonly employed terms for those who do massage: practitioner, technician and therapist. Most of what I will say is drawn from David Palmer's booklet *How to Choose a Massage School,* published by Thumb Press in 1986.

The three words replacing masseur/masseuse are practitioner, technician and therapist. I agree with Palmer that practitioner is the most comfortable to use; it is less cold than technician and less "loaded" than therapist. (You will still find the word "masseuse" used, outdated as it is.)

Palmer's explanation of the use of the word therapist and its political ramifications are interesting enough to mention here. The American Massage Therapy Association, the largest national organization of massage professionals in the country, wants to legitimize massage as a medical adjunct treatment so that, elevated to a "healing art," it would be subject to governmental controls. The goals make sense: The profession would be clearly extricated from its sexual uses and abuses, and as a regulated industry, it would permit development of training standards and uniformity of licensing and certification requirements. As Palmer points out, however, the word "therapist" draws its force from the connotation that you are sick and need massage as a therapeutic or corrective procedure.

As Palmer notes, the term bodywork has come into usage in the past 10 years as a "good, strong word which carries none of the sexual stigma of the word massage." For Palmer, it harks too much of auto bodywork. To me, it suggests a series of treatments that have some ultimate goal, as opposed to an occasional massage one indulges in for more immediate relief.

Palmer defines massage as "structured touching," meaning that it is done with purposeful intention. The practitioner's intention can be to make you feel better, to correct body alignment or to transform your life. Apparently, some practitioners hold all three intentions and bring all three to bear on their work, whereas others activate only the first.

In other words, you may want just a feel-good outcome and leave it to other forces to "transform your life." You might also, at certain times of your life—during a period of mourning and grief, for example—want more than a casual one-time, feel-good massage. You may want and need a series of treatments where both you and your chosen practitioner have talked about what kind of "release" you want and what the best strategies and potential benefits might be. In yet another scenario, you might be in psychotherapy and find that you are unable to get at your fears or other emotional blocks through talk therapy alone; professional bodywork is increasingly recommended by psychotherapists as a way to sidestep your mental censor and give you breakthrough experiences that ultimately shorten the time you need to spend in psychotherapy.

Palmer raises other interesting definitional approaches to massage: It can be named after a technique that uses, for example, heat (heliotherapy), ice (cryotherapy) or water (hydrotherapy), or it can be defined anatomically as related to feet, hands, face, cellulite, deep tissue, lymph system, etc. Still another category he notes is "client-identified" treatment, as in infant massage, perinatal and postnatal massage, geriatric massage and sports massage.

Infant massage groups are also proliferating. According to Tiffany Field, Ph.D., Professor of Pediatrics and Psychology at the University of Miami Medical School, "supplemental stimulation makes babies stronger, less fragile-looking and more responsive." She notes that premature babies treated with massage 45 minutes a day for 10 days showed "superior growth and development," gaining 47 percent more weight than a control group. They were also more alert and active, and were able to be discharged from the hospital six days earlier.

Finally, according to Palmer, massage can reflect geographic origins—as in Swedish massage, Japanese massage, Tibetan massage, Chinese massage, Hawaiian massage, Esalen massage or Philippine massage. According to Palmer, the work devised by Trager, Feldenkrais and Alexander, each of which combines touching with talk therapy, movement, breath work and other critical components, does not regard itself as either massage or bodywork.

What follows is a working glossary of the forms of massage and bodywork you are likely to encounter in California spas.

• *Acupressure:* Any form of bodywork that applies manual pressure to the vital points and energy meridians of the body. These points were identified by medical practitioners in China centuries ago and are believed to improve the flow of energy (ki or ch'i). Practitioners use fingers, thumbs and palms.

• *Amma:* Sometimes spelled "anma," it is the word for massage in both China and Japan. A gentle massage, it is based on principles of Chinese medicine and is over 5,000 years old. Amma encompasses a complexity of techniques (of which shiatsu is but one) in which the practitioner uses thumbs, fingers, arms, elbows, knees and feet to press, stroke, stretch and perform percussive manipulations of the client's body. The technique does not use oils and can be done through clothing with the client sitting up or lying down.

• *Aromatherapy:* In connection with massage, it is simply the use of any one of numerous scents in the form of essential oils or botanicals that are added to the massage oil. See the Glossary of Spa Treatments on page 53 for more on aromatherapy.

• *Breema Bodywork:* Breema originated in the mountains of Kurdistan. In the Breema method, the body is viewed as an energy system, although its meridians are not the same as those identified in the healing arts of China. Like others, Breema practitioners regard the body as a self-healing organism; Breema work is designed to create (or re-create) the natural balance and harmony that governs our mental, emotional and physical energies. The Breema system consists of thousands of bodywork sequences, and the practitioner uses hands, elbows, feet and knees to gently move the recipient's body through various stretches and postures. In doing Breema work, the practitioner always works with the natural weight of both bodies and in coordination with his or her own breathing. Breema is thought to relax the body to such an extent that the energy flows freely and gathers enough vitality to make it impossible for any health problem to take hold. The larger aim of Breema is to teach through experience the possibility of living with the full participation of the body, mind and feelings. Breema also teaches self-exercises.

• *Deep Tissue Massage:* This massage technique separates muscle groups and loosens fascia (a thin layer of connective tissue covering, supporting or connecting the muscles or inner organs of the body) so as to bring about the realignment of the body and freedom of movement.

A Glossary of Massage Terms

• *Esalen Massage:* As described by Arthur Munyer of the Esalen Institute, Esalen massage uses long, integrating strokes that enhance relaxation. Typical also of Esalen massage is that it maintains a sense of presence with another being throughout the massage, allowing full contact through hand touch. It is both energetic and relaxing because it releases muscle tensions and opens and harmonizes the whole body.

• *Hellerwork:* Named after its founder, Joseph Heller, Hellerwork™ is a series of eleven 90-minute sessions of deep tissue bodywork and movement education designed to realign the body and release chronic tension and stress. Verbal dialogue is used to assist the client in becoming aware of emotional stress that may be related to physical tension. It is regarded as preventive rather than curative, and reflects a holistic approach to health. Hellerwork is designed to produce permanent change.

• *Polarity Therapy:* The brainchild of Dr. Randolph Stone in the early 1900s, polarity therapy uses a four-part program to restore the body's proper energy balance: clear thinking (positive mental attitude), bodywork (to alleviate energy blockages), body movement (stretching postures combining movement, breathing and sound), and diet (fresh vegetables, fruits and natural foods). As in other forms of bodywork, the practitioner of polarity therapy is viewed as a nonjudgmental channel that the client can use to discover his/her own self-healing powers.

• *Reflexology:* Reflexology, also known as zone therapy, is a turn-of-the-century practice fostered by three American physicians (Bowers, White and Fitzgerald). In their view, energy travels from critical zones of the body and ends its journey in the feet. Charts are available showing which zones correspond to which internal organs. The theory is that when excessive granular texture is felt in the feet as pressure is applied, it indicates the presence of uric acid crystallization. By rubbing the crystals on the nerve endings in the soles, a reflex reaction is supposedly set up between that zone and its associated body part. Reflexology is one of the massage techniques a person can learn to self-administer.

• *Shiatsu:* A direct offshoot of Amma, shiatsu literally means "finger" (*shi*) "pressure" (*atsu*). Like acupressure, shiatsu works with vital points and energy meridians and uses finger-thumb-palm pressure. Unlike acupressure, shiatsu also manipulates other parts of the body in the course of treatment. Historically, shiatsu came into being in the early part of the century in reaction to a government order in Japan requiring Amma practitioners to be licensed. To avoid such regulation, massage therapists changed the name of the practice. In 1925, Tokujiro Namikoshi opened the first school of shiatsu in Japan, founded the Shiatsu Institute in 1940, and finally secured licensing by the Japanese government in 1957 after he and his son had traveled to the United States to popularize (and westernize) it in this country. From his tireless efforts, it became an accepted massage form in Japan (where Amma still predominates), and the "Japanese" form of massage in the United States, where most people, even massage practitioners, are unaware of Amma. Only two schools teach Amma in the United States, in contrast to more than 100 in Japan.

• *Sports massage:* Sports massage can be either preventive or corrective in approach. Because it is given to those whose body tone and condition is tied to performance, it can be as specific as working over of leg muscles (in a runner, for example), or kneading muscles to assure optimal flexibility appropriate to the sport the person is engaged in.

• *Swedish Massage:* This familiar massage form is a practice created by Henri Peter Ling, a student at the University of Stockholm at the turn of the 19th century. His intention was to duplicate the movements of Swedish gymnastics and other types of exercise as a means of stimulating circulation, increasing muscle tone, and creating an all-around balance to the structure and function of the musculoskeletal system. It was used preventively before an athletic workout and remedially to speed the body's recovery from injury. Swedish massage is done with the person covered by a sheet, where each part of the body to be worked on is exposed in turn and then re-covered. The massage practitioner uses kneading, stroking, friction, tapping and even shaking motions. Oil is used to reduce or eliminate friction and to facilitate making long, smooth, kneading strokes over the tissue and muscles of the body. From the recipient's point of view, it is a "feel good" massage, and certainly the most commonly offered and best known.

• *The Trager® Approach:* Developed by Milton Trager, MD, more than half a century ago, the Trager Approach uses light, gentle, nonintrusive movements to facilitate the release of deep-seated physical and mental patterns that can inhibit, block or distort free-flowing motion and full self-expression. A Trager session is from one to one-and-a-half hours long. No oils are used. The client lies on a padded table while the practitioner works on the body using gentle, rhythmic movements that do not involve any force or pressure. The practitioner works in a meditative state of consciousness which Dr. Trager calls "hook-up." Critical to the accomplishment of the work, this state of mind permits the practitioner to connect deeply and sensitively with the client without experiencing fatigue. A series of sessions are recommended because the benefits appear to be cumulative. For Trager, the transformation clients experience comes from the practitioner's success in having reached the client's unconscious mind and having brought to the surface an experiential awareness of what being well (graceful, light, etc.) feels like. Training in the Trager Approach is strictly governed by The Trager Institute.

•*Watsu:* An underwater massage where you are cradled in the arms of a massage therapist who gently stretches and massages your body using yoga-like movements.

How to Receive a Massage

*© by Sheila T. Cluff, owner of The Oaks at
Ojai and The Palms at Palm Springs*

Because massage is not a common part of
our contemporary cultural experience, many
people feel uneasy about receiving their first
massage. Here are a few guidelines to help you
feel at ease and gain the greatest benefit from
your massage therapy session.

To help you relax, a few minutes in the sauna
or whirlpool is recommended prior to the massage to unwind and loosen you up.

Tell the therapist about areas of your body
which are injured, tense or sore. Also mention
any medical conditions, such as high blood
pressure, a heart problem, chronic headaches,
varicose veins or recent surgery.

Close your eyes and allow yourself to relax
as completely as possible. Focus your attention
on your breathing, which should be slow, deep
and even.

When the therapist's hands locate areas of
pain or tension in the body, consciously try to
relax those areas. As you inhale deeply, visualize the breath flowing to the tense area and relaxing it. As you fully exhale, visualize the tension leaving the body with the breath.

Allow the therapist to move your limbs into various positions. Be limp, like a rag doll, and do not try to help move your arms, legs or head. The therapist is a trained professional who will not do anything to hurt you. However, feel free to speak up if anything the therapist does is too painful or ticklish, or uncomfortable in any way.

The best way to receive a massage is with the body completely unclothed. The therapist is sensitive to the need for privacy and will keep your body covered with a sheet or blanket, except for the area being massaged. If this arrangement is not comfortable for you, you may wear underwear or a swimsuit.

Many people fall asleep during a massage— an indication that the body and mind are releasing stress and tension. The therapist will gently wake you when it is time to turn over or end the massage.

The Beneficial Effects of Massage

*© by Sheila T. Cluff, owner of The Oaks at
Ojai and The Palms at Palm Springs*

Massage dilates the blood vessels, improving circulation and relieving congestion throughout the body.

Massage increases the number of red blood cells, especially in cases of anemia, plus it increases the respiratory function.

Massage acts as a "mechanical cleanser," stimulating lymph circulation, and promotes excretion and elimination by stimulating the function of each organ.

Massage relaxes muscle spasm and tension, and lubricates and tones the skin.

Massage increases blood supply and nutrients to muscles without adding to their load of toxic lactic acid, produced through voluntary muscle contraction. Massage thus helps to prevent buildup of harmful fatigue products resulting from strenuous exercise or injury.

Massage can compensate, in part, for lack of exercise and muscular contraction in people who, because of injury, illness or age, are forced to remain inactive. In these cases, massage helps return venous blood to the heart and so eases the strain on this vital organ.

Massage may have a sedative, stimulating or even exhausting effect on the nervous system depending on the type and length of massage treatment.

Massage can help tone the nervous system.

Massage, by improving general circulation, increases nutrition of the tissues. It is accompanied or followed by an increased interchange of substances between the blood and tissue cells, heightening tissue metabolism.

Massage aids in digestion and assimilation of nutrients.

Massage makes you feel good.

Massage for Seniors

by Dietrich W. Miesler, M.A.
Director, Day-Break Geriatric Massage Project
16216 Main Street, Post Office Box 1629
Guerneville, CA 95446
(707) 869-0632

Too many elderly people look a little incredulous when the question of massage comes up. They say that massage is for young people, especially for athletes.

While massage may not add years to anyone's life, it definitely adds life to years—not simply because it is pleasurable but because of the physical effects it has on the body. So let's take a closer look at massage and see what it has to offer.

Massage is effective in relieving muscle pain, joint stiffness, poor blood circulation, mental stress, sleeplessness and similar problems that are so prevalent among older people. Although the improvements experienced after just a few treatments often seem magical to the recipient, they are all scientifically explainable, particularly their effect on blood circulation. Blood not only carries oxygen to each individual cell in the body but also nourishment and hormones that the endocrine glands release as a way of regulating body processes. Another primary function of blood is to carry away the debris constantly produced throughout the body.

Simply stated, massage helps anyone who has circulatory problems to achieve blood flow adequate for maintaining proper cell nourishment and cleansing. Add to this the pleasant feeling that touch evokes and you have the explanation for the calming effect of massage on those who suffer from depression, sleeplessness and other common discomforts associated with daily living. The element of touch is particularly important for elderly people living alone and suffering from touch deprivation.

And massage accomplishes another little miracle: By kneading sore muscles and by gently moving arthritic joints, massage can literally "rub out" pain by loosening muscles that have become tight through a myriad of factors associated with living a long life.

Although many massage techniques can be executed by people who have little or no training, and even by oneself, a practitioner who is skilled in the specialty of geriatric massage can often be very helpful in working on some of the more severe conditions older people might experience. As trained professionals, they can work under the supervision of the client's physician, if necessary. Some of the conditions for which massage has shown itself to be surprisingly successful are in stroke rehabilitation, edema, severe impairment of blood circulation

Massage for Seniors in the legs, Parkinson's disease and similar conditions.

The effect of massage on health problems continues to be underestimated, perhaps for the very reason that it feels good. After all, every other health intervention seems to be connected with unpleasantness—cutting into flesh, drilling little holes in the teeth, giving pills that can make you drowsy or upset your stomach—and here is an intervention that claims to be successful and pleasureful at the same time!

To find a geriatric massage therapist, look in the Yellow Pages under "massage" or contact Dietrich Miesler at the address listed at the beginning of this article.

A Glossary of Spa Treatments

Each spa puts its own spin on these treatments, but, generally speaking, what follows is the basic menu of services you'll come across in those spas that offer more than a tub, sauna and massage.

Remember, you're the client—feel perfectly free to ask questions, and, if any aspect of a treatment makes you uncomfortable, let the attendants know. They'll be happy to modify it and/or answer your concerns.

• *Aromatherapy:* Reportedly founded in 1937 by a French research chemist, "the art of aromatherapy" remains popular in European countries and is fast gaining acceptance in today's spas in what has been called an "aromatic renaissance." It uses essential oils (concentrated vegetal extracts)—different ones for different conditions—to treat various physical ills from migraines to insomnia to colds, and beyond. Most spas limit their selections to a few standards—lavender and eucalyptus are popular—and claim only an enhancement of calming or energizing effects along with your body treatment, whether it is a mineral water bath, a body wrap or a massage. The oils are absorbed through the skin, inhaled or ingested. Aromatherapists have their own association: the American AromaTherapy Association (AATA) which has printed a comprehensive wall-mountable chart, a must-have for anyone interested in the benefits associated with this age-old therapy system.

Many articles and even books are fast becoming available because of the growing interest in the power of scent, and courses are being offered to spa personnel so that they can use them appropriately, singly or blended. The following list showing different aromatic substances and each one's purported health effect is a modification of one developed by Tiferet, a company in Eugene, Oregon that supplies health food stores and spas. I have not yet come across a spa that offers you anything like the choices shown here, and most spas refer to the aromas not by the specific botanical but by its purported effect.

aniseed: respiration and circulation
basil: depression, anxiety, colds, memory
bay: respiratory conditions
bergamot: anxiety, fever, skin care
birch: tension, muscle relaxant, pain relief
cassia: digestion
cedarwood: stimulant, skin and lungs
chamomile: calming effects
cinnamon: weakness, digestion
cypress: confusion, anxiety
eucalyptus: coughs, respiratory symptoms
fennel: digestion

frankincense: skin conditions
ginger: stimulant and aphrodisiac
grapefruit: circulation and cleansing
hyssop: grief
juniperberry: fear, apathy, nerves
lavender: calming, muscle relaxant, burns
lemon: tonic-stimulant, antiseptic
marjoram: calming, migraines, colds
mugwort: nervousness, period problems
orange (bitter): uplift, anxiety
oregano: calming, muscle relaxant
patchouli: confusion, indecision, depression
peppermint: stimulant, indigestion
pine: calming, muscle relaxant
rosemary: calming, muscle relaxant
sage: fear, panic
sandalwood: anxiety, skin care
spearmint: digestion
tarragon: muscle cramps
ylang ylang: calming, aphrodisiac

• *Aromatherapy Bath:* An essential oil is mixed in the water of your hot tub. An added pleasure/benefit associated with an aromatherapy bath is that you not only absorb the aromatic through the skin, you also breathe in the vapors.

• *Herbal Wrap:* You'll be wrapped in an herb-infused linen sheet (typically pine, rosemary or lavender). Snug and cozy, you'll lie quietly while the moist heat gently penetrates the skin. Some spas wrap you in an additional waterproof blanket and some place cool patches (cucumbers!) over the eyes to shut out light and distractions. Usually, you'll be relaxing in the same treatment

room but in some spas you're moved to a cur-
tained-off cubicle with quietly breathing others. Most spas follow with a luxurious Swiss
shower. (Tepid temperature is suggested to cool
you down slowly.)

• *Hydrotherapy:* The term covers many different types of water-immersion treatments that
profoundly relax muscles. Generally, you are
assisted into a tub of just-right-temperature
water (approximately 97 to 100 degrees) and
the attendant standing outside the tub moves a
high-pressure jet stream over your body to massage muscles. Some spas do hydrotherapy in
swimming pools and others have you recline
in a specially designed tub with guard rails and
high-tech accoutrements in a private or semi-
private room. Once the jet stream pressure is
adjusted correctly, the tub does the water massage all by itself. In all cases, an attendant is
there to assist and to monitor your time.

• *Loofah Scrub:* As with the wraps, you'll get
up on a table and the attendant, using a loofah
sponge and pine or other bath gel, will rub you
down vigorously. Once this cleansing process
is completed, she'll follow up with a honey-al-
mond or other "flavor" mixture to hydrate the
skin. Often, you are then moved to a Swiss
shower.

• *Mud Wraps and Packs:* Again, different
spas have different types of mud treatments. In
contrast to immersing your body in a tub full
of mud as in the traditional mud bath you find
at Calistoga spas, in "wrap" form, the mud or
clay mixture is smoothed over you as you lie

serenely on a treatment table (Lincoln Avenue Spa, Sonoma Spa and others). At Glen Ivy, you get to stand up in an outdoor pool of rich clay-colored mud and spread it over your partner or friend. At Mount View Spa and Eurospa, again in Calistoga, you can receive a Fango mud bath (the mud is in powdered form and added to your mineral water bath) or a Parafango mud pack—paraffin wax and imported Fango mud is applied to your back. At Spa de Jour and La Costa, Moor mud, which has no peat or clay and is regarded by some as the most therapeutic mud available, is featured. In whatever form, mud baths and mud treatments are thought to draw impurities and toxins from the skin.

• *Salt Glow Rub:* Similar to a loofah scrub, this is another full-body exfoliating treatment for the skin. Epsom salts and a blend of oatmeal and cornmeal are the ingredients commonly used.

• *Sauna:* As familiar as sauna is as a basic spa treatment, I like the information printed by Burbank Spa in Burbank (see appendix, page 405) which starts by reminding you that *sauna* is pronounced *sow* (like *how*) *nah* and means bath or bathhouse. In Finland, the sauna has been a way of life for more than 2,000 years. It was brought to America in 1638, apparently, by Finns who settled in Delaware. One of the first saunas was built where Philadelphia City Hall now stands.

According to the Finnish family who own Burbank Spa, the high heat (approximately 180 degrees Fahrenheit) and the low humidity

(about 25%) of the sauna creates an environment that, by promoting perspiration, has a
deep cleansing effect on the pores. During a
sauna, there is an increase in blood circulation,
breathing and pulse rate. Ten minutes of sauna,
they say, is like ten minutes of running.

• *Seaweed Bath:* Freeze-dried seaweed is
added to your hot whirlpool or tub.

• *Thalassotherapy:* Any of various treatments
that use sea products, such as seaweed, for a
relaxing or therapeutic effect.

Northern California Spas

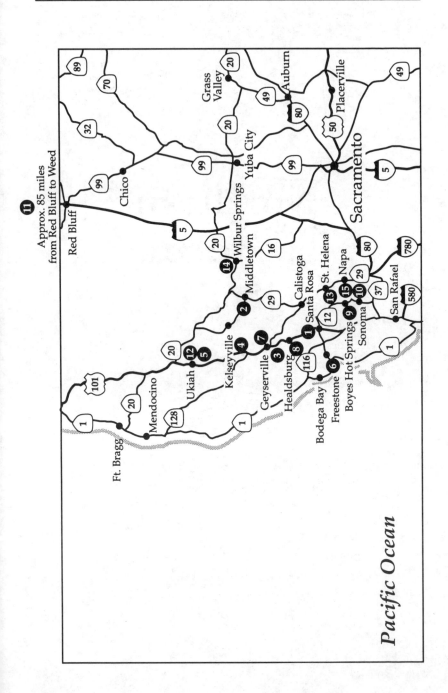

Essentials

1229 North Dutton Avenue
Santa Rosa, CA 95404
(707) 526-3766

Owner Eleanor Brodnansky is justifiably proud of her recent career shift into the world of day spas. It was from her three decades in the hair-care business that she conceived of Essentials as an urban retreat where women and men could enjoy a panoply of body and skin-care services designed to impart that elusive sense of well-being we all yearn for.

Her facility, serene and attractively designed, as is the business park in which it is located, is staffed by 12 professionals hand-picked by Eleanor as individuals who, in addition to knowing their craft, appreciate the importance of making each client feel truly comfortable and well-served.

Essentials was easy to find, and parking is conveniently located in the large lot shared by numerous businesses. The facility itself is very attractive. As I walked through the light, open, beige-furbished interior of this salon retreat, enjoying and commenting to Eleanor on how well it was laid out, I asked who was responsible for the design. She did every bit of it! This is clearly her baby. Later, when she gave me her brochure

Spa #1
map page 60

$$	Cost
☐	Overnight
☐	Program
■	Day Use
☐	Hot Springs
☐	Hot Tubs
☐	Sauna
■	Massage
■	Skin Care/Salon
☐	Exercise
☐	Meals
■	Spa Products
■	Workshops
■	Children
☐	Pets
☐	Weddings

and card, I asked again who (what firm) had done her lovely print materials, worthy of a spa ten times more costly. She told me they were done by a close friend. In short, it is very obvious that Essentials was done with *heart* and that Eleanor truly wants to do it right and to make sure that everyone enjoys being there, whether for a single service or for one of her spa packages.

The names of the packages she has designed reveal the scope of her services, so let me mention them briefly: A Day of Beauty, Quick Fix, New Mom's Day, Bride's Day, Groom's Day, Beauty Makeover, Men's Relaxation Day and Marvelous Morning. (Lunch, catered by the restaurant next door, is part of those packages that have you here for four or more hours.)

Obviously, you can also drop in for any one service from her menu of hair-care, nail-care, skin-care, and body-care treatments (all of which come with aromatherapy enhancement). On call are 8 to 15 massage therapists skilled in various massage techniques. A fully clothed neck and shoulder massage is available at a nominal cost and would be a great way for someone new to spa services to test the waters. Alternatively, you can try the Aroma Handscrub, the Hot Paraffin Hand (or Foot) Treatment, or the wonderful service offered to runners: the Jogger's Pedicure featuring the use of hot paraffin, hot towel and a whirlpool soak to "re-energize tired runners' feet."

When you register, you'll be given a light wraparound (if you're there for hair and nails only) or a thick, white terry robe if you're going for the extras that put "retreat" into this urban spa.

Essentials uses the Dermalogica line of skin-care products, particularly its alpha hydroxy acid products. Matrix and KMS skin-care and hair-care products are also displayed in the lobby.

Lest you think that is all, Eleanor plans to expand her list of seminars and workshops on various topics of potential interest to her clients. For that purpose, she has created a very comfortable lounge area situated away from the bustle of the main beauty salon area where you sit around on sofas and chairs as if you were in a friend's living room.

I fully expect to see everyone in the adjacent business park on her side and on the other side of North Dutton becoming regular clients. I certainly hope that the rest of the Rohnert Park, Petaluma, Sebastopol and Santa Rosa area will also drop in to this special place. Eleanor encourages working women and men, especially, to tour and try out her urban retreat.

HOURS
•9 a.m. to 6 p.m., Tuesday through Saturday.

INCIDENTALS
•No smoking.
•Children permitted on scheduled Kids' Days only.
•Cancellations appreciated at least 24 hours in advance of appointment.
•You are advised to register 15 minutes before your scheduled appointment.

Essentials   • Gift certificates are available.
• Credit cards accepted: all major credit cards.

Harbin
Hot Springs

Post Office Box 82
Middletown, CA 95461
(707) 987-2477
(800) 622-2477

Harbin Hot Springs is many things to many people. In a single visit, it is difficult to take in all of its personae—a New Age retreat, an educational center, a mineral springs spa resort, an intentional community and a school for massage—not to mention its sponsorship since 1972 by the Heart Consciousness Church, a nonprofit corporation organized by the resident community and supported by the hot springs operation and the conference facilities offered to outside groups and workshops.

To grasp all of that could be as difficult as traversing its "1,160 acres of secluded valley under the shadow of Mt. Harbin."

The area has been described as "serene," "lush," "sheltered," and even "sacred." Certainly it was sacred to the Native Americans who first came here for the healing properties of the hot mineral waters, and it probably still seems so to those who believe in universal acceptance—the only "doctrine" of the Heart Consciousness

Spa #2
map page 60

$$	Cost
■	Overnight
☐	Program
■	Day Use
■	Hot Springs
■	Hot Tubs
■	Sauna
■	Massage
☐	Skin Care/Salon
☐	Exercise
■	Meals
■	Spa Products
■	Workshops
■	Children
☐	Pets
■	Weddings

Church and one which, translated, means they turn no one away because of his or her beliefs or lack of them. And that the property is "lush" is absolutely true.

The physical beauty of Harbin is impressive. In trying to zero in on what makes Harbin stand out, particularly since it is not as superbly landscaped and tended as many of the pricey spas, I realized that it had something to do with the immediacy of the hills and valleys in contrast to the flatlands. You encounter it right at the entrance to Harbin where an information/security booth sits at a fork in the road—uphill veering to the left is Harbin, downhill to the right are the conference grounds.

From the main office (where a funky but fine "boutique" shares space with the registration desk, refrigerated juices and staff offices), you proceed up a gently graded hill that winds past Harbin's Little Theater, vegetarian restaurant and organic vegetable gardens, a tiny frame building that houses the School of Shiatsu and Massage, and elegant old California frame buildings with skinny verandas where guests can stay dorm-style or in private rooms.

After hiking just enough so that the calves of your legs begin to feel it, you finally come to rest at a stunning plateau where changing rooms with lockers are to your left, the main (60-degree Fahrenheit) swimming pool with its clear, blue water is off to one side, and a spacious lounging deck is across the way. Up a few stairs are the redwood sauna, graced by a massive fig tree, and the uppermost-level pools, the hottest pool (enclosed) at 112 degrees and the warm pools kept at a toasty 97 degrees. At the main swimming pool level is a juice bar (where you make your massage appointments) and, below you, a beautiful, spacious massage deck is nestled into the trees.

As you move around in this pool area, you'll see guests walking around, most of them nude, or lounging in the spring-fed swimming pool or in one of the hot or warm mineral water pools—some hand in hand, some with babies or children close by, some by themselves. (If you're not used to being among unclothed bodies, it's amazing what a 5- or 10-minute immersion among them will do. For one thing, you begin to feel quite self-conscious in your clothes.) You're as likely to hear different languages being spoken as to see every size, shape, age and gender talking, soaking, changing or practicing Watsu (the incredible water-immersion massage) in the pool.

Incidentally, Harbin's high-tech water filtering system is ensconced up here in the pool area behind closed doors. I stared at the pipes and valves and wires, recalling only that the owner of Vichy Springs, another historic hot springs facility now thriving in Ukiah, described it to me as the best system anywhere—state-of-the-art, as he says. His years of experience in the water-bottling business have educated him as to what works best and is environmentally safe.

If you look down from the pool area to the massage pavilion below, you are likely to see a body stretched out on a table in the open air, legs akimbo, enjoying a massage from a naked, Rubenesque massage practitioner. The sight is as sensual as it is nonsexual—and perhaps only spa "insiders" will understand and trust that oxymoron.

Harbin's large resident community works at various jobs that keep the place going: office reception, bookkeeping, housekeeping, landscaping, security, childcare, massage and various other projects. Our guide, a man who once devoted his life to computers, usually spent his time listing the week's films and writing reviews for Harbin's Little Theater—a good-sized room constructed in lecture-hall style with terraced and pillow-covered steps down to the stage, open nightly for free movies.

Those who make up the resident population at Harbin are of various dispositions, talents and backgrounds, and the purposes that brought them there also differ. Some came just to take time out and regroup and some to carve out a new life that has more meaning for them. It seems that many who came for the former soon joined the latter. As a resident member, you pay a nominal weekly rate for lodging. You can start a cottage industry and may even be assisted with it, depending on the decision of the community.

Harbin's doctrine of universal acceptance brings to it a diversity of people and interests and lifestyles. By welcoming all perspectives, Harbin is assured that it will not unwittingly slip into cultish philosophies. On the other hand, it is obvious that people who are attracted by Harbin's residential community are already bonded by certain values they hold in common—preservation of the environment, the human potential for self-understanding, acceptance, holism, and the possibility, if not presence, of universal spirituality.

Because the conference facilities are so elaborate, and because they constitute a major enterprise for Harbin, they deserve a full description here. At the entrance to the property, you take the high road to Harbin's main center and the low road to the conference area where you have wonderful choices of facilities depending on how many people you need to accommodate and what ambience you and your group are looking for.

In at least one of the buildings, you can throw down a sleeping bag on the well-padded floor and stay there at night, or, as many do, you can camp in the Upper Meadow and Fire Circle, a large area shaded by massive oak trees. The area will hold up to 500 people and has nearby parking and bathroom facilities. The meadow is a 15-minute hike through the woods to and from the pool area. (By the way, Harbin will provide you with a list describing its trails; it also will alert you to such things as deer hunting season in August and September when you are cautioned to wear BRIGHT colors while hiking.) A ceremonial fire circle adjoins this grassy meadow and has been used for gatherings and ceremonies for many years.

The largest building is the Conference Center which holds 35 to 300 people and contains a kitchen, dining room, bathrooms and showers, and a private apartment for the conference leader. This wood, stone and glass structure is next to two private 250-square-foot spring-fed pools which, with 24 hours advance notice, can be heated to the temperature you request.

The Meadow Building, situated at the foot of the mountain, has all of the same amenities as the Conference Center and accommodates 20 to 50 persons. The Stonefront Building, the only one located in the center of the main property, has easy access to both the mineral bath area and the restaurant (downstairs in the same building) and overlooks Harbin's organic vegetable gardens. Accommodating 14 to 30 people, this upstairs conference area has a carpeted workshop area (on the plain side) and a separate library meeting room (delightfully furnished and showing off lovely pastel pillow covers sewn by one of the residents).

The Mountain Lodge, nestled in the old oak trees, is a solar-heated redwood structure with a wraparound deck. Described as a hideaway at the top of a steep, forested hillside, it is apparently the perfect meeting spot for groups of 10 to 35 who want maximum privacy and quiet and who want to feel close to nature. In addition to the same general amenities as the others, it also has its own hot tub.

For those of us who don't mind Harbin's New Age rhetoric but don't "sing the song of oneness" ourselves, we can enjoy this beautiful retreat anyway. If you want to test that out,

Harbin's philosophy of acceptance and its very affordable rates certainly encourage it. For nominal rates during the week and even on weekends, you can get a day-visit pass, and, for very little more, you can reserve a campsite for the night. At a gently increasing rate, you can rent a private room with a half or full bath.

The Stonefront restaurant cooks up hearty and healthy meals described as "gourmet vegetarian," which are available at reasonable prices. Up in the pool area is Fern Kitchen, a great community space with a huge skylight over the sink area, massive refrigerators and storage cabinets for your food, and a row of long rectangular tables by the window overlooking the pathway to the pools. Here, there is to be absolutely no meat, fish or poultry. Fresh ingredients from Harbin's organic garden are for sale. The nearest supermarket is in Middletown, four miles away.

You also can get a feel for Harbin by reading a sample issue of its *Quarterly*. This 40-page publication is printed on newsprint, and an earlier newsprint publication, *Living the Future*, describes the New Age viewpoint in some detail. The *Quarterly* is filled with articles, poetry, recipes from Harbinites and advertisements, and is sent only to those holding memberships. (In addition to announcing its impressive array of workshops, the latest *Quarterly* I read had a provocative astrological profile of Bill and Hillary Clinton, as well as the reflections of massage teacher Diana Lonsdale on the staff of Harbin's School of Shiatsu and Massage.)

Harbin
Hot Springs

Harbin puts out various pieces of literature, and if you spread them out on a table in front of you, you might get a more comprehensive picture of the place. Its glossy PR piece captures the beauty of the site, its old and new buildings and its incredible oak trees and pools. As inviting as the photographs are, they do not communicate Harbin's warm, country vitality. Its one-page descriptive sheets in black and white give you useful information about the School of Shiatsu and Massage that offers weekend workshops leading to state certification. Other flyers provide maps of paths and trails, and announce one-day workshops.

Photocopied reprints describing Harbin as a "center for healing and growth" constitute yet another type of literature from Harbin, and more formal typeset reprints from *Mother Earth News* (1984) highlighting intentional communities in general and Harbin in particular are also part of their publicity handout material. Actually, this variegated array of literature simply affirms the community's intention to remain open, dynamic and heterogeneous, serving as a "springboard for the creation of an alternative society."

Speaking of its publications, Harbin published *Harbin Hot Springs: Healing Waters, Sacred Land* in 1991. In this fascinating book, Ellen Klages chronicles the retreat's 125-year history. I was impressed to learn that the serenity that characterizes Harbin was achieved only after much struggle.

HOURS

•Office: 9 a.m. until 10 p.m. on Friday and Saturday; 9 a.m. to 7 p.m. Sunday through Thursday. Open year round.

•The reception booth is open 24 hours a day.

INCIDENTALS

•Numerous seminars, gatherings and workshops (many directed specifically to men); conference facilities.

•Two-week state-approved certification program in massage taught at the on-site School of Shiatsu and Massage—with instruction also in Tantsu, Watsu, co-centering and Veechi. Call for price, which includes lodging (bring sleeping bag) and full use of Harbin's facilities.

•Memberships are available at three levels: trial, annual and lifetime. One person in each visiting party must hold one of these forms of membership.

•Children are allowed only at campsites and accompanied and supervised by adults; they must be closely watched at pool area. Children's rates apply to those under 18.

•Use of pools and main area from 10 a.m. to 5 p.m. (until 8 p.m. during summer months).

•Alcohol and drugs are not allowed.

•Smoking: only below the main gate and on the deck below the office.

•No campfires are allowed on the property due to fire danger.

•Credit cards accepted: MasterCard and Visa. Personal checks also accepted with I.D.

Isis Oasis
Retreat Center

20889 Geyserville Avenue
Geyserville, CA 95441
(707) 857-3524

Spa #3
map page 60

$$ Cost
■ Overnight
□ Program
□ Day Use
□ Hot Springs
■ Hot Tubs
■ Sauna
■ Massage
■ Skin Care/Salon
■ Exercise
■ Meals
□ Spa Products
■ Workshops
■ Children
□ Pets
■ Weddings

Among the changes that have taken place at this unique spa since the previous edition of *California Spas* was published are: Lora Vigne, owner of Isis Oasis, is now "Loreon;" a new suite has been opened, called (surprise) "The Suite;" elder hostel groups come to enjoy yoga and t'ai chi; geriatric massage is available; and ongoing and new workshops are thriving.

Other than that, this 10-acre wonderland still houses: the owner's private residence (a charming two-story red farmhouse, once used as a Baha'i school); a mini-zoo of exotic birds and animals (that started with two ocelots evicted from her San Francisco apartment); a therapeutic house for massage and facials; a theater for events presented by the nonprofit Isis Society for Inspirational Studies (with sound system, piano, dressing rooms and seating for 100); a lodge (with lounge and dorm-style rooms); a dining pavilion; a honeymoon cottage; a retreat house (built before the turn of the century and partially restored by Loreon);

several sleeping yurts; a tipi; a temple for meditation (decorated with her artwork); a 20' by 40' swimming pool at 76 degrees adjacent to a hot tub at 102 to 104 degrees Fahrenheit; and a sauna built into a cedar-walled barrel (California Cooperage) that holds four.

The 500-year-old Douglas fir, considered sacred by the Pomo Indian inhabitants of days gone by, is still an awesome presence on the property. Loreon, Paul and all their guests regard themselves as keepers of the tree and gather around it for group meditations.

The story of how Loreon found and developed this property over the years (as well as how she came upon her partner Paul Ramses) is filled with the kinds of synchronicities that befit one who honors Isis, the goddess of nature. But that is more appropriately the subject of a lengthy personal profile. For my purposes here, let me just say that Isis Oasis is a *trip,* and one that does not insist you be steeped in Egyptology to the extent that Loreon and Paul are.

Loreon is a pleasant, easygoing woman, both serene and playful, even mischievous—particularly when she cradles a bobcat on her shoulder and feeds a gargantuan emu from her hand.

The literature from Isis Oasis also shows that Loreon the goddess can be pleasantly silly. She writes about the wine barrel room—"cozy and a barrel of fun," and about the sleeping yurts— "everyone enjoys being inert in a yurt."

Loreon is adding bodywork to the massage and facial services already in place. Her facility can accommodate individuals and families (one

*Isis Oasis
Retreat Center*

of the yurts sleeps 10) as well as organized groups.

So lovely is the property (rolling hills and plateaus providing vistas of the Alexander Valley, the Russian River and surrounding mountains), so inviting and varied the accommodations (the "enchanted" honeymoon cottage, the roomy retreat house—one of the oldest in Geyserville with its own hot spa—the several charming yurts, and the free-standing wine-barrel room, most displaying Loreon's artwork and stained glass and all with scatterings of antique furniture), and so strangely thrilling her mini-zoo (pheasants with brilliantly colored plumage, peacocks, swans, ocelots, bobcats, servals, pygmy goats, llama, emu and probably more as time goes by) that I still urge you not to miss this experience.

If you're not up for a retreat weekend or a simple overnight with hot soak and massage, you can always get married there. Loreon's scrapbook bulges with photographs of the weddings that have taken place under the eye of nature's goddess. Loreon still does most of the cooking for these events, using fresh vegetables from her garden nearby, but she also employs a capable kitchen staff for the times when she is in San Francisco (frequently) or Egypt (whenever she can).

Isis puts on a great many workshops, too numerous and changing to include here, but you should call for a schedule.

HOURS

•Open year round.

INCIDENTALS
•Full conference facilities.
•Greyhound bus stop within walking distance.
•Smoking in outside areas only.
•Town of Geyserville, Lake Sonoma, wine country and recreations nearby.
•Early advance reservations advisable.
•Weddings performed (non-denominational ministers).
•Credit cards accepted: MasterCard and Visa.

Konocti Harbor Resort / Dancing Springs Spa

8727 Soda Bay Road
Kelseyville, CA 95451
(707) 279-4281
(800) 862-4930

Spa #4
map page 60

$$$ Cost
■ Overnight
■ Program
■ Day Use
☐ Hot Springs
■ Hot Tubs
■ Sauna
■ Massage
■ Skin Care/Salon
■ Exercise
■ Meals
☐ Spa Products
☐ Workshops
■ Children
☐ Pets
■ Weddings

Reopened after a six-month closure, Konocti is back in the game. The main lodge has been completely remodeled, as have its 250 rooms. The Dancing Springs Spa adds another dimension and a touch of class to Konocti Harbor Resort, owned by the San Francisco Plumbers Union.

The spa is housed in a spacious two-story building uphill from the clusters of buildings that, together with their beach cottages and other lake-level apartments, house some 280 guests of the resort. I say uphill only to suggest that it is closer to the two beautiful camel humps of Mount Konocti than to Clear Lake: The facts are that there is no hill to climb and lake views are available to every guest at Konocti, even those in the lowest-price rooms. What's more, a lovely foot bridge connects what are called the "deluxe" rooms (where spa guests on packaged programs stay) and the spa building.

Before describing the spa and its array of services, let me say that what really sets Konocti apart from others in this book is, first, that it caters to families with children, and second that, as in the past, leading musicians and groups are lined up to perform almost every weekend. (An all-country weekend will have taken place by the time you read this. As a country music fan, I hope these weekends will continue.)

To satisfy kiddy tastes (in children and in adults), Konocti provides an obstacle-strewn miniature golf course and shuffleboard as well as a beach playground and wading pools. In the summer, ask about their day camp for children. For Mom and Pop, choose basketball, softball, volleyball, horseshoes or tennis (eight courts!), then take a swim in one of their two Olympic-size pools, one open at ambient temperature and one "domed" at approximately 75 degrees Fahrenheit. Fishing, boating and golf are also available. At night, people come from near and far for the featured entertainers.

With all of that going on, the spa's philosophy—that we have to live in the world and learn to make healthy choices amid all of the temptations—is understandable. Once you leave the busy first-floor lobby area with its rack of T-shirts for sale and its serious Cybex-equipped co-ed gym (incidentally, new equipment has been added recently—a second stair climber, a rowing machine and a leg press), serenity reigns. The main spa, upstairs, is furnished in wicker with soft mauves and pale grays in carpets and on walls. A spacious meeting room/lounge area looks out to the lake, creating an oasis of peace amid the bustle.

Very impressive is the spa's 60-foot lap pool (80- to 83-degree water, four feet deep throughout) with its five huge rectangular skylights set into a high, polished-pine ceiling. The lap pool is situated between the men's and women's quarters so that both can use it. The basic spa facilities are duplicated on the men's side.

Once you register at the spa, whether as a day-use or spa program guest, you'll be given a locker, towels and a robe to start your journey. Then you'll proceed to one of several tiled shower stalls (one is wheelchair-accessible) for a good soapy shower and thorough rinse before you begin spa treatments. Here are your choices: a whirlpool bath (105 degrees), a dry cedar sauna (190 degrees) and a tiled steam room (set the temperature yourself) where you stretch out and inhale the continuous steam from a tiny cup of eucalyptus oil. (I noticed that large clocks seemed to be visible at many locations—a nice feature when you are doing any kind of heat therapy that unwittingly allows you to lose track of time!)

The spa features a one-hour aromatherapy massage, loofah scrubs, herbal wraps, hydrotherapy and seaweed and other "bubble baths." In addition to its massage rooms (again with skylights and beautiful polished-pine ceilings) and its "wet room" for wraps, scrubs, baths and hydrotherapy, the spa has a separate room for pedicures (elevating the pedicure to a position

I personally favor). In addition to more elaborate spa packages where you stay overnight, you can also sign up for a "Day of Pampering" that gives you an exercise class, massage, facial, herbal wrap and loofah scrub, or alternatively, a massage, facial, shampoo and style, manicure and pedicure.

An adjacent fitness room, reserved for aerobics, yoga and other classes that change seasonally, is very spacious and has a wonderful springy carpeted floor to absorb the impact that would otherwise jolt your body.

A full-service beauty salon, open to the public as well as to those staying at Konocti who are not on a spa program, is housed downstairs. The salon services offered, to men as well as women, are too many to list. Besides offering back facials in addition to mini-facials and deep-cleansing facials, and beard trimming for men and French braiding for women, you can get your ears pierced, your eyebrows shaped and almost every hair on your body waxed away! Not only that but when you spend money either in the salon or on a spa treatment, you get complimentary day-use of their spa facilities.

Before leaving the spa building, let me repeat that in the summer, for a small fee, children over five years of age can be in day camp, either from 10 a.m. until 4 p.m. or from 5 p.m. until 10 p.m. in the evening, depending on how you want to spend your adult time. Two counselors supervise the children's activities (arts and crafts, games, an evening movie, etc.) with assistance from a couple of high school seniors.

Konocti Harbor Resort / Dancing Springs Spa

Twenty children is usually the limit they will accept to be sure that the ratio of children to adults is reasonable.

Finally, right outside the spa is a small café (with outdoor and indoor seating) where you can have a "healthy" pizza (vegetarian, turkey) on a Boboli, frozen yogurt, orange juice, a smoothie and such. The fare here is purposely limited. For those on a spa program, you'll probably use the dining room in the main lodge for your main meal, but, if you want to maintain healthy eating habits, look for the notations the spa has made next to those entrées on the menu that are lower in fat and calories.

As long as you know that there are two very distinct atmospheres between the Dancing Springs Spa and the well-established Konocti Harbor Resort, and you're the kind of person who enjoys having a foot in both worlds, or you want to vacation with children and assure they won't be bored, I can recommend Konocti. Don't expect to zoom into Kelseyville at the speed limit, however. The road out of Middletown is a scenic winding road—just settle back and accept it as an opportunity to start slowing down.

HOURS
•Open year round. Monday through Friday, 6 a.m. to 10 p.m.; Saturday, 8 a.m. to 10 p.m.; Sunday, 8 a.m. to 6 p.m.

INCIDENTALS

•Day use, discount for hotel guests, no charge for guests using the beauty salon or having a spa treatment.

•A 15% service charge will be added to all services and spa packages (except for day-use fee and fitness classes.)

•Advance appointments required.

•Individualized spa packages can be designed.

•Special hikes and 5K runs scheduled.

•Cancellations for *à la carte* services is three hours prior; for package programs, 48 hours.

•Annual individual, family and corporate memberships available.

•Helicopter pad.

•Call or write for spa package information, accommodations and rate card, and a calendar of events (Monday night football, jazz champagne brunches on Sunday as well as weekend entertainment).

•Credit cards accepted: all major credit cards.

Orr Hot Springs

13201 Orr Springs Road
Ukiah, CA 95482
(707) 462-6277

*Spa #5
map page 60*

$$ Cost
■ Overnight
☐ Program
■ Day Use
■ Hot Springs
■ Hot Tubs
■ Sauna
■ Massage
☐ Skin Care/Salon
☐ Exercise
☐ Meals
☐ Spa Products
☐ Workshops
■ Children
☐ Pets
☐ Weddings

Orr Hot Springs is nestled in a canyon at the top of a winding mountain road in the Mendocino Coastal Range—certainly not a Californian's picture of Ukiah. In the springtime, the most dramatic feature of this laid-back country spa is its lush landscaping. Roses, wisteria, lavender, foxglove, stock, marigolds and a profusion of herbs greet you all along the way up to and into the property, with a few stone lanterns pretending to light the pathway. It is hard to imagine what Orr would look like without this "coat of many colors" that adorns an otherwise plain country retreat that resists leaving the good old flower-children days.

Like other Northern California country spas, many of Orr's staff people live on the 27-acre property, so there is a limit to the number of people that can be accommodated in its small stash of 13 cabins, built of locally milled redwood in the early 1940s. Eleven campsites are dotted around the surrounding hillside, however, and a large, carpeted, unadorned "healing room" with a loft is available for those who are content to bring a bedroll and share floor space with others.

Still more overnight space can be had if you have your own sleeping van, for Orr's management will permit you to park it in the lot outside the main gate. A community kitchen is in the main lodge and is available for all overnighters to use. Everything you need to work with (except your food) is provided, although they suggest bringing your own cooler. Orr also has a nice outside picnic area with a gas-fired grill.

It is clear at Orr, almost more than at other places, that you are there specifically to "take the waters." Several underground springs are tapped to bring this liquid silk water into the bath house, which harks back to 1863. (All other historic 19th-century buildings burned down.) Four private rooms lined along the bathhouse walkway have porcelain Victorian tubs that fill continually with hot mineral water. Bathers start here and then move to one of two communal tubs outside, each one strikingly different from the other and from most tubs you'll find.

One is made of redwood, eight feet in diameter, and is enclosed in a light, airy gazebo with picture windows and stained glass. The water from this tub ranges from 102 to 105 degrees and its overflow fills the second tub, unenclosed and completely open to the skies. This tub is striking because it is built into the bedrock and inlaid with tile. Here, the water is only slightly above body temperature.

Orr Hot Springs

The main swimming pool at the farthest end of the property is built into the rock of the hillside and, again, water flows continually and doesn't require chemicals. When we were there, a woman was blissfully nestled against the side, her head under the pipe so that the water flowing down from the hillside could cascade down over her head and body. This water is refreshingly cool, but even cooler water can be had in the wading pools of the creek a few feet away. (They even recommend using the river mud for a do-it-yourself face and body mask.)

A large gas-fired sauna is adjacent to the pool and can be used as a dry sauna or turned into a steambath by ladling water on to the rocks. Again, there is stained glass in this structure and a skylight that opens to the surrounding bluffs. Trilby Spring, marked with a small sign, pops up in a small area dug into the rock at poolside; it stays at body temperature and is just deep enough to encourage its long-ago use as a soaking pool for tired feet. (Beautiful tiled foot baths are also inside the bathhouse.)

A grassy stretch along the side of the pool was covered with stripped-down bodies the day we were there. As in other clothing-optional places, most people shed their clothes around the bath and pool areas only, although you might see an occasional nude body elsewhere.

A massage crew comes in from the outside in response to requests made at the front desk, where massage information—procedures and tips—are also available. As everywhere else, massage practitioners are all state-certified.

Orr was bought by a collective in 1974. When we were there, a staff of three were keeping things going, although there are 10 shareholders. Paradoxically, it seems that in places with the least structure—whether in terms of actual physical "structures" or in terms of activities, programs and services—the rules of the house must be more rigid if an easy cooperative atmosphere is to be maintained.

House rules also are interesting in that they call attention to the kinds of covenants people have broken in the past. Orr has a printed list that they give you when you arrive. Some of the "please refrain froms" are quite serious (smoking outside of designated areas, alcohol and drug use) and others are no less important but provoke more smiles (feeding the fat cats inside the lodge). Speaking of cats inside the lodge, Orr used to have a mascot rooster, Andy, who attached himself to the place and strutted around freely (and fully clothed at all times).

If the charm of Orr has not yet sunk in from my description, let me run down their "Please do's and don'ts" list to #7: "If you wish to maintain a period of silence while you are here, silence beads are available at the front desk. If you see someone wearing these beads, please respect this request for privacy." For anyone who has experimented with silence—from a simple turning off of a television set as a deliberate act, to a 20-minute meditation, to a flotation tank of sensory deprivation, to a serious "fasting" from all talk for a day or more, you know that the effects can be powerful and rewarding.

Orr Hot Springs

HOURS
- Open year round, seven days a week.
- Office hours are 10 a.m. to 10 p.m.

INCIDENTALS
- Private and communal baths.
- Discounted bath cards.
- Main swimming pool is closed from noon Tuesday to noon Wednesday for weekly draining and cleaning.
- Reservations advised for all accommodations, and you are asked to always call before visiting.
- Infants under two are free. Children are limited to three per night, two adults per child, with 100% supervision at all times.
- Handcarts available to transport luggage from parking lot to cabin.
- Hiking at nearby Montgomery Redwoods State Park.
- Credit cards accepted: MasterCard and Visa.

Osmosis

209 Bohemian Highway
Freestone, CA 95472
By appointment only
(707) 823-8231

Osmosis remains the only place in the western world, with the exception of International Spa in Calistoga, where you can enjoy an "enzyme bath"—a kind of heat therapy that the Japanese have enjoyed for a good many years. Osmosis' owner-founder Michael Stusser introduced it to John Cashman at International Spa, trained Cashman's staff, and continues to supply him with the bath ingredients. He may soon enjoy more competition.

Since Osmosis moved from the hills of Sebastopol to Freestone, it has become very popular. As at his previous facility, Michael has re-created a traditional Japanese garden—something he learned in Kyoto. (He also has taught organic gardening at the Farallones Institute, an ecological teaching, learning and demonstration center in Berkeley and Occidental.)

The term enzyme bath doesn't begin to capture the quirky charm of this substance, which is made up of enzymes from 60 kinds of plants that are extracted by a fermentation process and added to fragrant cedar fibers from the Hinoki

Spa #6
map page 60

$$	Cost
☐	Overnight
☐	Program
■	Day Use
☐	Hot Springs
■	Hot Tubs
☐	Sauna
■	Massage
☐	Skin Care/Salon
☐	Exercise
☐	Meals
■	Spa Products
☐	Workshops
☐	Children
☐	Pets
☐	Weddings

tree, used in Japan for building temples and, in this country, found only in southern Oregon. In preparing his own mixture, Michael adds fresh Douglas fir, rice bran and water.

As his brochure reveals, your visit to Osmosis begins with taking a cup of "enzyme tea." For the Japanese, the tea ceremony is an important ritual that honors four principles: harmony (*wa*), respect (*kei*), purity (*sei*) and tranquillity (*jaku*). The small tea room with futon seating looks out on a lovely Japanese garden with its scaled-down bridge, waterfall and fish pond.

Following the tea, you will be taken to a dressing room to undress. You can strip down or wear a swimsuit. You are then taken to one of the two tub rooms where an attendant will use an ordinary pitchfork to scoop out a body-sized opening for you in the mass of cedar particles. (The pitchfork is clearly a symbol of east meeting west, and I suspect that your graceful acceptance of its incongruity may speed you on your way to enlightenment.)

You will be told how to position your body and your head and, once you feel at ease, the cedar fibers piled high around you will be gently placed back over your body. (Incidentally, as the enzymes ferment, the essential oils are released from the cedar into the steamy vapors to waft gently around you.) Once in, it is best not to wiggle your toes and fingers because the movement opens up pockets of heat that can be uncomfortable if you're not expecting it.

Now you begin your journey in toasty comfort, by yourself or next to a friend. (You are never put in a tub with strangers!) The temperature of an enzyme bath is high—110 to 130 degrees. Because of its dense humidity, however, it feels quite comfortable. Nevertheless, it is important that you listen and heed the attendant's advice. Leaving your hands, feet or arms outside the bath, for example, or asking that your reclining space be on the shallow side, will keep you a bit cooler than immersing yourself entirely. The attendant will check you in seven to ten minutes, sponge off your forehead with a cool cloth, and make sure that you are not overheated. The maximum time to stay in the bath is 20 minutes.

Once settled down into this miraculous substance, too dry to look like porridge, too moist to look like sawdust, your attendant will slide open the *shoji* doors to reveal a feast for the eyes: in the foreground, Michael's Japanese rock garden with prized bonsai, and in the distance, the rolling hills of western Sonoma's countryside. Being able to look out to the mountains and sky and feel the cool breezes, which grace the area year round and especially in May and June, is not a serendipitous occurrence: Michael has carefully selected this design feature, knowing that one of the major resistances some people have to mudbathing is the sense of claustrophobia they feel in the typically dark, cavernous rooms that house most mud baths.

Another telling difference between the enzyme bath and the mud bath is the way you get into it: In a mud bath, you are "panned" into the tub on a wooden board with a handle—as if you were a giant pizza going into the oven; in the enzyme bath, you step in gracefully, like Botticelli's Venus returning to the sea.

What is similar to a traditional mud bath, however, is that an enzyme bath requires you to leave your independent do-it-yourself spirit outside the door with your shoes and gracefully surrender to the ministrations of the attendants. Well trained, they will assist you into and out of the bath, make sure you are steady on your feet before you try to move around, and help you brush off whatever sticky cedar stuff is clinging to your skin.

At this point, you are led to the shower where you are given a kimono to wear. From there, you move to the wrap room, where you will be blanketed like a burrito for 30 minutes of sublime transition. Here, you can lie still and quiet, or elect to listen to audiotapes ranging from their "metamusic" of peaceful nature sounds or their "hypno-peripheral processing" billed as "the most powerful behavioral change tapes in existence."

According to their literature on hypno-peripheral processing, this audiocassette program uses the powerful storytelling device initiated by the famed psychologist, Milton Erikson. Six subjects, each comprised of two tapes, are available through mail order. All of these audiotapes are sold in the front lobby.

Alternatively, you can go from your shower to a massage. Osmosis has eight massage rooms. As in most other spas where massage is a serious component, the massage practitioners all do Swedish-Esalen and individually specialize in other massage forms (deep tissue, shiatsu, etc.). Massage for pregnant women also is offered. You can choose to have a woman or a man as your massage practitioner. A massage at Osmosis is always one hour and 15 minutes of hands-on work. Michael feels strongly about full-body massage after a bath. Massage is not included with the bath, but I would highly recommend you treat yourself to both.

Whether you go directly to the wrap room or have a massage first, it is during these 30 luxurious minutes of tranquility that your body slowly cools down to normal temperature and the whole experience will come together, leaving you feeling light, peaceful, energized, refreshed, restored, invigorated and ready to tell all your friends about your discovery.

Having given you the poetry of the bath, let me now turn to a western version of Osmosis. First of all, as you know, the process of osmosis is "the tendency of a fluid to pass through a semipermeable membrane...so as to equalize concentrations on both sides." That process is really more than and less than what goes on in this enzyme bath.

In scientific terms, we know that heat is heat, yet we also know that the ways we experience the heat of water, the heat of fire, the heat of a heating pad, the heat of a sauna and the heat of the sun are quite different. The heat from these moist cedar fibers is likely to be more evenly distributed than is possible with the less porous mud, and more comfortable because of the cedar's different thermal, adsorptive and osmotic properties.

The science of the enzyme bath, however, is unlikely to matter much while you are reveling in your experience at Osmosis. When you leave, you not only have an extraordinary sensation that your body and mind have been elevated to an entirely different plane of being—a sensation that seasoned spa-goers come to expect—but you also leave with the special feeling of having been exquisitely cared for.

The historically preserved town of Freestone, although over in a minute, is pleasant to amble through. The Green Apple Inn, a restored Victorian farmhouse operated as a bed and breakfast inn by Rosemary and Rogers Hoffman, is still there. Charm envelops this plain, well-tended inn and its good-hearted owners, and room rates are modest as B&B prices go.

A visit to the Western Hills Nursery with its four acres of exotic and drought-resistant plants and trees is another must-see in this area. It is a feast for the eyes as well as a splendid place to buy plants for your own garden.

If you continue north on Bohemian Highway, you'll pass through Occidental, another sweet town for good food and good people. (I was recently told that Occidental also boasts of a world-famous chorus!) But if you haven't discovered Duncans Mills, keep going until you reach Monte Rio, then swing west (Highway 116). Besides the highly touted Blue Heron restaurant, there are other shops and cafés on both sides of the highway that are worth getting out of the car to visit.

The Blue Heron, known for its excellent menu, has a well-established supper-club following. In addition to their "house musicians" who play through brunch and weekend dinner hours during the summer months, the restaurant holds concerts every Thursday at 7:30 p.m. Their concert series range from folk-rock to jazz to Latin and back again. The Blue Heron also has a down-home bar with booths, separate from the dining area. If you're not up to a full-course dinner, drop in and hang out there for a bit before you head off for Point Reyes to the south or Calistoga to the east.

Finally, for the most beautiful country stretch I've ever traveled, there is the Coleman Valley Road that meanders around from Occidental to the sea, changing character several times en route. And of course you know that you are surrounded by wine country.

HOURS
•Open for day use, seven days a week, 9 a.m. to 10 p.m., by appointment only.

INCIDENTALS
•Be prepared to leave your shoes outside the door and to keep your voice down inside the facility.
•Available for purchase in the lobby: Osmosis herbal teas (peppermint, yarrow, nettleleaf, red clover); cedar body lotions, shampoo, conditioner; Japanese incense and incense burners,

Osmosis

rice crackers, robes (Yukata, 100% cotton flannel), meditation cushions in a variety of designs and fabrics, and more.

•Credit cards accepted: MasterCard and Visa.

Pocket Ranch Institute

Post Office Box 516
Geyserville, CA 95441
(707) 857-3359
(707) 857-3764 fax

Holding a unique position in the world of retreat facilities, Pocket Ranch is another exciting find for this guidebook to spas and urban retreats in California. Founded several years ago by Barbara Findeisen, a Marriage, Family and Children's Counselor (MFCC) at a time when she was in crisis and wanted a nurturing, therapeutic, compassionate community in which to recover, Pocket Ranch is now there for all to, in her words, "reconnect heads with hearts and set free the spirit within."

From the afternoon I spent there talking with staff and touring a tiny portion of its hundreds of acres (Barbara found a benefactor from whom to lease this near-perfect property in Alexander Valley) and, even more so, from the very credible testimony of those who have stayed there—individuals and groups from all over the country as well as caregivers themselves in need of care—Barbara's dream seems to have been profoundly realized. That Proustian sen-

Spa #7
map page 60

$$-$$$$ Cost
■ Overnight
■ Program
☐ Day Use
☐ Hot Springs
☐ Hot Tubs
■ Sauna
■ Massage
☐ Skin Care/Salon
☐ Exercise
■ Meals
■ Spa Products
■ Workshops
☐ Children
☐ Pets
■ Weddings

tence is to say I was mightily impressed.

The reason why I feel comfortable including this "nonprofit public benefit corporation" here in the company of profit-making spas and urban retreats is this: In addition to its array of on-site therapeutic counseling services, its residential care facility (certified by the California Department of Mental Health as an alternative to hospitalization), and its eclectic workshop offerings, Pocket Ranch welcomes individuals who prefer to be on their own "self-directed" quests. Whether you are interested in working on yourself or not, you can come and spend a night or two—or more—in this peaceful, remote, splendiferous wooded setting and simply "chill"!

If this facility were just a superb get-away-from-it-all retreat, however, I would have gone myself for a visit but I still would not include it here. But the fact is that Pocket Ranch incorporates bodywork into its programs and makes it available to workshop participants as well as individuals who have come by themselves. Well-trained therapists offer Swedish, Esalen, shiatsu and deep tissue work. A sauna is also available. A splendid swimming pool surrounded by lounge chairs appears like an oasis in the clearing between the dining room and the old swinging bench, on which I sat and scribbled notes.

If you do want to dip into the Ranch's therapeutic services (individual counseling with a licensed therapist, individual or group sessions in breath work, art therapy, hypnosis, and other such adjuncts to treatment), you can. These services, as well as bodywork and massage, are billed separately, of course, but the rates conform to respective rates in other facilities. Incidentally, the credentials of the therapy staff are impeccable and those who know of UCSF clinical professor Ken Pelletier's work, *Mind as Healer, Mind as Slayer*, will be pleased to read his strong endorsement of the work they do; it has been reprinted in their brochure materials.

Although some of the workshops can be pricey ($$$$), if you are not attending a workshop and just want to go to the Ranch and be on your own, for under $100 a night (well under if you share a double room), you can. Whatever you personally want and need to renew your energies for daily living—get a massage, take a swim, eat well, walk about, meditate, hike, swim, write or hang out in a hammock—it's yours. And three meals and snacks are included in the nightly rate. Both vegetarian and non-vegetarian dishes are always available, special dietary needs are accommodated, and the kitchen is open 24 hours a day for late-hour snacking.

During the day, everyone takes meals at the same appointed hours and joins each other at round tables in a large comfortable dining room where, the day I was there, a construction crew was busily adding what will be a stunning, glass-enclosed pavilion whose roof will peak in the center at 16 feet. (In fact, carpenters were everywhere, completing repairs to the main lodge and building all sorts of wonderful additions to fulfill Barbara's vision. A hilltop meditation cottage was in process and will be in place by the time you set forth for Geyserville.)

As for your accommodations, you will be housed in one of the many four-unit cabins dotted about the property, each accommodating eight people. On the outside they look like barns that have been sliced off 10 or 12 feet below the roof line and plunked down on the ground. Because they flange out at the sides, it made placing the furniture a bit of a design problem, but what you will notice more than that is that each one has been furnished with an eye for simplicity (pine furniture), elegance (high, hand-crafted bedsteads with recessed built-in lighting), and comfort (private baths, desks, inviting bedding). I found out in the course of asking questions, for example, that the Ranch's Renaissance man, Phil McPherson, who serves as architect, designer, graphics artist, builder and more, couldn't find a fabric and pattern that he felt was appropriate for the bedspreads and so just set about designing his own. This is the kind of spirit, ingenuity and dedication you find throughout Pocket Ranch.

Pocket Ranch also has a fine ropes course all set up for corporations and other groups who want to offer their employees or members a challenging, team-building experience. In addition, the Ranch lives harmoniously, it seems, with its animal kingdom—bobcats, wild boar, snakes (in season) and coyotes. Listening to the wail of coyote herds in the night air, I was told, is an unforgettable experience. I was moved enough by the sight of horses and cows roaming freely and munching their hearts out down in the canyon. (Is this a reflection of the kitchen staff's philosophy in staying open all night?)

Without going into detail about its workshops (Pocket Ranch will send you one of its handsome press kits as well as a schedule of upcoming workshops), let me say that the "STAR" program is the principal draw. Formulated by Ms. Findeisen (and adapted from the Fischer-Hoffman system, for those of you who know this work), it is a 17-day intensive program designed to assist you in looking at deeply rooted childhood issues which, if not confronted, can keep you stuck. The participant-therapist ratio is almost one-to-one and, although the work is accomplished in a group setting, as a participant you are assigned a staff person who works closely with you throughout the program on issues of your choice and at your pace. Indeed, there is no coercion in any of the activities at the Ranch. Writing exercises and bodywork sessions are an integral part of this workshop. At the end of the intensive, a number of participants have gone home to form and join STAR support groups in their respective cities.

David Gaskin, the Ranch's workshop coordinator who toured me around (and answered my millions of questions), is a "graduate" of the STAR program, which, he told me, absolutely turned his life around. Out of that workshop, he walked away from his unsatisfying corporate life and, eventually (serendipitously) was invited to join the staff at Pocket Ranch. I found David to be one of those individuals

whose warm, open face is one of those I describe as having no secrets—the best advertis-
ing I know of for any institute dedicated to personal transformation. He also repeated often
enough that he is not a "woo-woo" person about
all of these growth experiences that are at the
heart of Pocket Ranch, and I, for one, appreciate that one need not be of that disposition to
benefit. I was interested to learn that your own
therapist from home is invited to join you at
the Ranch and work with you there whenever
possible.

By the way, a Christmas holiday retreat for a
maximum of 24 participants is given annually
starting the day after Christmas. This workshop
introduces you to Native American traditions,
including the use of the "sweat lodge" and crafts
projects where you can fashion a ceremonial
drum and go into the woods to find your own
"intention stick" which you will then decorate.
Speaking of these activities, David showed me
a wonderful totem pole now lying on its side,
waiting to be painted (and weathered). When
completed, it will stand between two distinctive trees down in the canyon, a perfect spot
for a totem pole.

I feel I could go on endlessly about this "place
of rest, place of healing and place of opportunity" but I invite you to write for their printed
materials and talk to one of the staff members
about the range of offerings that are available
for you and your family, colleagues and friends.
In its early days, Pocket Ranch was used largely
by women. Today, men and women are repre-

sented about 50-50 and come from all over the country and world.

I should also let you know that to get to the Ranch means that, after you make it to Geyserville (and pass Isis Oasis on the main street), you will be driving for some five miles over a hills-and-dales dirt road in an area called "Pocket Gorge" on geological maps. In other words, you don't get there by mistake and you don't drop in. (You can't; there is a coded security gate to protect the privacy of guests.)

HOURS
•Open year round.

INCIDENTALS
•Presently accommodates approximately 40.
•Handicapped accessibility.
•24-hour emergency staff is on call; two-way radio and helicopter pad for emergencies.
•Outside groups can rent the facilities for their own workshops and conferences.
•Small retail store for sundries. VCR, music tapes, books in main lodge.
•No smoking allowed.
•Write for brochure, names of clinical staff, quarterly newsletter, three-minute videotape, workshop schedules and registration information for STAR Intensives (given six times a year). STAR participants are picked up at the airport and taken to the Ranch.
•Six-month work-exchange programs available.
•Credit cards accepted: MasterCard and Visa.

A Simple Touch

239C Center Street
Healdsburg, CA 95448
(707) 433-6856

Spa #8
map page 60

$$ Cost
☐ Overnight
☐ Program
■ Day Use
☐ Hot Springs
■ Hot Tubs
☐ Sauna
■ Massage
■ Skin Care/Salon
☐ Exercise
☐ Meals
■ Spa Products
☐ Workshops
☐ Children
☐ Pets
☐ Weddings

This sweet day-use-only spa is tucked away behind the Windsor Wine Tasting Room close to the center of the historic town of Healdsburg. Settled by the Pomo Indians, Healdsburg was incorporated in 1867. Like Sonoma, the heart of the town is marked by its Spanish-style plaza which, again like Sonoma, is now surrounded on all sides by shops and businesses that tourists like me can't resist. The day I visited A Simple Touch, I found myself buying a gorgeous Panama hat while my friend picked up a charming clay cat dish with a mouse face on the bottom of the bowl.

Owned and managed by two professional young women, runaways from years of working in Calistoga spas, A Simple Touch has attracted a significant local following. The facility itself is small, attractively furnished and nicely laid out. The lobby area, for example, is spacious and airy, the colors are soft peaches (walls) and blues (carpeting), and the art work on the walls was gathered from the area's local artist population.

In addition to massage (Swedish, shiatsu and

sports massage) are aromatherapy tubs, one-hour and mini-facials, seaweed baths, herbal wraps and, the latest addition, a rose petal wrap. A main distinction here is the Fango mud bath. The only other spas to feature this dehydrated mud powder from Europe are Eurospa in Calistoga (Pine Street Inn) and Mount View Spa. Beth LaBree, who toured me around and had me smelling jars and bottles of wonderfully odiferous substances, was perfectly happy to let me take a pinch of the Fango mud and rub it between my thumb and forefinger. It felt silky fine. Not yet having soaked in it, I can still say with certainty that for anyone who finds the traditional mud bath too hot, too heavy or too claustrophobic, this method of detoxifying the body of impurities is an elegant way to experience the "unbearable lightness of being" open to those willing to take small, delicious watery risks.

Incidentally, you can select an essential oil to be added to the Fango mud or you can "take it neat." Similarly, you can ask to soak in the essential oil of your choice and omit the mud altogether. Select one that best suits your state of mind/body at the time (see the listings under "aromatherapy" in the Glossary of Spa Treatments on page 53). If you aren't sure, tell them how you feel and let them decide; Beth and Karen are walking storehouses of information about aromas and their therapeutic effects and seem delighted to share what they know. (My goal is to someday soak in every one of the essential oils, one at a time, to see for myself whether a given aroma actually does relieve the particular stresses and strains it is purported to do.)

Their one tub room is a good size and, like the lobby, has a light airy feeling. The tub itself dominates the room. It is large and round and, as at Eurospa, once the tub has been drawn for you and the Fango mud has dissolved, you can alter the temperature at any time by just turning on the hot or cold water faucets. Whatever bath you choose, be sure to use the adjacent quiet room to rest and cool down after you exit the tub and before you dress to face the world again.

In each of the two smaller rooms where massages, facials and wraps are done, the massage table is equipped with thick separable cushions that allow a pregnant woman, for example, to do what she thought she'd have to forgo— lie face down without fear of squishing her tiny resident guest. Another innovation Beth and Karen are pleased to have found is a waterproof insulated blanket used for the final stages of the wrap. After you've been swaddled in warm herb-soaked cheesecloth, for example, you'll be wrapped in this special blanket designed to retain the heat of the soaked cheesecloth and spare you any sensations of clamminess.

Whether or not these treatments "detoxify" the body, or "remineralize" the skin or enhance brain and memory has never been a deciding issue for me when I go to a spa. Whatever else it is, an hour or two in this soothing, "scentuous" ambience with a skilled attendant ministering to you throughout and New Age music quietly wafting through the walls is definitely worth making room for in your day.

If your visit to A Simple Touch is part of a day or weekend getaway, you are in luck, because Healdsburg's town plaza now embraces a number of different and equally fine eateries. I especially enjoyed the Ravenous, an unpretentious place next to The Raven theater where you and the children will find something home-cooked and delectable (veggies are all organically grown). When I was last in Healdsburg, I had an early dinner with my friend at the Charcuterie right on Healdsburg Avenue at the edge of the plaza. I had an Italian dish and I found the taste delicious, the presentation elegant, and the service impeccable. My next culinary venture in this gentrified country town will be Matuszek's, featuring Hungarian and European continental dinners, located in the same corner complex as the Charcuterie.

HOURS
•Sunday through Thursday, 9 a.m. to 6 p.m.; Friday and Saturday, 9 a.m. to 9 p.m.

INCIDENTALS
•Reservations must be guaranteed with a credit card.
•Bed and breakfast referrals are available.
•Credit cards accepted: MasterCard and Visa.

Sonoma Mission Inn & Spa

Post Office Box 1447
Sonoma, CA 95476 *or*
18149 Sonoma Highway 12
Boyes Hot Springs, CA 95476
(800) 862-4945 (within CA)
(800) 358-9022 (outside CA)

Spa #9
map page 60

$$$ Cost
■ Overnight
■ Program
■ Day Use
■ Hot Springs
■ Hot Tubs
■ Sauna
■ Massage
■ Skin Care/Salon
■ Exercise
■ Meals
☐ Spa Products
☐ Workshops
■ Children
☐ Pets
■ Weddings

Everything I described in the last edition of *California Spas* remains, and I repeat: Sonoma Mission Inn is like a Southern California spa plunked down in Northern California, offering you the best of both worlds.

The exciting news is that a two-year search for the legendary mineral waters that made this spot famous in the 1800s has paid off. A new source of 135-degree natural, hot, Artesian mineral water was discovered 1,100 feet beneath the Inn. All of Sonoma Mission Inn's pools now boast of this skin-caressing liquid that we in the Bay Area usually had to travel much farther to find. All the more incentive for us to zip over to Sonoma for a weekend, a romantic dinner in the evening, a day of solid R&R, or a beautiful finale to an afternoon tour of the vineyards.

Although it has a history not unlike that of a great many spas throughout the state—once a healing ground to Native Americans, a flashy resort for the post-WWI Charleston set, a charred ruin after a 1923 fire, and a restoration project in 1927 to "replicate a California mission complete with arcade and bell tower"— after WWII, it again fell into desuetude (that wonderful word which conveys so much more elegance than "disuse"), until it was purchased in 1980 by Edward Safdie and transformed by interior designer John Dickenson. It was Dickenson who blended its early Mission architecture (outside) with the best in 1920s decor and 1980s use of color (inside).

The Inn was bought in 1985 by Rahn Properties of Fort Lauderdale. In the year that followed, 70 guest rooms were added, the restaurant, bar and kitchen underwent major remodeling, conference facilities were expanded, and a country-style market was constructed adjacent to the spa-hotel.

The major renovation program accomplished in 1985-1986 earned for Sonoma Mission Inn the four stars issued by Mobil Travel Guide, whose criteria for the award are apparently stringent enough to make it a coveted one among those in the hotel/restaurant business.

Like Rancho La Puerta, Sonoma Mission Inn is a spa whose doors are open to men and women—alone or together—on a year-round basis. According to SMI's literature, guests and visitors range in age from 30 and up and are comprised of singles as well as couples.

Sonoma Mission
Inn & Spa

As with other spa facilities where fitness is a serious part of what they have to offer, SMI designs its programs—both the exercise and the nutrition portions—so that you can take them with you. No one need be told in the 1990s that one week a year of living "right" is not going to do it. The task of a good spa is to compress into a short period of time everything it takes to energize you—physically, mentally, emotionally and sometimes even spiritually—so that you'll continue to take good care of yourself not out of a "have to" decision but out of a "want to" feeling.

If you go to the Inn specifically to take advantage of the spa programs, you'll be given a "spa fitness calendar" that shows what you can look forward to from morning to night. Like other good spas with structured programs, SMI also starts its day with a hike and follows with yoga, aerobics classes, step classes and stretch classes that last until 11 a.m. when tennis (for fun) is part of the schedule.

After a two-hour lunch/leisure break, you are ready for "poolercize," low-impact aerobics, a stretch-and-relax class and advanced or endurance low-impact aerobics. And of course you'll find steam and sauna, herbal wraps, hydrotherapy, facials and massage (Swedish and shiatsu) as well as a fully equipped weight room with Lifecycles and Cybex weight equipment—not to mention complete salon services for women and men. These services can also be had on an *à la carte* basis. Incidentally, SMI has added two treatments fashioned specifically for men: a Swedish massage and a "rejuvenating facial."

Sonoma Mission Inn offers a romantic atmosphere as well as on-purpose fitness regimes. On any given day, you might find a celebrity or two soaking next to you in the warm (cooled to 82 degrees) mineral water pools or working out by your side. For the folks coming up from the southland who want Sonoma's and Napa's famous wine country, a rural atmosphere and slightly cooler weather, but don't want to sacrifice the panache (and conveniences) of a Southern California full-service hotel, SMI is your place. From its wonderfully comfortable lobby providing complimentary fruit and bar service to its gourmet restaurant (with an award-winning chef and a wine list featuring 200 wines), its country-style market with gift selections and café, its tennis courts, sumptuous spa facility, outdoor pools and full-service beauty salon, it is a hands-down winner. Not only that but the staff tell me that Sonoma is a bicycler's heaven.

All of this elegance awaits you in the small country town of Boyes Hot Springs in the scenically rich and wine-beautiful Sonoma Valley.

HOURS
•Open year round.

INCIDENTALS
•Gift certificates are available.
•Spa memberships are available.
•Check for special packages and rates before you go, because they change frequently and re-

Sonoma Mission Inn & Spa

turn clients often are given special discounts.
•Convention facilities are available and wedding parties are welcome.
•Credit cards accepted: MasterCard, Visa and American Express.

Guest enjoys a quiet moment in the natural surroundings of Skylonda Retreat in the Northern California town of Woodside.

Above: *Pedicure at Spa de Jour in Palm Springs.*

Left: *The communal hot tub at Kabuki Hot Spring, San Francisco.*

Below left: *An outdoor evening massage at Marriott's Desert Springs Resort & Spa in Palm Springs.*

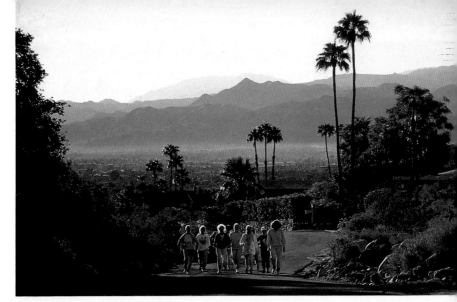

Above: *An early morning walk at The Palms in Palm Springs.*
Below: *Water exercise classes at Skylonda Retreat, Woodside.*

In the Northern California hot spring capital of Calistoga, Roman Spa offers soothing natural mineral pools in a beautiful setting.

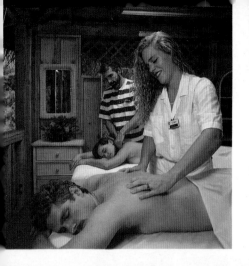

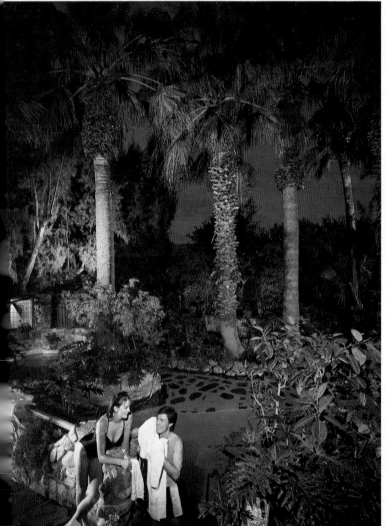

Above left:
Guests lay side by side while being massaged at Two Bunch Palms in Desert Hot Springs.

Above right:
Woman relaxes in a luxurious bath at Mister Lee's Beauty, Hair and Health Spa in San Francisco.

Left:
The often-photographed outdoor mineral pool at Two Bunch Palms.

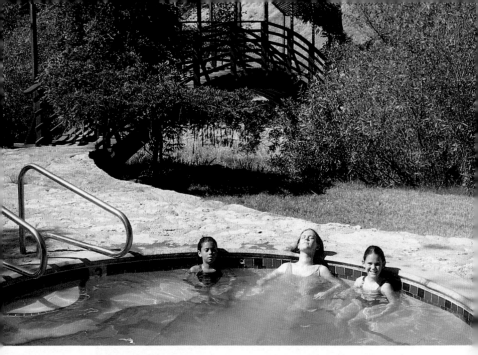

Above: *Families can bathe together in the hot mineral tubs at Vichy Springs in Ukiah.*
Below left: *The elegant accomodations and pool at Sonoma Mission Inn and Spa in Sonoma.*
Below right: *A manicure at Norma Jean's The Beauty Studio in Marin County.*

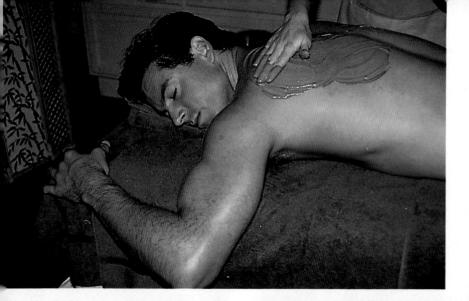

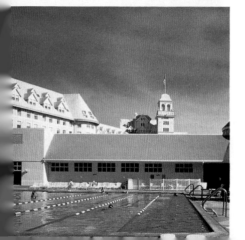

Top: *Thalassotherapy treatment using seaweed at Cal-a-Vie in Vista.*
Above left and right: *At Osmosis in Freestone, you can unwind with an enzyme bath (much different from a traditional mud bath) after sipping tea in the beautiful Japanese gardens.*
Left: *One of the two pools at the Claremont Resort in Oakland.*

Next page: *Above: Spa cuisine at Pocket Ranch Institute, Geyserville. Below: A combination manicure, pedicure and facial at Norma Jean's in Larkspur, Marin County.*

Sonoma Spa

457 First Street West
Sonoma, CA 95476
(707) 939-8770

No longer a brand new spa—the paint wasn't dry when I first reviewed it—the success of Sonoma Spa is no surprise. In the able hands of Bruce Kendall and his sister Lea, owners of Golden Haven and Lincoln Avenue Spa in Calistoga, of course it would thrive.

Sonoma Spa is located right off the plaza in the center of Sonoma, next to other elegant shops that will surprise anyone who hasn't been to the town of Sonoma in awhile. Inside the building, which we were told is a fine example of Greek Revival architecture, you'll walk into a light and airy reception area done in mauves, teals and pinks. The front windows face the historic park and, if you are waiting for a room to open up, sit where you can look out and people-watch.

Six lovely spa treatment rooms are lined up along the corridor that runs from the front of the facility to the back (two rooms are wheel-chair-accessible). Here you can opt for wonderful choices of body treatments, facials and massages corresponding to those offered at their Calistoga spas. There are five body treatments,

Spa #10
map page 60

$-$$ Cost
☐ Overnight
☐ Program
■ Day Use
☐ Hot Springs
☐ Hot Tubs
■ Sauna
■ Massage
■ Skin Care/Salon
☐ Exercise
☐ Meals
■ Spa Products
☐ Workshops
☐ Children
☐ Pets
☐ Weddings

Sonoma Spa

all lasting one luxurious hour:
- a rose petal body masque
- an herbal mineral body mud
- an herbal sea mud
- a cooling body mud (it's all in the mint)
- an herbal wrap

For facials, Sonoma Spa offers:
- special herbal facial (75 minutes)
- a mini-facial (25 minutes)
- an acupressure face-lift (50 minutes)

Massages are classified as "full-body massage" (three types from 50 minutes to $1^3/4$ hours) and "specialty massage" (again, three "flavors," all 25 minutes in duration): back, neck and shoulder massage, a special facial massage (head, face and feet) and foot reflexology. (Incidentally, none of the specialty massages require you to strip down.)

Sonoma Spa has put together various treatment packages for you, or you can customize a package to your own body's yearnings. As at Lincoln Avenue, these treatments can be enjoyed privately or with another. A cedar sauna is also available, whose aromas are worth a deep sniff even if you don't choose to hang out there.

There are wonderful places to eat and shop in this rejuvenated town so I suggest you make a day of it.

HOURS
•Open year round, seven days a week, 9 a.m. to 9 p.m.

INCIDENTALS

Sonoma Spa

•Gift certificates for spa treatments are available at the desk or by telephone.
•California Spa and Facial products are for sale.
•Credit cards accepted: MasterCard, Visa and American Express.

Stewart's Mineral Springs

4617 Stewart Springs Road
Weed, CA 96094
(916) 938-2222
(800) 322-9223

Spa #11
map page 60

$-$$ Cost
■ Overnight
☐ Program
■ Day Use
☐ Hot Springs
■ Hot Tubs
■ Sauna
■ Massage
☐ Skin Care/Salon
☐ Exercise
■ Meals
■ Spa Products
☐ Workshops
☐ Children
■ Pets
■ Weddings

Weed is a small, historic lumber town with a population of some 3,000 and an altitude to match. When you go to Stewart's Mineral Springs on the outskirts of town, I suggest you do as we did and drive into Weed first. It is quite attractive. Everything you need—banks, pharmacies, markets and so forth—seems to be there, and, despite its tourist information office being in a sweet little self-contained building set at a jaunty angle for visibility, Weed is not one of those "cutesy" towns that suffocates you with gift shops and tourist nonsense. A new mural for the downtown area was on the town's agenda for discussion, and there was some talk about the injured bear that had recently shocked people driving south on Interstate 5. (We city folk love things like that. What can I say?)

What is also interesting about Weed is the presence of a thriving "black enclave" as *San Francisco Chronicle* writer Glen Martin put it in his article of July 27, 1993. Apparently, this long-established rural African-American community has lived harmoniously in the town of Weed for a good many years (some since the 1920s). Charles Byrd, an African-American and Siskiyou County's sheriff since 1986, speaks of the "unique social contract that exists between the races in northern Siskiyou County." Apparently, African Americans, Caucasians, Native Americans, Latin Americans and Southeast Asians all live and work side by side in the county and, according to Byrd, don't talk "color" but, rather, "friends." Like all small, rural towns, however, the youngsters evidently are restless and want to move on after high school to at least see the bigger cities.

If you take the Edgewood exit off I-5 and drive on Stewart Springs Road for about five, beautiful, cow-studded miles into a forest canyon of cedar, fir and pine, you'll come to the collection of old wooden structures that tells you you've arrived at Stewart's Mineral Springs. Once inside the bath house that also houses the reception area, I was about to ask my first question—which was how hot their water is when it comes out of the ground. Before I got to it, the person who showed me around announced that the mineral springs water is not hot; they heat it (to about 180 degrees) and store it in a 1,500-gallon holding tank. The next interesting point of information was that their 120-year-old bath house is not insulated and so they remain closed from December 1 to March 1.

The bath house is very appealing. Just beyond a few display cases of Native American-inspired jewelry and vaguely New Age literature and "objets," is a large "Sarah-plain-and-tall" room heated by an old wood-burning stove. The floors are worn wood plank that have yielded to many a weary foot over the years, and a large braided rug covers the main floor area. Straight ahead are showers and dressing cubicles. You'll be given a soft sheet to wrap yourself in as you walk about the common areas; nudity is not permitted. ("We'd like to but the eyes of the world are simply not ready.") To the left are two identical rows of tub rooms, six on each side.

Each small room has a nondescript porcelain bathtub; the only "descript" feature is a heavy rope that hangs over each tub. The mineral water is a slippery friend, and you are encouraged to pull yourself up and out with the help of the rope. (Incidentally, the water is also high in silica, which is abrasive; accordingly, you are advised to sit quietly in it, not to rub it into your skin. The chemical composition of the water is available at the desk if that interests you.) Once in the tub room, you adjust the water temperature yourself. (Instructions are posted on the walls and with water heated to such a high temperature, I would be sure to read the instructions first.)

At the end of this tub corridor is a large redwood sauna. Unique to the sauna is that it houses a wood-burning stove (using cedar logs), something you won't see anywhere else that I know of.

Large outdoor decks around the bath house overlook the marvelous mineral springs that run all through the property. Besides relaxing or sunning yourself on a chaise here, the deck also gives you access to the rushing creek below where you can take a cold plunge any time you want. (The hot dip/cold plunge alternation is standard in Europe, Australia and Japan, and Stewart's apparently sees many of these foreign visitors.)

Stewart's has two massage rooms and four massage therapists. One of the rooms on the outside deck is so close to the rushing creek that no additional music is piped in. Stewart's has just started to do European body wraps and facials. (Somehow they seem incongruous in this rustic facility, but hey!)

Now to the rest of this beautiful property with its lovely, covered walking bridge and foot bridges over Parks Creek leading to its varied accommodations, outdoor Jacuzzi, restaurant and conference hall. The sound of rushing water in Parks Creek is everywhere and accounts for a large measure of Stewart's Mineral Springs' appeal, at least for me. The housing—small one-room cabins with wood-burning stoves, apartment units with kitchens and baths, dormitory units with bath, an A-frame house with five bedrooms, three baths and a fully equipped kitchen, and "authentic Native American style teepees"—are dotted throughout the canyon. Wood is supplied for a nominal charge. No effort has been wasted on color coordinating and putting chocolates on the pillows, but everything is clean and serviceable.

I had earlier read about the unusual Serge's Restaurant in a Bay Area paper, and so enticing was the description I would almost have driven up here for it alone. Serge's, however, was just about to open in town at the time I was there, but another fine restaurant (I was assured) is there now. The restaurant is open on weekends only. If you come to Stewart's Mineral Springs, I would try both eating establishments.

Another unique feature here is the Sweat Lodge where a Karuk medicine man offers "purification sweats." Mount Shasta, peaking at 14,164 feet and visible all around you in Siskiyou County, has long been revered by Native Americans for its spiritual power and healing influence, and many still come to the Springs every Saturday. The Spa Hotel and Mineral Springs in Palm Springs, now managed by the Agua Caliente Band of Cahuilla Indians, shares with Stewart's its unusual contemporary homage to their spa's earliest settlers.

Indeed, according to the folklore, when Southern Pacific put in the railroad in the 1870s, they came up and slaughtered the Native Americans—men, women and children—who occupied the land here. It was when Henry Stewart, near death, was brought to the medicine ground and his health restored that, in reverence and gratitude, he founded Stewart's Mineral Springs. That was in 1875.

Today, Stewart's describes itself as a "famous therapeutic mountain retreat" and invites individuals and groups, large and small, to enjoy its mountain air and healing waters. In addition to its mineral springs, massage therapies and soothing European body treatments, many other recreational activities are available in the area, including skiing, hiking, fishing and river rafting.

HOURS
•Sunday through Wednesday, 10 a.m. to 6 p.m.; Thursday through Saturday, 10 a.m. to 8 p.m.
•Closed December 1 to March 1 annually.

INCIDENTALS
•Available for day use, overnights or extended stays.
•No one under 18 allowed in bath house.
•No smoking.
•Restaurant on site (serves beer and wine).
•Gift certificates are available.
•A variety of accommodations are available, including teepees with rings of fire.
•Conference/meeting/wedding accommodations are available. Special group rates.
•Pets are allowed with a deposit.

Vichy Springs Resort

2605 Vichy Springs Road
Ukiah, CA 95482
(707) 462-9515

Spa #12
map page 60

$$ Cost
■ Overnight
☐ Program
■ Day Use
■ Hot Springs
■ Hot Tubs
☐ Sauna
■ Massage
■ Skin Care/Salon
☐ Exercise
■ Meals
☐ Spa Products
☐ Workshops
■ Children
☐ Pets
■ Weddings

When I first visited the undeveloped property of Vichy Springs in 1987, this spa resort was little more than a gleam in Gil Ashoff's eye. He told me then that his bottling plant would soon be in operation so that Vichy Springs' historic water could be imbibed. That accomplished, his long-range plan was to restore Vichy Springs to its turn-of-the-century heyday when famed artist Grace Hudson, along with Jack London, Mark Twain, Ulysses S. Grant and Teddy Roosevelt, among other luminaries, came for the healing waters then touted as "The Famous Champagne Baths." A full century later, the new Vichy is thriving.

The bottling plant is capable of turning out 24,000 bottles of Vichy Springs mineral water every day. This "pure naturally carbonated alkaline mineral water" flows from its deep spring source 700 feet away at the rate of 150,000 gallons a day, and is bottled within seconds. The decision to take on this massive project came after Gil and Marjorie completed a world-wide tour of mineral water resorts. "We found the water at Vichy Springs simply the best there is," Gil said.

It's very exciting to see the restoration of a site like this, and to read a brochure from 1915 with its ornate prose ("leave behind the follies of fashion, the unnatural life of town and city") and its extravagant claims ("...the water checks the excessive secretion of acid, neutralizes the excess of acid already present, stimulates intestinal action, promotes digestion and the local and general well-being of the patient.") The recreations Vichy boasted of at that time ranged from lawn tennis to billiards to trap shooting at the Vichy Gun Club.

But the water! In these historically rich hot springs areas, it is always about the water—its healing properties, chemical composition, drinkability or the simple luxuriant feel of it on your skin. Whether you regard it as "sodic, calcic, magnesic, bircarbonated [sic], alkaline-saline, borated and carbon-dioxated" or as "closely resembling the famous waters from Grand Grille Springs of Vichy, France," or as "simply the best there is," what makes Vichy, and has for some time, is its water.

Vichy Springs takes up approximately 700 acres that was once part of 35,000-some acres known as the Yokayo Rancho in 1845. The site is now registered as California's 980th historical landmark. In addition to restoring a dozen rooms and two historic cottages, the Ashoffs took one of the old structures and turned it into a private school now run by Marjorie.

Vichy Springs Resort

Vichy Springs Resort invites conferences, weddings (October to March, only) and other large outdoor events, and has been very popular with men and women for its excellent massage, foot reflexology, herbal facials and, of course, hot mineral water baths. It also has charming picnic areas in a pine forest near Little Grizzly Creek and, a 30-minute hike away, a lovely waterfall.

Now let me tell you about the unique 130-year-old tubs on the hillside. It's not that they look 130 years old—with the rainbow of discoloration from years of mineral deposits, they do—but what totally intrigued me was that each tub has a large stopper, which, when removed, allows this splendiferous water to come gushing in. I love the paradox of using a stopper to keep the water from coming in rather than to keep it from draining out. These outdoor tubs are lined up in a row overlooking the property. Besides these old mineral baths, the Ashoffs have put in a new (round) hot mineral spa "set in an ancient travertine onyx formation." And, of course, there is an Olympic-size swimming pool filled with luxuriant spring water—a favorite for lap swimming. (The pool is unheated and so is open in the summer only.)

Like some of the other spas in this guidebook, Vichy has much more to rave about. But one has to draw a line somewhere. (I didn't tell you about the French government sending geologists to Vichy in 1979 to test the water, nor did I mention the awards that Vichy Springs water has won, nor the presidential dinner receptions the Ashoffs once attended in Washington, D.C. where their water was served, nor the educational foundation they have started. The list goes on.)

Vichy is one of a dwindling number of spas that are open for day use. My recommendation is that locals use the day trip as a sampler, and then come back for a relaxing week or more. As I said in the earlier edition of this book, "Gil and Marjorie have elaborate plans for the future, so don't be surprised when you visit if there's even more to show and tell."

That still goes.

HOURS
•Open during daylight hours.

INCIDENTALS
•Expanded continental breakfast and use of all mineral baths included in lodging price.
•Baths open 24 hours for overnight guests.
•Bathing suits required.
•All rooms have private baths and all buildings are designated no smoking.
•RV parking available.
•Facilities for weddings and large parties.
•Direct-dial telephones in all units.
•All accommodations have individual heating and air-conditioning units.
•Close by: Mendocino coast, wineries, Grace Hudson Museum and the Skunk train to Fort Bragg. Lake Mendocino is 10 minutes away for watersports.
•Credit cards accepted: all major credit cards.

White Sulphur Springs

3100 White Sulphur Springs Road
St. Helena, CA 94574
(707) 963-8588
(707) 963-2890 fax

Spa #13
map page 60

$$ Cost
■ Overnight
☐ Program
■ Day Use
■ Hot Springs
☐ Hot Tubs
☐ Sauna
■ Massage
■ Skin Care/Salon
☐ Exercise
■ Meals
■ Spa Products
☐ Workshops
■ Children
☐ Pets
■ Weddings

Big changes at White Sulphur Springs! It is now being leased to the same people who just completed the Mount View Spa in the historic Mount View Hotel in Calistoga. Under the knowledgeable hand of Reinhard Bergel (former owner of Valley Spa and Rehabilitation Clinic in Castro Valley) both Mount View and White Sulphur Springs provide two great additions to the Calistoga area. For White Sulphur Springs, the renovations mark yet another chapter in the rich historical life of this retreat.

A 330-acre property of redwood, fir and madrone, White Sulphur Springs is another of those spa resorts whose history dates back to early Native American settlers and, later, at the turn of the century, evolved into a sought-after hideaway for such celebrities as Clark Gable and Kay Spreckels. Before owners Betty and Buzz Foote purchased it as a healthy place to raise a family, it was occupied by a boys' camp (1951), the United Methodist Conference (1957), and a Hadassah youth center (1974).

An Illustrated Guide to White Sulphur Springs resides in U.C. Berkeley's Bancroft Library for history buffs to read about the resort as it was in the late 1800s when all of its buildings and cottages—including the music hall, the laundry and baths, the stables and the original hotel—were flourishing. In this guide, M.L.W. Towle devotes many stanzas to what was described in local newspapers of the day as "the most select and fashionable of our watering places." The saga of the Springs, exciting as it is, is too long to reprint here. The Footes have collected an enormous amount of memorabilia, however, with plans to assemble it all into a book.

The structures that remain in this splendid wooded area—the original bathhouse, the Carriage House, the former dance pavilion and the creekside cottages originally built in the 1920s—have all been modernized to the right degree. There has been no attempt to turn White Sulphur Springs' simple country digs into a citified facility. (Although I do miss the pungent smell of sulphur that used to hang in the air.) And the future plans are exciting.

Right now, for example, only one of its several free-flowing mineral water springs has been opened up for use. This rock-lined pool stays at approximately 85 to 92 degrees year round. But the Olympic-size pool will be open soon, as will its new Health Center, which was still under construction when I was there. There are to be six or seven massage/treatment rooms, each one with high windows looking out to the steep hillside. Also in Bergel's vision is to have tubs nestled into the hillside for open-air soaking.

Until this shift in management, White Sulphur Springs was a quiet, rustic retreat for hikers, meditators and groups looking for a serene meeting space (or wedding site) away from the clamor and clatter. As a spa, it had the one outdoor pool and one massage practitioner. Now, the Health Center will be staffed by a strong massage therapy staff and will offer facials, herbal wraps and volcanic mud wraps. Bergel feels that nothing less than a full-hour massage makes sense, so don't skimp on this one.

All of its varied types of accommodations— a room at the Inn (the old Dance Pavilion), an upstairs bedroom with shared bath in the Carriage House, or one of its creekside cottages, each with its own little front patio area—are very simple. Clean sheets, good beds, ceiling fans and small sitting areas are it—no chocolate on the pillow. (Unless something has been done to fix it, the floor of one cottage is so tipsy that the Footes dubbed it "The Titanic.") This section of the property also has picnic tables and a large basketball court.

For conferences, White Sulphur Springs offers the old lodge, a 2,000 square-foot building with a massive stone fireplace. Smaller groups are invited to use the Creekside Room and the Carriage House lounge. In good weather, the Indian Meadow and large lawn area are also perfect for groups. The old dining hall, the building that suffered the most in past disasters, has been refurbished and is reserved mostly for groups who bring in their own caterer. (The staff will also make catering arrangements for you.) The hall accommodates 120 guests.

Further up the drive is a nifty grandmother's cottage that the Footes restored beautifully for the use of Buzz's mother. It looks so crisp in its coat of gleaming white paint that you would not guess it was the very first building constructed on the property in 1852. Built for the owner and subsequently used to house White Sulphur Springs' managers through the years, it is designated in early photographs simply as "the owner-managers' cottage." A plaque was installed to name the cottage the "Alstrom House" after Sophie Alstrom Mitchell, a famed local watercolorist who lived there and raised her six daughters from 1862 to 1882.

Above the Alstrom House is a beautiful redwood grove with benches and picnic tables and, off to one side, a volleyball court. This romantic grove is another place that lends itself to outdoor events. In fact, the Footes' nephew wanted his wedding to be there and so he and Buzz worked hard, by themselves, to put in the massive wooden bridge that takes you across the little stream to the grove. (According to Betty Foote, this "little stream" was a raging river in the floods of 1986.)

As a guest, when you're not being facialed, wrapped and massaged, soaking in the waters or playing volleyball, you can take time out to enjoy the miles of hiking trails in the immediate area. Then, when you've had all the physical exertion or serenity you can endure, the Napa Valley wineries and other wisps of civilization are a short car trip away.

The new management has put out its own brochure, which includes directions for getting to White Sulphur Springs. Somehow I prefer the advice given in 1868: "From San Francisco, take the steamboat at Market Street Wharf..."

HOURS
- Open daily 9 a.m. to 6 p.m.

INCIDENTALS
- Day use is available for a nominal fee.
- Private rooms, shared baths, creekside cottages.
- Continental breakfast.
- Catering can be arranged.
- Weekly and monthly rates are generally available.
- Wedding "destination site" accommodations are negotiable.
- Advance deposit is required with reservation. 72-hour cancellation notice is requested for refund of deposit.
- Two-night minimum stay is not required on weekends and holidays.
- No room telephones or televisions.
- Credit cards accepted: MasterCard, Visa and American Express. Personal checks are also accepted.

Wilbur Hot Springs Health Sanctuary

3375 Wilbur Springs Road
Williams, CA 95987
(916) 473-2306

"Wilbur Hot Springs is the site of a turn-of-the-century hotel, 22 miles from the nearest town." So introduces Wilbur's very nicely presented flyer with its appealing logo depicting the soles of a contented man's feet—or rather the appealing feet of a contented and soulful man! Whatever, Wilbur is my kind of country spa. It fits my picture of what a country spa should be without going too far in either direction—the rustic or the precious.

All of the pictures you're likely to see of Wilbur's main lodge, restored many times since the original structure went up in the 1800s, are deceiving. I have to say this for the handful of people out there who, like me, visualize themselves driving into Wilbur and having the postcard view of the lodge in the distance. Not possible. The pictures were taken from across Sulphur Creek, whereas you will be driving parallel to it and pulling up alongside the build-

Spa #14
map page 60

$$ Cost
■ Overnight
☐ Program
■ Day Use
■ Hot Springs
■ Hot Tubs
■ Sauna
■ Massage
☐ Skin Care/Salon
☐ Exercise
☐ Meals
☐ Spa Products
☐ Workshops
■ Children
☐ Pets
■ Weddings

ing to unload before moving your car to an out-of-sight lot down the road. The only way to get the postcard perspective on this historic lodge is to cross the creek yourself (and brave the snakes).

Wilbur's evolution was similar to that of many hot springs in the northern and southern parts of the state: first used by Native Americans and much later developed as a place that outsiders from all over could come to take the supposedly curative waters. Different in this spa's history is the period when Wilbur was a stage stop for the goldrushers. In its more recent history—the property was bought in the early 1970s by psychologist Richard Miller who had worked closely with Fritz Perls—it is described as a "health sanctuary." Miller had come to agree with Perls that years of psychotherapy with clients across a desk couldn't hold a candle to what could be accomplished in weeks of a residential treatment program.

In those early years at Wilbur, Miller focused on providing psychologically oriented seminars and workshops in this tranquil hot springs setting where the body could be as engaged as the mind in the healing process. That "focus" is no longer present. Miller then went to work with substance abusers, maintaining an office at Wilbur where he came once a month to give a CokeEnders seminar.

If you want to know more about Wilbur's evolution, you'll find a huge scrapbook laid out on the coffee table in the enormous group room (with billiard tables, guitars, a piano, wood flutes and a fireplace) that leads into the dining room and community kitchen. It takes a little muscle to turn its oversized pages, but the energy expended is worth it.

A major change from when I was here last is Wilbur's conversion from kerosene lamps to solar power. They are very proud that converted sunlight is now their power source throughout the hotel.

The baths at Wilbur are different from any you'll see elsewhere. They are situated immediately across the gravel driveway from the lodge, hiding behind a long shoji-like fence put into the ground at staggered heights to follow the contours of the terrain instead of forcing it into submission. This design was worked out by the staff after much consultation about what would be the most pleasing way to screen the nude bathers from the main drive.

The complex of "watering holes" you'll find on the other side of the fence includes a small free-form swimming pool, a terraced area for sunbathing and a gracefully roofed bathhouse that holds three long trough-like pools whose water temperature ranges from a gentle 98 degrees to a hot 112 degrees. You have 24-hour use of the waters (hushed voices here at all times).

You can wear a swimsuit in the pools if you want to, although we noticed that the naked folks left our pool for another as soon as they spotted the fabric on our bodies. Or so we imagined. Everyone must wear a cover-up walking across from the lodge to the baths and back.

Nudity is not permitted on the lodge side of the fence, and food is not permitted on the bath side.

The charms of Wilbur are too many to fully describe here, but the highlights must be mentioned. In first position is the huge, well-stocked (cookware, dinnerware, utensils, spices, etc.) community kitchen, where you would not believe the elaborate meals some people were cooking up while we were there. Somehow I had imagined a homogeneous group of raw vegetable eaters and certainly not gourmet gourmands doing pasta, salad, wine and laughter from 7 p.m. to 10 p.m.—and I won't even talk about the breakfasts.

Second in my book of warm memories is the sweetness of the rooms (20 of them) with their wicker tables, old spring beds, softly worn oak dressers and lace curtains; the bright sunlight that streams down from the skylight over the penthouse area and steep, narrow staircase below; the very attractive 18-bed community sleeping room, inviting even to a cranky loner like me; the charming second-story verandas; the artist-in-residence program that does not judge your art but, rather, you and your commitment to and rapport with Wilbur; yesteryear's velvety parlor just off the lobby area in the lodge; and the staff, who are present and available to just the right degree. My only plea would be to have a shower installed in a couple of the bathrooms in the main lodge instead of only in the outdoor bathhouse area. Having to walk across the roadway to shower—well that, to me, is where precious leaves off and rustic begins.

Individual massages available to guests are the commonly requested Swedish, Esalen and shiatsu, plus the trademarked Tragerwork, deep tissue work and lymphatic massage. Interestingly, Wilbur recommends that tall people (5'9" and over), overweight people and anyone under considerable stress sign up for an hour-and-a-half session.

If you like walking, there is no shortage of hiking trails. And, while you can ride into town if you're willing to take the four-mile bumpy gravel road in and out, there's really not much town to see.

You would be better off using Wilbur as a retreat—one that you design yourself, whether it means unwinding with good food, hot soaks, long walks and all the massages you can afford, or curling up by the fire with a good book or three and/or meeting new people over the sharing of good food and hot mineral water soaks. I don't need to tell city folk that just gazing up at the lacy coverlet of stars in country where no electric light is around is like watching the aurora borealis.

Incidentally, the artwork on the walls in the dining room and elsewhere is wonderful. Take note of the papercuts that give a surreal, almost high-tech impression of the actual site of the old geothermal springs you'll see marked along the dirt road as you go back toward the (out of sight) parking lot.

Besides comfortable clothing, bring extra

shoes regardless of whether you're a hiker. You are requested to leave your "outdoor" shoes outside on the porch to keep down the dust in the lodge. (Besides the high temperature of that one tub, the other Japanese motif you'll find here is the lineup of assorted shoes and boots on the front porch.) I also would suggest you bring a thermos so that you can have hot cocoa in your room at night or have your coffee ready for you in the morning. Wilbur adds that you should bring towels, soap, a flashlight (definitely), a robe and some warm clothes for cool nights. Other things to bring, whether for your kitchen use or for the community sleeping quarters if you opt for that over a private room, will be communicated to you at the time you reserve a space.

If you want, you can even reserve the whole hotel for a four-figure dollar amount per night. (Wilbur staff and a variable number of artists-in-residence live on the property, and so even if you take up the entire lodge, you won't be alone.)

Because of the relative remoteness of Wilbur, you might like to know that the fire station is at the crossroads of Highways 16 and 20, right at the entrance to the four-mile gravel road into Wilbur, and that ambulance and paramedics arrive in three to four minutes. Helicopters also are able to move into the valley if the access road is blocked for any reason.

HOURS
•Open year round.

INCIDENTALS
•Holiday reservations require one-month advance notice.

•Free use of all pools to overnight guests.

•The very attractive Group Room is approximately half the price of private room accommodations. Only children 13 and over are permitted in the Group Room, and they must be accompanied by an adult.

•For the serenity of the other guests, Wilbur places a maximum on the number of children it will allow at any one time. Check when you make your reservation. Families with children staying in private rooms are housed on the first floor only. Children two years old and under are free. You are expected to supervise children attentively. They are not allowed in the library.

•A private apartment at the rear of the lodge also can be rented, and the entire hotel can be reserved for group use.

•Bottled waters and juices, snack foods, T-shirts, postcards, insect repellant and sunscreen lotion sold in lobby area.

•You can reserve refrigerator space in the kitchen.

•Smoking in designated outside area only.

•No nudity except in bathhouse and pool area.

•Credit cards accepted: MasterCard and Visa. Credit cards are necessary for telephone reservations. All credit card transactions add a 5% surcharge to your bill.

Willow

6517 Dry Creek Road
Napa Valley, CA 94558
(707) 944-8173

Spa #15
map page 60

$$ Cost
■ Overnight
☐ Program
■ Day Use
☐ Hot Springs
■ Hot Tubs
■ Sauna
■ Massage
☐ Skin Care/Salon
☐ Exercise
☐ Meals
☐ Spa Products
☐ Workshops
■ Children
☐ Pets
■ Weddings

Willow is most comfortable regarding itself as a retreat. It has no fitness program or elaborate spa services, it is not a resort (no restaurant, salon or horseback riding), nor is it a historical landmark or a Native American healing ground.

With its solar-heated swimming pool, lovely outdoor hot pool (102 degrees), massage pavilion, redwood sauna, hillside tennis court, vineyard, hiking trails, fruit trees, fully equipped community kitchen and dining room that are sparkling clean, not to mention its adorable bunny rabbits, its chickens, and its cats (Molokai—"Molly"—rules the house), whatever kind of spa it is, Willow deserves the highest possible rating.

Its 40-acre facility, owned, managed and tended by Liz, Leslie and Christina (and Leslie's daughter Natasha, who tends the animals among other chores), exudes *womanness*. Don't ask me what that quality is. I do know it's not simply that each of its nine distinctive guest rooms is named after an accomplished woman—from Joan of Arc to Geraldine Ferraro. It is more a gentle, nurturing presence that seems to linger over every inch of this hillside retreat.

The quiet care these women take of the property and their guests is expressed in a myriad of details. You feel it in the comfortable and spacious living room with its fireplace (where a piano and guitar are there for you to play), in the light pine furniture of the dining area, in the carefully selected photographs and other art work on the walls, in the decorative touches and color combinations that distinguish each room, in the diffused light from the many skylights throughout the main building, in their special vegetable garden (Leslie and Christina cook a brunch on those weekends when groups are not having their own caterers) and everywhere outside. In the evenings, tiny Christmas lights draped over the bushes and trees illuminate the grounds. Guests are asked to observe quiet time after 10 p.m. and before 8 a.m.

If you don't stay in one of the rooms inside the main house, you can reserve the Barn, a spacious self-contained building with its own kitchen, wood-burning stove, bath and deck, or the Bunkhouse, a long, narrow structure that sleeps up to four—great for those who want to spend the least possible, although all of the room rates are very affordable. Willow can also accommodate groups: 32 overnighters and, for wedding and birthday celebrations, as many as 100 day-users.

Four massage therapists are on call. Swedish massage is the most requested, but each thera-

Willow

pist has been trained in other bodywork forms as well, so if you especially want foot reflexology or polarity therapy, mention it when you make your reservation.

HOURS
•Open year round. Reservations from 8:30 a.m. to 8:30 p.m.

INCIDENTALS
•No smoking in buildings.
•No portable stereos.
•No camping.
•Wheelchair-accessible.
•The TV in the dining room is used only for significant happenings (Wimbledon tennis match, for example).
•Clothing optional in pool/tub area only.
•Day use (when not reserved for a group).
•Group meeting space in living room and dining room. Can bring in catering service.
•Work-exchange available: five hours of work gets you one free night's lodging.
•Credit cards accepted: MasterCard and Visa.

Calistoga
Spas

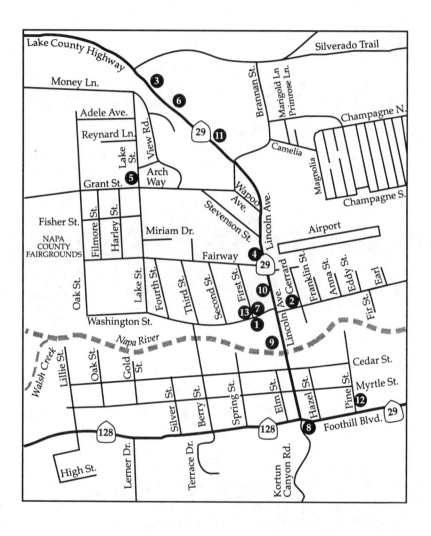

Down Lincoln Avenue: An Introduction to Calistoga

Changes have taken place in Calistoga since I last wrote it up, but, happily, Calistoga has a way of absorbing change with style and grace. Nothing, to my eye, at least, has disturbed the easy country feel of this very special place which, long before Sam Brannan founded it in 1859, has been giving up its healing waters and volcanic mud for our health and pleasure. As the story goes, it was Brannan who inadvertently called this goldmine of mineral water and volcanic ash "the Calistoga of Sarifornia" instead of what he intended—"the Saratoga of California." History buffs can drop in to the Sharpsteen Museum and learn about the early days when the Wappo Indians had it to themselves.

Although a few more facilities have popped up in recent years, what remains the same, remains the same. My favorite eatery, Checkers, I found to be thriving. The old-timers—Nance's (where changes are deliberately few and far between) and Doc Wilkinson's (where modernizing is accomplished as gracefully as in the town proper)—still staunchly uphold Calistoga's traditions, and the visiting populations still shift from the beer-and-pretzels bunch in the summer to the wine-and-cheese set in the winter. I love it all, and I still find Calistoga to be a town I can move around in by myself without feeling alone. True, there has been a major marketing push in most of the spas here to cater to couples, but I do not have the feeling that I have to be coupled to enjoy my stay.

Calistoga has long attracted people who come for the presumed curative powers of its hot mineral waters and the detoxifying effects of its mineral-rich volcanic ash mud baths. As decades passed and medical practices became increasingly more scientifically based, the healing powers of the waters and the mud were regarded more as folklore than fact.

From the '70s on, however, with the resurgence of interest in alternative healing, it seems that what the older folk have held to all along—common-sense preventive care, family doctors and do-it-yourself remedies—are now part of the general conversation about health care at both the personal and policy level. (Did you know that social scientists have found that, on average, it takes 19 years for a new social concept to become part of mainstream thinking?) At any rate, Americans are beginning to recognize that Western medicine and folk medicine, or alternative medicine, are not mutually exclusive: they can and should coexist harmoniously.

All of that preachy talk is to say that, whatever language we feel most comfortable with—

neuralgia and lumbago or tension and stress or therapy and healing—it does not really matter to a body neck deep in hot mineral water or in a tub of steaming mud. Common sense says to listen to your body, to be cautious about high heat therapies, to know when it's time to cool down, and, as the Greeks told us millennia ago, to do all things in moderation. Calistoga's spas provide a superb balance of traditional and new, and of do-it-yourself and be-done-to treatments.

The upscaling that has gone on in Calistoga over the past several years—first the refurbishing of the old Mount View Hotel and now its addition of a spa in the best European tradition, the opening of the Lavender Hill Spa by John Cashman of International Spa, the appearance of the Calistoga Massage Center and Doc Wilkinson's continual expansion of services—are, as I said in the previous edition, as important for what they have *not* touched as for what they have.

I noted then that when Lincoln Avenue Spa went in, care was taken to preserve the basic brick structure of the old bank building in which it is housed, that the Calistoga Gliderport still has its big, lumbering gliders lolling about like huge sleeping birds, and that if Funke's department store isn't as funky as it once was, neither are we. All of that is still true.

If you are a twosome or group wanting to spend a romantic day or two of pleasure in this area, I still suggest you call (as far ahead as possible) the Château Montelena Winery on Tubbs Lane and reserve one of their two small picnic islands for lunch. The only charge the winery makes is your Scout's honor to treat the area as you would a gift of priceless value, which is what it is. The rules for its use are strict (no more than 10 people per island) and must be if they are to continue to open these areas to the public. Next, make a reservation to stay at one of the spas that appeals to you, or the Mount View Hotel, or the delightful Brannan Cottage Inn on Wappo Avenue near the end of town, or one of many bed and breakfast inns on the outskirts of town.

Once in the car and on your way to Calistoga, stop at the Oakville Grocery in Oakville (two miles north of St. Helena) and select cheeses, pâtés, olives, breads, fruits and wine from an outrageous choice of fine produce and deli foods. After you've registered in the place of your choice, go out and explore the town. Pick up Mattioli's *In Your Pocket Guide* to Calistoga; it lists just about everything except the newest places I want you to see: the Calistoga Massage Center and the Calistoga Bubble Shop (separately owned but housed together in the old hardware store) and the fantastic garden café-restaurant, Wappo's. Both are on Washington Street just off Lincoln Avenue. Wappo's is visually wonderful—warm wood and copper-topped tables inside and a lush garden patio outside where you look up from your table to see thick clusters of grapes hanging down from the lattice work overhead. More important, the food is exquisite. Wappo's also serves wines and beers, but I recommend the Javanese iced coffee—"exquisite" does not begin to describe it.

As you stroll up and down Lincoln Avenue, pop into the new Mount View Hotel and tour its spa. Drop into the lounge for a drink. Then browse through the bookstore and the many small stores selling art, ceramics and jewelry (unexpectedly high-quality work for a small country town). At the top of Lincoln Avenue is a bicycle rental shop, a second-hand store I never can resist and, around the corner on Foothill, the new Lavender Hill Spa created especially to attract couples who want to enjoy their treatments together.

Cross over to the Chamber of Commerce housed in the old train depot (the shops in the Depot are a tourist attraction themselves) and gather up more information on what's available to you in this wonderful northern country area.

For example, the Petrified Forest is not that far away—continue a little north on Highway 29 (which becomes 128) and turn left on the Petrified Forest Road that comes in at the sign indicating Santa Rosa. They have some amazing specimens of excavated trees and marine life preserved over thousands of years. (If you missed out on Château Montelena's islands, the Petrified Forest is also a pleasant place to take a picnic lunch—and it's FREE.)

Or for more adventure, talk to the Once in a Lifetime Balloon Company about a sunrise balloon ride. (They describe themselves as the "Cadillac of balloon companies" because, unlike others, their after-the-ride breakfast is a brunch at one of the local restaurants.)

I already told you that I can't "do" Calistoga without stopping at Checkers, either to get a designer pizza, a great sandwich or a construct-it-yourself "healthy" sundae of non-fat or low-fat frozen yogurt and fruit and nut toppings. (Some more decadent toppings are available if you are entirely without shame.)

There's much more here—wineries and the Old Faithful geyser, of course, and the lovely Pioneer Cemetery for those who take pleasure in meandering through historic graveyards. Suffice it to say that Calistoga has many faces, and with a little planning and ingenuity you can put together a surprising variety of vacations or day trips, each one distinctly different from the one before.

On to the spas…

The Calistoga Massage Center

1220 Washington Street, Suite 5
Calistoga, CA 94515
(707) 942-6193

Calistoga, Northern California's hot springs mecca, continues to find room for entrepreneurs to expand or start new ventures. The Calistoga Massage Center, small, sweet and different (it focuses on massage, leaving the mineral water pools to its neighboring businesses) offers "quality bodywork in the heart of town."

Open for almost two years as of this writing, the facility's three treatment rooms are on the second floor of one of Calistoga's old hardware stores (whose brick walls and heavy wooden steps remain). When you first walk in, you might see people in the lobby area waiting to see others who share these premises, but, before you turn to go upstairs, do take the path of least resistance directly in front of you and walk through the Calistoga Bubble Bath. This adorable shop sells everything you need to create your own spa experience at home (including music and relaxation tapes) and/or to pick up as gifts for those who envied your taking this trip to Calistoga.

Spa #1
map page 142

$$ Cost
☐ Overnight
☐ Program
■ Day Use
☐ Hot Springs
☐ Hot Tubs
☐ Sauna
■ Massage
■ Skin Care/Salon
☐ Exercise
☐ Meals
■ Spa Products
☐ Workshops
☐ Children
☐ Pets
☐ Weddings

The Calistoga Massage Center

Now to the upstairs haven. Owner Michelle Satur's main concern is that each client receive friendly, individualized service. If you want to "zone out" or keep the massage therapist focused on a problem area, or talk to her as she works to learn more about your body, it's up to you. For your therapeutic massage, you can select a half-hour massage focused on your back, neck, shoulders and feet; a half-hour acupressure massage; one hour of foot reflexology or full-body massage; or a longer (one-and-a-half-hour) "leisurely full-body massage." In the trend toward accommodating couples traveling together, she offers a "massage for two" (one hour each at a slight discount) and, something I have not seen elsewhere, two hours of massage instruction which includes a half-hour of massage and a half-hour of instruction for each person in the twosome.

You can also take advantage of one of her "pamper packages"—"The Cocoon" (an aromatherapy blanket wrap including foot bath, mini-facial and foot and scalp massage), "Head, Hand & Foot Heaven" (an aromatherapy foot bath and scrub along with a foot, ankle, head, neck and scalp massage), and an "Herbal Facial Treatment" that gives you a hand, foot, neck and shoulder massage. I understand from Michelle that she also works on people with special concerns, such as frail elderly or those with osteoporosis.

It was Michelle who led me to the fantastic new restaurant-café next door, the Wappo. Don't leave Calistoga without trying it.

HOURS
•Open Sunday to Thursday, noon to 8 p.m.; Friday, noon to 10 p.m.; Saturday, 10 a.m. to 10 p.m.
•Morning hours available by appointment.

INCIDENTALS
•Discounts for students and seniors, Upper Valley residents and employees.
•Tuesday through Thursday specials.
•Credit cards accepted: all major credit cards.

Calistoga Spa Hot Springs

1006 Washington Street
Calistoga, CA 94515
(707) 942-6269

Spa #2
map page 142

$$ Cost
■ Overnight
☐ Program
■ Day Use
■ Hot Springs
■ Hot Tubs
■ Sauna
■ Massage
☐ Skin Care/Salon
■ Exercise
☐ Meals
☐ Spa Products
☐ Workshops
■ Children
☐ Pets
☐ Weddings

Calistoga Spa remains a favorite of those who head to Calistoga on a regular basis. It has been under the same capable management for many years. A major attraction here are the four mineral pools, always happily peopled by motel guests and day-trippers (although guests still get priority on busy days). You have your choice of an 83-degree L-shaped swimming pool for lap swimming (82^1/$_2$' by 24'), a 100-degree soaking pool (40' by 20'), a 105-degree octagonal jet pool (24') for adults only, and a 90-degree wading pool, 12" to 18" deep (20' by 13'). The area around the pools is nicely landscaped and provides ample seating and tables. A refreshment stand is also in close range. Overnight guests can use the pools from 8 a.m. to 10 p.m. and day-users can drop in from 8:30 a.m. to 9 p.m.

The bathhouse, separated into women's and men's quarters, houses the mud baths and Jacuzzi mineral water tubs in a light airy space laid out so that the attendants can work from the center of the room. A steam room, blanket wrap and massage areas, and dressing room/ locker space are also located here. As elsewhere in Calistoga, mud baths are sterilized after each use by flushing with mineral water at 180-200 degrees Fahrenheit.

Beyond the reception area and lobby is a large exercise room equipped with Universal weight machines, exercise bicycles, a rowing machine and dumbbells that can be used for a fee. Aerobics classes are held here, led by instructors from the City of Calistoga's Recreation Department. On a second story of this wing are conference facilities for up to 40 persons. Amenities here include a wet bar, kitchen, Swedish fireplace and an outdoor deck from which one can look out to Mount St. Helena.

As in many Calistoga spas, the unspoken convention seems to be that the spa will provide you with the best they have to offer in services, but you are expected to manage your own stay according to your own needs and desires. The attendants are there to monitor your time in the mud and steam baths, to provide you with the space and towels you'll need, and to show you where to go next—but don't expect anyone to "hold your hand" or to put together a "package" for you.

HOURS
•Open year round, 8:30 a.m. to 9 p.m.

INCIDENTALS
•All rooms are equipped for light housekeeping

Calistoga Spa
Hot Springs

with cooktops, refrigerators, dishes, utensils, etc., and all have color cable TV, telephones and air conditioning.

•Family units are available and so is a unit called The Suite.

•A three-night minimum stay is required from June 15 through September 15.

•48-hour cancellation notice is required.

•Special seasonal and other discounts apply.

•Series tickets for use of pools and aerobics classes are available.

•Daily and monthly rates.

•Gift certificates are available.

•Call for rates on Palisades Conference Room.

•Credit cards accepted: MasterCard and Visa.

Calistoga Village
Inn and Spa

1880 Lincoln Avenue
Calistoga, CA 94515
(707) 942-0991
(800) 543-1094

The relatively new Calistoga Village Inn and Spa has now found its place in the Calistoga community. Its location, at the very end of Lincoln Avenue within inches of where the lovely Silverado Trail comes in, has distinct assets: It is away from the bustle of town and, unlike any of the other Calistoga spas, the area just behind the facility looks out to an unobstructed view of the mountains in the distance. Another unique feature is its adjoining restaurant, now called the Lincoln Avenue Grill.

When I was last there, I was impressed with the upgrading and beautification that had taken place since my previous visit—in its 32 units, in the charming garden-encircled spa facility in the back, and in the deck and picnic area around its pools. Adults looking for primo spa treatments, and families with children looking for a place to splash and picnic, can be very comfortable here.

Most of the small row-cottages facing Lin-

Spa #3
map page 142

$$ Cost
■ Overnight
☐ Program
☐ Day Use
■ Hot Springs
■ Hot Tubs
■ Sauna
■ Massage
■ Skin Care/Salon
☐ Exercise
■ Meals
☐ Spa Products
☐ Workshops
■ Children
☐ Pets
☐ Weddings

Calistoga Village Inn and Spa

coln Avenue (41 of them) have pleasant sitting/ dining rooms adjacent to the bedroom. If you're staying with someone who wants to sleep when you want to be up reading a paper, this is a welcome arrangement. In any case, it gives you room to spread out. Village Inn owners have designated some of their units as exclusively no smoking units, so those sensitive to cigarette smoke can be assured that the drapes and carpets will not harbor tobacco odors.

The spa building, adjacent to the Inn's large mineral water pool, smaller wading pool (two-foot water level) for the kiddies, and enclosed Jacuzzi and sauna room, has been very nicely refurbished since I was here last: much white wicker furniture, thriving plants, a tea dispenser, Hansen's and Crystal Geyser juices, and—something I like to see—conveniently placed tip envelopes in the lobby.

Their services include mud baths (great in cool weather), salt scrubs (great in hot weather), mineral baths, steam baths, facials, mini-facials and herbal wraps (great any time). On their menu of services, the breakdown is by time: one-hour treatments (salt scrubs, facials and wraps), one-and-a-half-hour treatments (various combinations of mud baths, salt scrubs and facials), and two-hour treatments (various combinations of mud baths, salt scrubs, facials and wraps with massage).

Excellent massage is available here, ranging from Swedish-Esalen, deep tissue, acupressure, shiatsu and reflexology, alone or in combination. Your massage practitioners (a man or a woman, your preference) are all skilled in aromatherapy.

Catering to the couples' population that has discovered Calistoga, the Inn offers a co-ed mud bath during the week in the winter months. (Winter is a great time for a spa vacation.) They also have put together interesting packages: The Calistoga Experience (one night's lodging with basic spa amenities and complimentary breakfast; The Works for Two at the Spa (including mud bath, steam, blanket wrap and half-hour massage); and Dinner for Two (your choice from the menu up to $40 a couple). If you are a golf buff, you can try their Calistoga Golf Experience which limits the spa treatment to a half-hour massage for two and replaces it with a day (unlimited) for two at the Mount St. Helena nine-hole golf course, capped off with the Dinner for Two package.

Finally, for those who would prefer to stay in a motel that is separate from the spa but close by, the Comfort Inn across the road is under the same ownership.

It was fun to see this place evolve from a series of false starts by other hopeful owners into what it is today. Nice job!

HOURS
•Office: 7 a.m. to 11 p.m. daily.
•Spa: weekdays from 9 a.m. to 9 p.m.; Saturday and Sunday 8 a.m. to 9 p.m.

Calistoga Village
Inn and Spa

INCIDENTALS
•No general day use.
•Minimum stays required on holiday weekends only. Inquire when booking.
•No-smoking rooms and rooms with private whirlpool tubs, micro-fridges and VCRs are available.
•Families with children welcome. (Under 16 at no cost if in parents' room.)
•Conference and meeting rooms also available.
•Color TV and telephones in all rooms.
•Room rates include complimentary continental breakfast.
•Reservations guaranteed with credit card number; 48-hour cancellation notice is requested.
•Gift certificates are available.
•Credit cards accepted: MasterCard, Visa, American Express and Diners' Club.

Dr. Wilkinson's Hot Springs

1507 Lincoln Avenue
Calistoga, CA 94515
(707) 942-4102

Dr. Wilkinson's, under the able management of the doctor's son, Mark, is one of the older spas that is synonymous with Calistoga. Right down on Lincoln Avenue, across from the Soaring Center, it is a Calistoga landmark spa that will probably always be the first choice of the Wilkinson family's dedicated following.

As with many in the spa business, "the Doctor" as he is referred to almost reverently by staff, had a chiropractic practice for many, many years. Having reached his 80th year, Doc now has time to concentrate on some of his other endeavors. The same vintage as Frank Hughes, Jr. of Nance's, Doc Wilkinson landed in Calistoga in 1946 as a young chiropractor. His deep concern for health remains the hallmark and legacy of Dr. Wilkinson's. ("Doc Wilkinson has been in the business so long," their brochure states, "that the mere mention of his name can relieve stress and relax the soul.")

In times when corporations are frequently represented in what is blithely referred to up

Spa #4
map page 142

$$ Cost
■ Overnight
☐ Program
☐ Day Use
■ Hot Springs
■ Hot Tubs
■ Sauna
■ Massage
■ Skin Care/Salon
■ Exercise
☐ Meals
■ Spa Products
☐ Workshops
■ Children
☐ Pets
☐ Weddings

and down the state as "the spa industry," it is satisfying to walk into a facility that is family owned and operated. Even the outside staff who work here regard the Wilkinsons as family.

Not caught in a time warp, however, son Mark has accomplished a lot in recent years. Next to the spa, for example, is The Salon at Dr. Wilkinson's, which offers a stunning array of facial and body treatments (check out the "Cerofango," an application of Calistoga volcanic ash and clay, herbs and paraffin created to permit deep hydration of the hands and feet.) Aromatherapy treatments (and products) have been added since I was last here gathering information. The salon also offers mini-facials, a grapefruit/aloe face-lift, and the increasingly popular acupressure face-lift. Personalized consultations are also available. Right next to that is Edy's Art House, where Mrs. Wilkinson has opened a shop of collectibles. Next in line is their Victorian House, just one of the many lodging choices the Wilkinsons can give you. Mrs. Wilkinson made an effort to keep a Victorian flavor to the five rooms here (all have private bath, refrigerator and TV) and, as Mark says, it has the feeling of a B&B without the second "B".

This little Wilkinson row of pink and white turn-of-the-century cottages is not the end of the Wilkinsons' contribution to the town. Around the corner at 1412 Fairway, the Wilkinsons also own and operate Hideaway Cottages where they put up their guests when their other accommodations are full. The cottages are nestled behind the main Victorian house, vintage 1875—an eye-catcher with its gingerbread and other turn-of-the-century features nicely restored. Sadly, however, no rooms are available in the main house. The rental units, 17 of them, almost all with kitchenette and bath, are sweet, no-frills accommodations typical of Calistoga. All units are air-conditioned and have TV, but, by design, none have telephones. The lush surrounding grounds and pools, available to guests only, are so serene and quiet that you'll forget you're within walking distance of the main street. (And remember, you also have the choice of a room behind the spa facility near sundecks, lounges and garden patios as well as individual bungalows in a garden setting.)

Like many others here and in Desert Hot Springs, the Wilkinsons made the difficult decision not to open the pools to a day-use public so that they could assure access and privacy for their overnight guests. Like other spas in Calistoga, they have three mineral water pools—one outdoor pool kept at a refreshing 82 degrees for swimming and another at 92 degrees for easy soaking. The hot pool (104 degrees) is located inside a large, glass-walled room adorned with tropical plants and ferns. Water exercise and stretch class is held every Saturday morning (in season) under superb instruction.

Spa services offered include traditional mud baths, mineral whirlpool baths (that will demonstrate for you Doc Wilkinson's Whirlpool

Dr. Wilkinson's
Hot Springs

Dr. Wilkinson's Hot Springs

Machine), steam rooms, blanket wraps and massage (Swedish-Esalen, acupressure and deep tissue). Men's and women's bath house facilities are separate—women move to the left of the reception desk and men to identical quarters on the right.

Wilkinson's offers a "Stress-Stopper Package" that is available Sunday through Thursday between September 15 and May 15. A midweek getaway, this special includes overnight lodging, unlimited use of pools, choice of one full treatment per person ("The Works"—mud bath, mineral whirlpool, steam room, blanket wrap, and half-hour massage, or a variant that excludes the mud bath and extends the massage to one hour, or a relaxing one-and-a-half-hour facial).

For newcomers who want to know a little more about a mud bath before they take one, ask at the desk for the printed card that answers the questions the Wilkinsons have been asked for the more than 40 years they have been in Calistoga.

HOURS
•Open year round.
•Baths offered from 8:30 a.m. through 3:30 p.m. daily.
•Massage from 9 a.m. through 4:30 p.m. daily.

INCIDENTALS
•Appointments strongly advised.
•Deposit required, as is 48 hours' cancellation notice.

•All rooms (except those at Hideaway Cottages) are equipped with color TV, telephones and coffeemakers, and permit unlimited use of pools.

•No children are allowed at Hideaway Cottages.

•Weekly rates (with daily maid service) are available.

•Conference room available.

•Gift certificates are available.

•No pets allowed.

•Credit cards accepted: MasterCard, Visa and American Express.

Dr. Wilkinson's
Hot Springs

Golden Haven
Hot Springs

1713 Lake Street
Calistoga, CA 94515
(707) 942-6793

Spa #5
map page 142

$$ Cost
■ Overnight
☐ Program
■ Day Use
■ Hot Springs
■ Hot Tubs
☐ Sauna
■ Massage
■ Skin Care/Salon
☐ Exercise
☐ Meals
■ Spa Products
☐ Workshops
■ Children
☐ Pets
☐ Weddings

Golden Haven Hot Springs is just off the beaten path, tucked away in a quiet residential neighborhood just minutes from the main thoroughfare. It is one of the early spas of the '50s and continues to attract old-time regulars, although with its purchase by native Alaskan Bruce Kendall in 1983, it is showing distinct signs of moving into the '90s. The European body wrap, for example, which guarantees that you will lose a minimum of six inches off your total body measurement, is now one of Golden Haven's regular offerings to men and women.

Kendall also owns Lincoln Avenue Spa (see page 178) and Sonoma Spa (see page 113). Each facility has its own distinctive look and style. When you write for a brochure, you'll also receive a four-page promo newspaper, with color photos, that reflects the particular ambience of each one.

Like Calistoga's spas in general, Golden Haven has a totally unpretentious look to it; only the Mercedes, BMWs and Porsches in the parking lot suggest that this quiet little Calistoga spa is a top choice for those with enviable liquid assets as well as for the Toyota set. (Prices have remained very affordable.)

Although Calistoga is known for its mud baths, at present only Golden Haven, International Spa and the new Lavender Hill Spa are set up so that you can enjoy the experience in a private room with the person accompanying you. The same with their mineral baths.

In addition to the mud bath, Golden Haven offers Swedish-Esalen massage, foot reflexology, acupressure face-lifts and all-natural herbal facials. All guests at Golden Haven, whether overnight or day-use only, have access to the lovely mineral water pools, the large warm-water one for swimming (80 degrees) and the adjacent hot pool (with Jacuzzi) for that special make-me-well experience.

In the lobby/reception area, you will find T-shirts for sale as well as the California Spa and Facial health and beauty product line that was introduced by the spa in 1991. Some of the enticing products I wanted to scoop up are their oatmeal facial scrub, an herbal body mud and a cooling body mud. (All of their products, I was told, were developed without relying on animal testing.)

Their more than 30 rooms, all with color TV, many with kitchenettes and several with private sauna or Jacuzzi, are air-conditioned. There are no telephones in the rooms. Dishes and utensils are available from the front office with a refundable deposit.

Golden Haven
Hot Springs

HOURS
•Open year round, 8 a.m. to 11 p.m.
•Spa services from 9 a.m. to 9 p.m.

INCIDENTALS
•Open to the public for day-use of spa and pools.
•Children under 12 are not permitted on Friday and Saturday and in all cases must be strictly supervised by an adult.
•Gift certificates can be purchased at the desk or by telephone and may be used for lodging, spa treatments and items sold in the lobby.
•Credit cards accepted: MasterCard, Visa and American Express.

Indian Springs
Resort

1712 Lincoln Avenue
Calistoga, CA 94515
(707) 942-4913

For those who haven't been to Calistoga in recent years, Indian Springs Resort is what was formerly Pacheteau's, then Brannan's Original Calistoga Hot Springs. The interim owner had decided to turn back the hands of time and capitalize on the fact that it is the original Calistoga spa from the days of Sam Brannan. The present owner wants to recall the time when hot springs were the exclusive healing waters of the local Native Americans.

Historians tell us that Robert Louis Stevenson, who did bits of his writing in hotels and boarding houses from San Francisco to Monterey, wrote parts of *Silverado Squatters* when he stayed here in 1880.

Delving even further back in time, it has been since 1865 that this 60 acres of rich volcanic ash from centuries of Mount Konocti eruptions has been used for its healing and pleasure-giving properties. Mud baths here use only pure volcanic ash, which, I was told, retains heat better and is odorless. It is not mixed with peat

Spa #6
map page 142

$$ Cost
■ Overnight
□ Program
■ Day Use
■ Hot Springs
■ Hot Tubs
■ Sauna
■ Massage
■ Skin Care/Salon
□ Exercise
□ Meals
■ Spa Products
□ Workshops
■ Children
□ Pets
□ Weddings

moss, as at other spas. Nance's is the only other Calistoga spa having enough pressure for the mineral water to spring from the ground without having to be pumped.

Actually, I miss the pungent smell of sulphur that used to be more pronounced here than at any other spa in Calistoga and, for me, added to its unique character. When you first breathe in the fumarolic sulphur smell you want to run the other way, but it grows on you and soon you'd follow it anywhere. Besides that, the characteristic odor served as a reminder that I was in real hot springs country.

Other distinctive features of this spa are its long, graceful driveway to the bath house entrance, its charming row of free-standing guest cottages, its grassy picnic area where tables have been sturdily tented against the hot wine country summer sun and its spectacular pool.

Near Olympic in size and notable for its stunningly bright blue-green water, the pool is situated on a rise that takes up the length of the entrance-way to the spa. "Oh, that one!" people less familiar with Calistoga will say once you describe the pool. If that doesn't recall it, remind them of the huge holding tanks sitting up in the hills behind the spa. Incidentally, the water temperature in this pool is 88 degrees in summer and 100 degrees in winter—not designed for lap swimming.

Families gravitate to this spa, and justifiably so. Not only is it well-situated—the area has no immediate spa neighbors, and you feel more comfortable about letting loose—but its picnic grounds, tether ball, play area (sandbox and slide), tennis court, and clean, spacious stucco cottages provide comfortable living for parents with children.

Treatments available to you at Indian Springs are the traditional mud bath (which includes a hot soak, sulphur steam and a heavy blanket sweat), a mud bath with massage, a sulphur steam bath (which includes a mineral water tub, sulphur steam and a blanket sweat), or a simple and simply wonderful massage and shower alone. You can also get a facial, either the standard or a "repechage" (four-layer facial).

For all of the changes that have been accomplished here, it is soothing to know that Evelia Fernandez, who came to the United States from Mexico in 1978 and has been with the spa through all of its renovations, still presides over the mud baths. Since she joined the staff in 1981, this wide-eyed diminutive woman has managed to establish herself as queen of the mud bath ritual.

HOURS
•Open year round.

INCIDENTALS
•Discount "series cards" available for pool; day use of the pool is free to children two years old and under. Free swim with any spa service.
•Credit cards accepted: MasterCard and Visa.

International Spa

Post Office Box 856
Calistoga, CA 94515
(707) 942-6122

Spa #7
map page 142

$$ Cost
☐ Overnight
☐ Program
■ Day Use
■ Hot Springs
■ Hot Tubs
☐ Sauna
■ Massage
■ Skin Care/Salon
☐ Exercise
☐ Meals
■ Spa Products
☐ Workshops
☐ Children
☐ Pets
☐ Weddings

International Spa is a day-use spa facility located just behind the Roman Spa, a motel/pool complex where guests take advantage of the proximity of International Spa for their treatments. Both spas are immediately north of Lincoln Avenue at the corner of Washington and First streets.

For more than 10 years, this facility, stretched out like a railroad car along the length of the parking lot, has been a popular services-only spa. Reservations must be made three weeks in advance and secured with a MasterCard or Visa. As described in detail in the write-up of Osmosis on page 89, the Japanese enzyme bath is a specialty here at International Spa—and it still is only here and in Freestone that the enzyme bath can be found.

The various other treatments available are therapeutic massage, which combines Swedish-Esalen, foot reflexology and acupressure; foot reflexology alone, which includes an herbal essence foot bath and a neck and shoulder massage; and an acupressure massage alone, which they describe as a full finger-pressure massage that penetrates deeply into the muscles and helps to release old tension-holding patterns.

For its herbal facials, International now uses the owner's own creation, "Quan Yin Essentials." Based on aromatherapy healing principles, facials include application of a Dead Sea mineral mud mask, followed by hydration of the face with pure rose water, and a regenerating, anti-aging facial gel mask followed by steam and moisturizer. A 20-minute massage of the neck, shoulders, feet and hands is an integral part of the treatment.

The herbal blanket wrap, which International offers as an alternative to the mud bath or enzyme bath, involves soaking for 15 minutes in hot herbal mineral water and then being wrapped in warm blankets saturated with selected herbs. An alternative is the seaweed bath where powdered seaweed is dissolved in the mineral water along with the essential oils, and your soak is followed with a blanket wrap. They still offer a "plain" mineral bath infused only with herbal essence.

For the mud bath (which couples enjoy taking side by side in adjoining tubs), you are immersed in the familiar mix of volcanic ash, peat moss and hot sulphur water for 10 or 15 minutes. You then shower and relax in a hot mineral water tub, again infused with herbal essences—eucalyptus, lavender, cinnamon and clove. For the last 30 minutes, the attendant wraps you snugly in blankets of flannel and wool that permit you to sweat out toxins and, with them, any remaining cares. As soft, relaxing music plays in the background, the attendant periodically applies cold compresses to your face. Mud baths are available for individuals, couples and groups.

The enzyme bath is described in the write-up on Osmosis (page 89). Whatever heat treatments you select, International is careful to alert you to the fact that women who are pregnant and anyone with high blood pressure should avoid these high-heat therapies. This is a generally accepted caution.

John Cashman, the spa's owner, concentrates on giving high-quality, individualized attention to those who use his facility and welcomes your letting the staff know what you prefer in terms of the depth of massage and the temperature of your heat treatments. Furthermore, he is always on the prowl for new treatments that promise his clients the sense of peace and well-being they come to Calistoga to find. Since *California Spas* came out in 1992, he has installed hydrotherapy tubs and has new plans in the works. Cashman also just opened his Lavender Hill Spa (see page 174).

HOURS
•Open seven days a week, 9 a.m. to 9 p.m.

INCIDENTALS
•Reservations for services should be made three weeks in advance and can be held with a MasterCard or Visa; 72-hour cancellation notice is strictly adhered to.

•The skin products used at the spa are sold in

the lobby along with "Backhuggers," relaxation tapes, herbal toothpaste and soaps.
•Credit cards accepted: MasterCard and Visa with a surcharge. Personal checks also accepted.

Lavender Hill Spa

1015 Foothill Boulevard
Calistoga, CA 94515
(707) 942-4495

Spa #8
map page 142

$$ Cost
☐ Overnight
☐ Program
■ Day Use
■ Hot Springs
■ Hot Tubs
☐ Sauna
■ Massage
■ Skin Care/Salon
☐ Exercise
☐ Meals
■ Spa Products
☐ Workshops
☐ Children
☐ Pets
☐ Weddings

While many Calistoga spas are now pitching their services to couples, John Cashman of International Spa has taken the concept a step further in his new Lavender Hill Spa. Once a small bed and breakfast inn right on Foothill Boulevard (Highway 29), this sweet, single-story yellow house and its charming "outbuildings" have been furbished with couples in mind every step of the way. Although singles are certainly not discouraged, most of John's design effort is aimed at making it easy for two people to take their treatments in tandem and to do so in a romantic atmosphere.

The lobby area is furnished with my favorite dark-toned wicker pieces, nicely placed ferns and exotic plants, and a cooling ceiling fan. The work of local artist "Toni," who paints Renoir-ish ladies and gentlemen of a more romantic era, is displayed throughout Lavender Hill. Softly polished Mexican pavers here and in the bath areas complete the warm ambience Cashman has created for Lavender Hill.

So brand-new when I was there (grand opening festivities had not taken place although customers were already registering for appointments), Lavender Hill was still putting the finishing touches on the facility. Beyond the current work in progress is a soon-to-be-realized plan to install a large community hot pool at the lower end of the terraced area and to place outdoor cabanas in the upper reaches so that guests can enjoy mineral water plunges and massage in the open air. (Always pack a suit for those places, like Calistoga, where communal nudity is a NO.)

The entrance to the spa is on the side of the building which allows its lovely apse-like room facing Foothill Boulevard to be used to full advantage. As you walk into this wide, semicircular space, you'll find massage tables, for body work or facials, on either side of the front window facing Foothill Boulevard. For a twosome wanting to begin and end their treatments at the same time but not needing to hold hands every minute, this semi-private arrangement is ideal.

Between the lobby and this front treatment room is a charming inner parlor that serves as a pre-treatment room, a quiet space where you can sit in your robe (provided by the spa) as you wait for your spa attendant. Two other treatment rooms, one on each side, and a large bathroom take up the outer space surrounding this soundproofed waiting area. A fourth private treatment room is by itself on the other side of the lobby, at the entrance to the facility.

For your baths—salt, seaweed, aromatherapy and mud—you will leave the main house for

Lavender Hill Spa one of the two adjoining bath houses, one across the deck from the main house, the other in the back nestled against the terraced hillside. Here, you *will* be within whispering distance of each other. In both buildings, the tubs are right next to each other as are the tables where you will be wrapped snug as bugs in rugs to drift off into that incomparable mental space these luxurious heat therapies provide.

You'll find that aromatherapy is now standard in almost every spa as an adjunct to your massage, hot soak or body wrap—wherever the use of aromas is appropriate as an enhancement to your treatment goals, whether you are looking for healing, calming, energizing or general stress-relief. Lavender Hill, in addition to its strong appeal to twosomes, emphasizes aromatherapy in its treatments. Although the botanicals and essential oils available are many, each one with its own special promise (see pages 54-55), most facilities rely on a basic few. A quick consultation with your spa attendant or massage practitioner will determine which one is right for your state of being at the moment.

Finally, Cashman is quite excited about the "VibraSound," a biofeedback system in the form of a waterbed—massage table-size—designed to transport you gently into a meditative alpha state and hold you there for 45 timeless minutes. It had not yet arrived when I was there, but from the description I was given, soothing music vibrates through the water, starting at your feet and moving gently up your spine while you lie still, dressed only in goggles designed to flood you with healing color images. This description might not have done justice to this technological wonder, so do ask questions about it when you make your reservations—or just be adventuresome and do it!

HOURS
•Open year round.
•Monday to Thursday, 9:30 a.m. to 5:30 p.m.; Friday, Saturday and Sunday, 9 a.m. to 9 p.m.

INCIDENTALS
•Advance registration and 72-hour cancellation notice required.
•Credit cards accepted: MasterCard and Visa. Personal checks also accepted with I.D.

Lincoln Avenue Spa

1339 Lincoln Avenue
Calistoga, CA 94515
(707) 942-5296

Spa #9
map page 142

$$ Cost
☐ Overnight
☐ Program
■ Day Use
☐ Hot Springs
☐ Hot Tubs
☐ Sauna
■ Massage
■ Skin Care/Salon
☐ Exercise
☐ Meals
■ Spa Products
☐ Workshops
☐ Children
☐ Pets
☐ Weddings

Lincoln Avenue Spa, Bruce Kendall's second acquisition (he now has Golden Haven, Lincoln Avenue, and the latest, Sonoma Spa in Sonoma), introduced a new look to Calistoga's main street when it opened several years ago.

While other Calistoga spas have spruced up and expanded, they still retain a kind of no-nonsense muslin character for which this historic country town is known. That a "scrap of lace" has appeared on Lincoln Avenue is a delight. In fact, the Lincoln Avenue Spa could not be so genuinely welcomed if the old landmark spas and businesses were not still alive and flourishing.

One reason why the Lincoln Avenue Spa is so much at home on Calistoga's main street is that it lives in the town's first bank, an old hunky rock building that went up in 1890. "Lives in" is not as whimsical as it may seem: The fact is that the spa facilities—from reception desk to massage rooms, dressing areas and mud wrap rooms—were set into the building in such a way as not to break into the original rock shell. Even the old safe has been preserved.

One of the specialties you'll find only here is a new way of using mud. The "body mud" treatment, as they call it, takes care of those people who are squeamish about immersing themselves in mud. For the old-timers, however, not only is the traditional mud bath a glorious experience, but they will swear it draws out of their bodies all the impurities, aches and pains that human flesh is heir to.

In this version, you are not immersed; instead you are given a beautiful-to-behold "mud" preparation consisting of potter's clay to which 34 ayurvedic herbs have been added. (Ayurveda—literally meaning "knowledge of life"— is an ancient health system from India, and ayurvedic herbs are those selected as cleansing and detoxifying and thus suited for use in mud therapy.)

Couples particularly enjoy this mud wrap since they can smooth it over each other's bodies (a bit reminiscent of Glen Ivy's outdoor mudpool fun). If you came alone, don't worry. You can slather it on yourself or take advantage of the attendant's presence. She stays in the room taking care of details and is happy to assist you on request. As she will tell you, the clay is not put on the face or on the feet—the former because it is too tightening to facial skin and the latter because you could slip walking.

Once lathered in clay, you will be wrapped in a light cotton sheet and helped into one of two side-by-side steam boxes with curved plexiglass covers that afford you room enough to bend your knees. Here you will stretch out for 30 minutes in soft, steamy splendor as vapors from below envelop you.

The steam is controlled by a wall switch that the attendant turns on once you are happily inside. Your head—shoulders, even—can be outside if you prefer. Some people like the steam all over their face; others don't. If your head is outside, you'll have a towel draped over your face that you can remove for a quick cooling effect. The line-up of the two boxes allows you to take a head-to-head position with your companion so that you'll have someone to whisper to and giggle with if it's your first time. As I mentioned earlier, the attendant is in and out of the room constantly to monitor the whole process and to help you step out safely when it is time to emerge and hose down.

Owner Kendall designed this massive creation himself, based on those used therapeutically in ayurvedic clinics throughout India. He had the final product handcrafted by a shipwright, who used Honduran mahogany because of its ability to withstand moisture.

The pipes, valves and all the technological goodies that make this unique design work are encased in a cabinet that takes up the lower half of the box. So beautiful is this steam bed that one expects to open its doors to neatly stacked linens and laces, surely not pipes and tubes.

The other services offered are herbal wraps, herbal facials and acupressure face-lifts. The herbal wrap is for those who want the cleansing, rejuvenating effects of the mud bath but without the mud. The herbs used in the wrap, different from those used in the body mud treatment, are infused into a cotton flannel blanket that is placed on the steam bed. The attendant wraps the warm blanket around you, closes the plexiglass cover, and starts the steam magic that makes the world go away.

When you have an acupressure face-lift, the facialist will give you a diagram of the pressure points on the face and printed instructions showing you how to do it yourself at home. It is always satisfying to be able to take one of these self-nurturing treatments home with you.

Lincoln Avenue Spa offers Swedish-Esalen massage, shiatsu and foot reflexology. Like many of the pricier spas in the state, Lincoln Avenue Spa also "packages" its treatments so that you can have a taste of each delectable service—facial, body, mud and massage—in different combinations that range from one-and-a-half to four-and-a-half hours.

HOURS
•Open year round, seven days a week, 9 a.m. to 9 p.m. Walk-in appointments are welcome.

INCIDENTALS
•Gift certificates are available.
•Kendall's line of spa products are for sale.
•Credit cards accepted: MasterCard, Visa and American Express.

Mount View Spa

1457 Lincoln Avenue
Calistoga, CA 94515
(707) 942-5789

Spa #10
map page 142

$$ Cost

■ Overnight

■ Program

■ Day Use

☐ Hot Springs

☐ Hot Tubs

☐ Sauna

■ Massage

■ Skin Care/Salon

☐ Exercise

■ Meals

☐ Spa Products

☐ Workshops

☐ Children

☐ Pets

☐ Weddings

The experienced hand of European-born Reinhard Bergel (former owner of Valley Spa and Rehabilitation Clinic in Castro Valley and a real pro in this business) shows up throughout the new Mount View Spa. Many people have asked me where they might find a European-style spa, and I have referred them to his Valley Spa. When it went out of business, I thought I had lost Dr. Bergel. Imagine my delight when I found him ensconced here at Mount View. I should have known he was involved in developing this facility as soon as I saw the gleaming white cleanliness that pervades all the treatment rooms, the breadth of services offered, and the inclusion of steam baths as well as the "Fango" mud bath, heretofore available only at Valley Spa and at the Eurospa (Pine Street Inn).

The spa is nicely situated in the back of the hotel overlooking the pool. It is very convenient to hotel guests, of course (who, incidentally, can opt to have a massage in their own room), but it is also easily accessible for walk-in day users. Day-use spa clients can also take advantage of the hotel pool and Jacuzzi. Its six treatment rooms are all quite "roomy." There is a steam bath in each tub room, and spa attendants are there to move you through your *à la carte* or programmed services. As popular as massage and body treatments now are in this country, there are still many who remain unsure of it all. Mount View Spa, with its spa attendants and intensive menu of European-styled services, will walk you through every step. This is not a do-it-yourself kind of city spa where regulars go for a simple sauna or tub and know the ropes. Men who don't eat quiche might be especially comfortable in its clean and simple—no frou-frou—decor.

Following a trend toward making the use of spa services attractive and easy for twosomes to use, Mount View Spa was designed to accommodate those who travel together and want to take their spa treatments at the same time. Whether for the convenience of it, the romance of it, or for the benefit of newcomers who feel more comfortable going through their first spa journeys together, this new development is everywhere. (Nonetheless, singles and those content to separate and meet each other later can still have it their way.)

For its body and facial treatments, Mount View offers: aromatherapy massage, Swedish-Esalen massage, shiatsu "lifeforce" massage (fully clothed, 55- to 75-minute treatment), and sports massage as well as seaweed toning baths (wonderful in combination with other treatments), aroma steam baths (state-of-the-art steam cabinets), herbal wraps, Fango mud baths (dehydrated mud combined with Salicyl and pine oil and dissolved in your hot mineral water tub), detoxifying mud wraps (warm Moor mud applied to the body), a "seaweed revitalizer," a "rejuvenating" facial, a back facial, a European deep-pore cleansing facial, mini-facials, a mask (personalized to your skin's needs) and reflexology in a 20-minute sampler or a 55-minute session.

Some of the unusual touches you can expect to find here are having cool hand towels available for use before and after your treatment, pitchers of mineral water with fresh-fruit slices in your treatment room and a selection of soothing music for your massage.

As elsewhere, Mount View Spa has created special "day spa packages" (available Sunday through Thursday) that combine steam, mud, massage and wraps in different combinations, some including a spa lunch and/or a spa T-shirt. They even offer a "Romantic Breakaway" for couples traveling together.

As if this mineral water-rich town did not already offer us an array of choices, from the old-time Mom-and-Pop facilities to the newer spas designed by the next generation of entrepreneurs, the addition of Mount View Spa, Lavender Hill Spa, and the sweet little Calistoga Massage Center, seems to say that this town has as much energy for its own regeneration and renewal as for ours.

Stop in for a quick tour. The Mount View Spa is excitingly different.

HOURS

•9 a.m. to 9 p.m. (Last treatment at 8 p.m.)

INCIDENTALS

•Credit card deposit required for all advance reservations. Cancellations must be made at least 24 hours in advance to avoid full charge.
•Gift certificates available.
•Credit cards accepted: MasterCard, Visa and American Express.

Nance's
Hot Springs

1614 Lincoln Avenue
Calistoga, CA 94515
(707) 942-6211

Spa #11
map page 142

$$ Cost

■ Overnight

☐ Program

■ Day Use

■ Hot Springs

■ Hot Tubs

■ Sauna

■ Massage

☐ Skin Care/Salon

☐ Exercise

☐ Meals

☐ Spa Products

☐ Workshops

☐ Children

☐ Pets

☐ Weddings

Nance's is one of Calistoga's "old reliables." A strong segment of the tourist population comes here for the good old spa town Calistoga has always been, where a room is a place you "hang your hat," as my Uncle Roy used to say, and where you don't have to put up with people "fussing all over you." According to Nance's management, "We try *not* to change, but every two years we do have to spruce up the place."

Under the same ownership for ages, Nance's only notable concession to modern times is to accept the three major credit cards and offer HBO. As their brochure proudly tells you, Frank Hughes, Jr. has been at the spa since 1946, when he came to work for his father, then a partner with Earl Nance at Nance's Hot Springs. Daughters Sara and Debbie are the active third-generation managers of the spa, and yes, Frank is still around giving massages "sometimes to third-generation customers."

Many of the spas in Calistoga, as in Desert

Hot Springs, like to show you the chemical composition of their water. At Nance's, the chemical chart has a prominent display position by the reception desk, and if you know what to make of the varying amounts of magnesium, soda, iron, alumina, chloride and silica that are in the water, here's your opportunity to jump up and down with joy or to frown in dismay. We still just scratch our heads in wonderment. Displaying the chart shows, however, that Nance's takes seriously the claims made by the old-time docs that this mineral-rich water could heal your aching bones and ailing flesh.

In its separate-but-equal men's and women's quarters, Nance's offers traditional mud baths that include a mineral water tub, steam and blanket wrap with massage if wanted, and various combinations of these services, including a whirlpool bath. In addition, "specific corrective massage" is now on Nance's menu of spa treatments. These are body-alignment sessions, one or more, depending on need, and are done only by Frank. Three staff members take care of moving clients in and out of mud, steam, water and resting areas. A quiet efficiency hovers over the bathhouse operation. A large and inviting hot mineral water pool (enclosed) is right at the entrance to the spa—you'll pass it on your way to your room—and many people spend most of their time here in and out of its warm embrace.

HOURS
•Open year round. Spa facilities open 9 a.m. to

Nance's
Hot Springs

5 p.m. weekdays and to 7 p.m. on weekends.
•Last mud bath is at 3:30 p.m.

INCIDENTALS
•Ticket rate is a 10% discount on six baths paid in advance.
•Advance reservations are recommended. 48-hour cancellation notice is necessary. Bath house appointments are guaranteed with deposit.
•Gift certificates are available.
•Air-conditioned rooms with color cable TV, HBO, kitchenettes and telephones.
•Senior citizen discount on lodging and services (10%) applies Sunday through Thursday, excluding holidays.
•No children or pets allowed.
•Credit cards accepted: MasterCard, Visa and American Express.

Pine Street Inn
and Eurospa

1202 Pine Street
Calistoga, CA 94515
(707) 942-6829

Pine Street Inn and its resident companion, Eurospa, are located on a quiet back street overlooking the vineyards.

Like the relationship between Roman Spa (for lodging) and International Spa (for body treatments), visitors to Pine Street Inn and Eurospa can use either or both, as they wish. Unless you're devoted to the traditional mud bath, or you go to Calistoga expressly for its 100-year-old ambience, you'll be delighted with what Eurospa has to offer.

Before describing its more typically European body and skin-care services, let me impress on you the prettiness of the spa. You walk into an airy waiting room of soft peach, pink and blue pastels. A *shoji* screen a few feet behind the reception desk and a window to the greenery outside adds a feeling of dimension and lightness. The space is relatively small, but designed by someone who enjoys the challenge of making small beautiful.

The "European Fango Mudbath" is their spe-

Spa #12
map page 142

$$ Cost
■ Overnight
☐ Program
☐ Day Use
■ Hot Springs
■ Hot Tubs
☐ Sauna
☐ Massage
■ Skin Care/Salon
☐ Exercise
☐ Meals
■ Spa Products
☐ Workshops
☐ Children
☐ Pets
☐ Weddings

cialty. Like the "lightweight" mud wrap you get at Lincoln Avenue Spa, this treatment does not bury you under the heavy, hot weight of the classical mud bath. Eurospa's dehydrated "mud" is imported from Germany and added to a tubful of natural mineral water and herbal extracts in proportions that keep its texture thin. What you step into looks like a tub of dark chocolate liquid.

The tub room reserved for this treatment is serene and relatively spacious. When you enter, you'll see in the center of the room a large porcelain tub, the size of a double bed. The head cushion placed at the near end of the tub indicates that, once immersed, you will be looking out toward the garden, a lush black fig tree and the vineyard beyond. The peacefulness of the room and the orientation of the tub to the outside reminded me of Osmosis in Freestone, where the enzyme bath is oriented to the outside to give you a visual treat and add another dimension to the experience.

The Fango mud bath is a 25-minute therapy. You can let the attendant know how hot you want the water, and you can also adjust it yourself since the faucets are right there. (Incidentally, the Eurospa staff is very friendly, very helpful and very well informed about the services they offer. I recommend having a heart-to-heart with manager Diane Byer.) When you have finished your mud bath, you are free to lounge in the room next door or wander out through the French doors to the back where you can alternate taking a plunge in their outdoor free-form pool (unheated) and immersing yourself in their 104-degree Jacuzzi. Or you can just settle back into one of the poolside chaises and gaze at the mountains and vineyards that surround Calistoga. Eurospa will provide you with a terry robe for moving from one area to another.

If the Fango mud bath is too newfangled for you, Eurospa offers several other more familiar, but still elegant, spa treatments: a seaweed body wrap, an herbal wrap, one of three types of aromatherapy facials, an herbal whirlpool bath, a milk-whey bath and/or one of five massage therapies their experienced practitioners provide. Eurospa also has special "packages" that mix and match these wonderful treatments.

The inn has 15 air-conditioned cottages, simply furnished, with gleaming pinewood floors. Four of the units have full kitchens and all have baths and color cable TV; none have telephones. An outside area with tables and a coffee-tea-juice bar is immediately behind the main reception area.

Owners Tom and Jean Lunney also led us to local pleasures such as Safari West on Franz Valley Road, a well-run wildlife preserve.

HOURS
•Open year round.
•Eurospa: Monday through Thursday, 10 a.m. to 6 p.m.; Friday, 10 a.m. to 9 p.m.; Saturday, 9 a.m. to 9 p.m., and Sunday 9 a.m. to 8 p.m.

INCIDENTALS
•No telephones in rooms.

*Pine Street Inn
and Eurospa*

•Gift certificates are available.
•Reservation confirmed with credit card or full payment in advance.
•Credit cards accepted: MasterCard and Visa. Personal checks are also accepted.

Roman Spa

1300 Washington Street
Calistoga, CA 94515
(707) 942-4441

Roman Spa is located just off Lincoln Avenue, and caters to a regular clientele who reserve year after year. (Newcomers are welcome, of course.) Roman Spa invites its guests to use the spa services of International Spa, just 50 feet away. Read the write-up on International Spa (page 170) and you will see that it offers a stunning array of individual and couple's services and is beautifully managed. When you call Roman Spa for a brochure, you'll receive an insert showing the varied offerings of the International Spa.

What I like about Roman is a few nice distinctions, such as its outdoor free-form pool, lovely landscaping—lush greenery and bright flowers everywhere in addition to a small rock garden and lily pond—and the placement of several chaises and picnic tables in shaded areas.

This seemingly small facility actually comprises seven pseudo-Spanish-style, two-story, balconied buildings that provide 60 rooms, two of which are equipped to accommodate disabled persons. Two others have their own large Jacuzzi

Spa #13
map page 142

$$ Cost
■ Overnight
☐ Program
☐ Day Use
■ Hot Springs
■ Hot Tubs
■ Sauna
☐ Massage
☐ Skin Care/Salon
☐ Exercise
☐ Meals
☐ Spa Products
☐ Workshops
■ Children
☐ Pets
☐ Weddings

tubs in the bathroom, one-third are designated as non-smoking and approximately one-third have kitchens. All rooms have refrigerators and telephones and are air-conditioned.

The outside pool, always filled with happy bodies of all ages, swimming and splashing about as well as lounging around talking and playing cards poolside, is kept at 92 degrees (95 in the winter months). The outside hot tub is a hotter 104 to 105 degrees. The indoor pool is maintained at 100 degrees. The sauna room has an adjoining sitting area with men's and women's changing areas and lockers.

Like most other Calistoga facilities, Roman has closed its doors to drop-in guests so that those who have reserved will be sure of having access to everything they paid for. Older people appreciate the close proximity of some of the rooms to the pool area.

HOURS
•Open year round, 8 a.m. to 10 p.m.

INCIDENTALS
•Weekly rates are discounted 10%. Off-season rates apply, except on weekends and holidays.
•Self-service barbecue and picnic area.
•Remote control color TVs in rooms.
•No children under four allowed in pool area.
•48 hours cancellation notice required.
•Gift certificates are available.
•Credit cards accepted: MasterCard, Visa and American Express. Personal checks accepted for telephone reservations only.

Bay Area
Spas

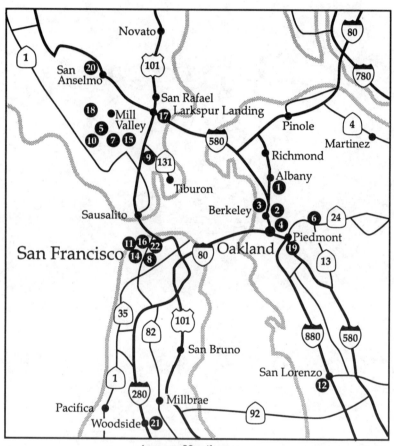

Approx. 22 miles to
San Jose
13

Albany Sauna & Hot Tubs

1002 Solano Avenue
Albany, CA 94706
(510) 525-6262

Albany Sauna, with its lovely reception area, skylights, T-shirts and Dr. Hauschka skin-care products for sale, has been a favorite among the locals for more than three decades.

Although still a reliable neighborhood spa located on Solano Avenue four blocks below San Pablo, people now come from all over the Bay Area to enjoy its authentic Finnish sauna. The huge central oven that holds court in the center of the facility, spewing out a spray of steam in response to a gentle tug of a chain on the trap door, is what gives Albany Sauna its unique standing among spas.

Instructions for adjusting the heat are printed on the wall of the spacious sauna room and should be read as soon as you enter so that you'll get the most out of your time. You can start with a cool shower, then relax at a lower level for a bit before moving up to the topmost bench where the heat is highest. Moving back and forth between shower and bench keeps you from "cooking" too fast. If you are two or more,

Spa #1
map page 196

$-$$ Cost
☐ Overnight
☐ Program
■ Day Use
☐ Hot Springs
■ Hot Tubs
■ Sauna
■ Massage
☐ Skin Care/Salon
☐ Exercise
☐ Meals
■ Spa Products
☐ Workshops
■ Children
☐ Pets
☐ Weddings

Albany Sauna
& Hot Tubs

filling the waiting bucket with water to pour over each other is still the sport it always was.

Two private dressing rooms lead into the one large sauna. Unless you made a group reservation, which gives you both dressing areas, you will move back into one of the rooms when the timer bell rings so that the party in the adjoining room can use the sauna.

If you prefer tub to sauna, Albany Sauna offers three open-air tub rooms each with the typical free-standing shower and plants around the decking area. All tubs are redwood. The water is continuously filtered to maintain cleanliness and the temperature is kept at a high bacteria-killing 106 degrees. Mineral water is for sale at the front counter and can be brought into the tub room. There is no piped-in music, but you can bring your own radio or tapes as long as you keep the sound at a volume that doesn't bother others.

Two massage therapists are on duty as long as the spa is open; others are called in as needed. Swedish-Esalen combination massage is the favorite here.

HOURS
•Noon to 11 p.m., seven days a week.

INCIDENTALS
•No smoking.
•Half-hour sauna included with any one-hour massage.
•Two-person minimum for tubs on Friday and Saturday after 6 p.m.

•Senior discount, Monday through Thursday before 5 p.m.

•Special prices for children.

•Credit cards accepted: MasterCard, Visa and American Express.

Albany Sauna & Hot Tubs

Berkeley Massage and Self-Healing Center

1962 University Avenue
Berkeley, CA 94704
(510) 843-4422

Spa #2
map page 196

$$ Cost
☐ Overnight
☐ Program
■ Day Use
☐ Hot Springs
■ Hot Tubs
☐ Sauna
■ Massage
☐ Skin Care/Salon
☐ Exercise
☐ Meals
☐ Spa Products
☐ Workshops
☐ Children
☐ Pets
☐ Weddings

A woman-owned and managed collective in its 23rd year, Berkeley Massage and Self-Healing wants to share its experience, knowledge and skills to "facilitate integral healing." Unlike other commercial facilities, they include hypnotherapy, homeopathy and psychic readings to accomplish their mission.

Right on busy University Avenue between Grove and Milvia Streets, Berkeley Massage has taken over an upper flat. When you arrive for your appointment, you'll be buzzed in. In other words, people don't wander up there by mistake.

This is one of the few places where diverse types of massage and bodywork are offered. If you know what you want, you'll find it here, and if you don't know, you'll be able to sample the differences between the more familiar Swedish-Esalen and acupressure, deep tissue, foot reflexology, polarity, shiatsu, Trager®, the Rosen Method, Reike and even cranial work. If you ask for a tub first, the water will be drawn for you just before you arrive and your massage practitioner will take you into one of two simple bathrooms where an old clawfoot tub (and an inflated plastic headrest) awaits you. Sit back and soak without concern for time; she will come for you and take you to one of three adjoining or close-by massage rooms. The massage rooms are done in pastels and reinforce the feeling you have of being at grandmother's house.

Their new brochure is in the works, but I still like the previous one and hope they retain their compelling invitation. "Call us when you want to feel your best: asking for a raise, closing the big deal, entertaining that important someone, or getting ready for a major event. Call us also when life seems overwhelming, chaotic or downright unfair."

I also like their first-person account of what you might experience when you walk into their "healing oasis," and with their permission, I quote it here:

"As I enter into the arched doorway, I am ushered into a space of peace and tranquility. I leave the hustle and bustle of downtown Berkeley behind, finding myself surrounded by soothing pastel colors and a spacious, airy atmosphere. My practitioner is attentive and caring. She offers me herbal tea, plum wine or spring water while I settle into a hot mineral bath in the old-fashioned clawfoot tub. She asks me what brought me in today and explains a bit about the work she feels might be appropriate for me.

Berkeley Massage
& Self-Healing
Center

"I am surrounded by plants, and as I soak, I begin to feel at home here. In 10 or 15 minutes, my practitioner leads me into a comfortable Victorian-style massage room. I breathe a sigh of relief, realizing that for the first time in weeks, I have made the time and space for myself, to take a real pause from my hectic schedule. I look around me and appreciate the thoughtful touches of fresh flowers, candlelight and the artwork on the walls.

"As I lie down on the large comfortable massage table, my practitioner asks me to share with her any needs that may come up for me during the session. She also lets me know that a choice for silence is fine. I feel the total focus of her attention on me, creating a safe and nurturing place for me to let go. My body gratefully accepts the firm and gentle pressure on my muscles. My mind is quieted by the soothing music. All the while I am aware that the masseuse is sensing and responding to the changes in my body.

"Now that my session is finished, my practitioner encourages me to take a few moments for myself before getting up. I sink a little further into the table, closing my eyes again, finding a new sense of self. I feel relaxed and whole. My masseuse takes a few minutes to offer suggestions of how I might carry aspects of this experience out into my normal workday. I am refreshed and revitalized. I realize the value of this session for me is on the inner level, a true gift to myself."

HOURS
•Open year round, every day from 10 a.m. to 10 p.m. and by special appointment.

INCIDENTALS
•Gift certificates are available.
•Credit cards accepted: MasterCard and Visa.
Personal checks also accepted with I.D.

The Berkeley Sauna

1947 Milvia Street
Berkeley, CA 94704
(510) 845-2341

Spa #3
map page 196

$-$$ Cost
☐ Overnight
☐ Program
■ Day Use
☐ Hot Springs
■ Hot Tubs
■ Sauna
■ Massage
☐ Skin Care/Salon
☐ Exercise
☐ Meals
■ Spa Products
☐ Workshops
■ Children
☐ Pets
☐ Weddings

The Berkeley Sauna has remained constant amid many construction projects that have taken place around it over the years. You'll still walk in to a small lobby where you'll find a bicycle or two, a bulletin board crammed with business cards and announcements, and *New Yorker* magazines and Berkeley's well-known local paper, *The Express*, on the tables. The cotton kimono on the wall is a sample; they are available for purchase.

The major change here since I last wrote it up is that they no longer have the Samadhi Float tank. I didn't ask why they took it out. (Floating in an isolation tank never did appeal to me.)

Saunas (there are three) are clean and attractive with Finlander open charcoal stoves, stand-up and low foot showers, and—commonly seen in good urban spas—wood buckets, scrub brushes and sitting stools. Also typical is the design of having two private rest areas opening into the sauna room so that on busy days two separate parties can be accommodated. The staff will orchestrate the timing so that when one group has finished the first half hour in the sauna and is cooling down in the dressing room, another party can move into the sauna. (Sound-proofing here is excellent, by the way.) Buzzers are in the dressing rooms and you can ring the desk for a bottle of juice (Knudsen, Calistoga and Hansen's), a hair dryer or an extra towel. Good information and precautionary statements are posted clearly in each dressing room. Read them through before you start.

The tubs, blue fiberglass in redwood-paneled, skylighted rooms, hold a maximum of four people and also contain the standard open shower. (One redwood tub has been added.) Tub water, maintained at 104 to 106 degrees, is constantly filtered with a bromine solution to maintain proper pH, and tubs are drained daily for thorough cleaning.

The massage rooms are located up a few stairs in a pleasant loft area. Two massage practitioners are on call, and Berkeley Sauna maintains a long list of others who come in on weekends and any time the spa is at peak capacity or when different types of bodywork are requested. While Swedish-Esalen is popular here (as everywhere), you can request reflexology, shiatsu, Trager®, deep tissue massage and special massage for pregnant women if you call ahead and tell the receptionist what you want. (Berkeley is filled with knowledgeable people in all fields.)

The Berkeley Sauna has a special reservation card system that allows you to pay a nominal fee so that you can call in a reservation for a tub

The Berkeley Sauna

or sauna; it helps on busy weekends. Otherwise, for tubs and saunas, you can take your chances on a walk-in or make a reservation in person. Appointments for massage can be made by telephone without your being registered, and anyone with a gift certificate also can call in for an appointment.

HOURS
•Monday through Thursday, noon to 10 p.m.; Friday, noon to 11 p.m.; Saturday, 10:30 a.m. to 11 p.m.; Sunday, 10:30 a.m. to 10 p.m.

INCIDENTALS
•Plastic child-sized tubs are available at the front desk for sauna or tub room so that young fry can be in cooler circumstances.
•Discount cards and senior rates available.
•Credit cards accepted: MasterCard and Visa. Personal checks also accepted with I.D.

Body, Mind and Spirit

6206 Claremont Avenue
Oakland, CA 94618
(510) 547-6716

Body, Mind and Spirit is the realization of a dream for John Vito, owner of this massage therapy center housed in what was once the Balance Point and the New Balance Point.

Formerly a massage therapist at San Francisco's posh health clubs, the Telegraph Hill Club and the Bay Club, and on the sports massage team for the 1990 Goodwill Games, ex-New Yorker Vito hopes to move Body, Mind and Spirit in the direction of a health center, bringing an acupuncturist and a chiropractor into his new venture in this relatively small second-floor facility over the Claremont Diner.

Still refurbishing (he took over in January 1993), the paint was dry when I visited (light mauve-gray tones to soften the angularity of this pseudo "flatiron" shaped building where College and Claremont Avenues come together). John is proud of his staff and the spirit in which they work together on many of the decisions that affect the Center's operation. He now has about 15 massage therapists, most of

Spa #4
map page 196

$$	Cost
☐	Overnight
☐	Program
■	Day Use
☐	Hot Springs
☐	Hot Tubs
■	Sauna
■	Massage
☐	Skin Care/Salon
☐	Exercise
☐	Meals
■	Spa Products
■	Workshops
☐	Children
☐	Pets
☐	Weddings

whom are graduates of the National Holistic Institute, an AMTA-accredited school in Emeryville where John also received his training.

John conducts a three-hour interview when he hires a massage practitioner, to be sure that everyone will pull together in this highly independent and portable profession. They frequently do trades on each other and John is always delighted with the individuality each person puts into what is otherwise the same technique they all learned. He is looking forward to having continuing workshops for his staff and their clients—on basic massage (clothes-on, seated), back and neck care, couples massage, and prenatal and infant massage.

In the ongoing renovations (new ergonomically designed furniture for the reception room was scheduled to arrive the day I was there), so far all of the pads on the massage tables have been replaced; all flannel sheets, in different patterns and pastel-colored solids, grace the tables in the Center's five treatment rooms; and *shoji* screens have been installed to allow light to filter in the windows facing the street. Picasso and Impressionist prints and mirrors were about to be hung. (Incidentally, music is more than a soothing nicety here; it is important to mask the city noises that waft upward from the street.)

The old Kenmore washing machine in the back room apparently is still going strong. There are no tubs at Body, Mind and Spirit, and the one sauna is a complimentary service for massage clients.

John likes to use the local "Charlie Sunshine's Secret Formula" for his massage oil (it's a new one to me) and intends to make it available in the reception area, although selling products, as you might be able to surmise at this point, is not what John is about.

The massage therapy staff is capable of handling nearly every modality that might be requested but, as John told me, he is gradually building a reputation for doing deep-tissue therapeutic and sports massage. Many of his clients are sports figures and/or individuals who have suffered chronic pain. The literature in the front reception area—*Natural Health*, *Treat Your Back* and the like—reflects the health-centered focus John is striving toward.

I asked about how he selected the name Body, Mind and Spirit—specifically whether "Spirit" had any special significance that you and I might want to know about. In response, he showed me the newly designed logo that will appear on his brochures and staff business cards, indicating that the "spirited" stick figure leaping up in the shaded background is intended to convey—and these are my words— the magical feeling that comes over us when we manage to unite our sometimes disparate selves. I hope John agrees with that bit of poesy.

Incidentally, this is a place where you get a hug before you leave, even when you're just updating a guidebook.

Body, Mind and Spirit

HOURS
•Monday through Friday, 11 a.m. to 8:30 p.m.; Saturday and Sunday, 11 a.m. to 7 p.m.

INCIDENTALS
•Gift certificates are available.
•Call about upcoming workshops.
•Member of the Bay Area Barter Exchange.
•Credit cards accepted: MasterCard, Visa and American Express. Personal checks also accepted.

Cheek t' Cheek Face and Body Salon

329 Strawberry Village
Mill Valley, CA 94941
(415) 383-FACE

One of the delights of updating this guidebook is that I find people in the spa world whom I thought I had lost forever. Gail Schwartz is one. She once owned Floating World in Sausalito, a lovely urban retreat that folded a few years ago. I had used Floating World and loved it. When I went back, there was a veterinarian's office where Floating World should have been. I made a number of efforts to find her and it, all to no avail. Then, when I decided to include body salons and similar "urban retreats" in this edition, I spied Cheek t' Cheek on the marquee in Mill Valley's Strawberry Village and dropped in. There she was!

Gail's salon, done in peaches and blues and white wicker, has a light, airy feeling. It is on a much smaller scale than Floating World, but, as she says, she is much more comfortable operating at this level. Whatever it amounts to in square footage, Cheek t' Cheek's array of ser-

Spa #5
map page 196

$$ Cost
☐ Overnight
☐ Program
■ Day Use
☐ Hot Springs
☐ Hot Tubs
☐ Sauna
■ Massage
■ Skin Care/Salon
☐ Exercise
☐ Meals
■ Spa Products
☐ Workshops
☐ Children
☐ Pets
☐ Weddings

Cheek t' Cheek
Face and Body
Salon

vices matches those you'll find anywhere. She specializes in European facials (basic deep cleansing and deluxe versions), nonsurgical face-lifts (a series of treatments with dramatic effects on sagging skin, droopy eyelids, lip lines and more), herbal deep peels (using all Asian herbs as an alternative to chemical peel), lash and brow tinting, waxing, a special "anti-wrinkle" treatment series and therapeutic massage. As at most other salons and spas, aromatherapy is a key part of the facial or massage you will find here.

Three facialists and three massage practitioners are available. Highly skilled, trained, experienced massage practitioners abound in the San Francisco Bay Area, so you can really ask for exactly what you would like when you call for your appointment. Cheek t' Cheek also offers a series of cellulite treatments and advice on home care, especially helpful for those on weight-loss programs who find they need extra toning to combat newly sagging flesh. (If the spa sounds very woman-focused, men should know that they are quite welcome. Here as elsewhere, men are beginning to use spa services, particularly facials, waxing and massage, and men are among Cheek t' Cheek's regular clients.)

It is worth noting that Gail's philosophy is that all skin-care and body treatments need to be performed in a quiet, healing atmosphere. Every salon has its ambience, its philosophy, its emphasis and, as David Palmer notes in his advice about selecting a massage practitioner (see page 33), it is to your advantage to be aware of the spa's philosophy and intention to see how it jibes with your own, whether generally or in the moment.

Gail is devoted to the Système Avancé line of products, which she uses and makes available for sale. She also provides good product literature in the waiting room, including a useful Q&A printout on glycolic acid, now a mainstay in salon and at-home skin care and touted by every esthetician with whom I spoke. (See appendix write-up on glycolic acid, page 417.)

HOURS
•Monday to Friday, 10 a.m. to 5 p.m.; evenings by appointment.

INCIDENTALS
•All cruelty-free products.
•Gift certificates are available.
•Credit cards accepted: MasterCard and Visa.

The Claremont
Resort and Spa

Ashby and Domingo Avenues
Oakland, CA 94623
(510) 843-3000 (hotel)
(510) 549-8566 (spa)

Spa #6
map page 196

$$-$$$ Cost
■ Overnight
☐ Program
■ Day Use
☐ Hot Springs
■ Hot Tubs
■ Sauna
■ Massage
■ Skin Care/Salon
■ Exercise
■ Meals
■ Spa Products
■ Workshops
■ Children
☐ Pets
■ Weddings

The post office places the Claremont Hotel in Oakland, but those of us who have lived many years in Berkeley claim it as our own. Of course, there are some who look at this eclectic Victorian structure that both sprawls and towers over the south end of the city as that "white elephant" once owned by the famed cowboy of cowboys, Gene Autry. Actually, the hotel has a rich history that predates Autry's acquisition of it. Indeed, the new fitness center stands on what was once the site of the original owner's horse stables.

When I first visited The Spa at the Claremont, housed in a charming building on the Berkeley side of the property and nestled between two of their ten championship tennis courts, what impressed me most was how at home it seemed—as if it had been there since 1915 when the hotel opened, instead of since 1989.

For years, as with other major hotels throughout the state, the Claremont has offered memberships permitting access to the tennis courts and swimming pools, and providing lockers and shower facilities. As the redone and renamed "Claremont Resort and Spa," the hotel/spa complex now competes with the best of its kind. It offers a state-of-the-art fitness center, a combination European-style/holistic health spa, a beauty and hair salon, two heated outdoor pools (one strictly for lap swimming and the other for aquatics), a wading pool for the kiddies, a whirlpool (kept at 104 degrees), a pro shop and an indoor-outdoor cafe with a panoramic San Francisco Bay view.

The Claremont Resort and Spa

Services are available to hotel guests, of course, but the spa is also a terrific day-use facility for those wanting a little more luxury and a little more "there-there" than you'll find in other urban spas.

The Claremont employs approximately 30 massage practitioners and tries to maintain a 50-50 balance of men and women so that they can respond to your preference. Whatever your choice—Swedish, shiatsu, sports massage, neck and shoulder massage, reflexology, even underwater massage—you will find it available here. They also offer hydrotherapy massage. And yes, aromatherapy has become an integral part of the spa's body and skin-care treatments. They are one of the very few places offering workshops on aromatherapy.

In addition to massage, the Claremont offers the familiar loofah and salt glow rubs, herbal wraps, aroma and seaweed baths as well as European facials and acupressure facials. Their packaged programs include unlimited use of the fitness center (classes, weight room, whirlpool, sauna, steam room) and various combinations of spa and/or beauty services. At the time of this writing, the packages range in price from $75 to $295. By the way, each one of these massages and treatments is described in their brochures. (You can also design your own package of treatments.) All spa and fitness center activities are available to hotel guests and members of the Pool and Tennis Club. If all you want is a dip in the pools and a workout, you can pay a nominal day-use fee and go at it.

The café is situated at pool level and has a superb view. It serves two menus, one "NC" (nutritionally correct) and the other for those who want to eat whatever they want to eat. (This "crossover cuisine," as they call it, is elaborated in the Claremont's main restaurant, the Pavilion Room, where not only are there more spa food selections, but the menu lists the number of calories and the sodium, fat and cholesterol content for each one.) Providing a dual menu is especially convenient for hotel guests where one is taking full advantage of the fitness programs and the other is simply there for a conference. The Claremont has 28 meeting rooms with a total of 32,000 square feet of meeting space.

The Claremont is a gender-friendly spa. The male partner of a woman executive can feel perfectly at ease using the fitness center, the tennis courts, the pools and all of the spa services.

Not all spas have achieved the co-ed comfort of the Claremont, which I would guess comes from the hotel's long-standing tennis and pool club memberships that hark back to a time when men were major users and women tagged along. The men's section in the spa duplicates the layout in the women's section, but it is decked out in color combinations regarded as more masculine. The amenities provided are obviously geared to men's needs. For all of that, however, men are becoming major skin-care clients, especially in spas attached to major hotels.

Describing all of the spa's many features would fill pages. Suffice it to say that it competes with the very best of its kind in the state. For my personal taste, these are the details I appreciated: In addition to being given a wonderfully thick white cotton robe and *zoris* when you check in, the changing area is splendidly equipped: besides the standard items—blow dryers, lotions, face cloths, shampoo—there are razors, deodorant, shower caps, mouthwash, tampons and a telephone. I also appreciated that three private changing rooms were available.

The colors throughout the spa area—rusts, beiges and teal blues—are quite attractive, and the artwork on the walls is worth a closer look. Each piece was thoughtfully selected by the present owner's wife.

There are many other indications of the care and taste that pervade the spa: The lounge area where you wait for your massage practitioner to come and get you, or where you sit and relax before and after any treatments, provides fruit,

The Claremont Resort and Spa

The Claremont Resort and Spa

tea and juices; the front desk sells the various body-care products used in the spa (as well as its own line of health and beauty aids); the full-service hair and beauty salon is right there at your toe-tips (their pedicures are one-and-a-half hours of wonderfulness); and it is the only spa I know that has a high-tech swimsuit dryer.

Their aerobics room has suspension cushion flooring designed specifically to absorb impact and decrease body shock and fatigue. The claim is that it also lessens ankle rollover. Their weight room equipment is the highly regarded Pyramid line. Personal training is available to those willing to pay the extra fee. Both the aerobics and weight room areas are large, light and airy, so drop any picture of those dark, dungeon-like gyms so often touted as amenities, even in the better hotel and apartment complexes.

Whether hotel guest or daytime visitor to the area, be sure to stop in at The Bread Garden and Peet's, side by side on Domingo Avenue, for a taste of Berkeley's gourmet best in breads and coffees. Since Peet's opened up shop in this location, it has had the same comfy spill-over-into-the-courtyard-and-sidewalk clientele that has long distinguished its original Walnut Square shop. Rick and Ann's excellent restaurant opened several years ago and is still flourishing next door. Call or write for their colorful, descriptive literature and price lists.

HOURS

•The Spa is open Monday to Thursday, 8:30 a.m. to 8:30 p.m.; Friday to Sunday, 8:30 a.m. to 6:30 p.m.

•The Fitness Center opens at 6 a.m. during the week and closes at 10 p.m. It opens at 7 a.m. on Saturday and Sunday.

•Bayview Cafe hours depend on the season, but are generally 11 a.m. until 5 p.m. in cool months and 11 a.m. to 7 p.m. when days are warmer and longer.

INCIDENTALS

•Make spa reservations in advance and check in 30 minutes before scheduled treatment.

•A gratuity (17.5% as of this writing...take note) will be added to all listed prices for services.

•Cancellations made less than four hours before scheduled appointments will be charged in full. On packaged programs, 48-hour notice is required.

•Day use is available for a nominal fee.

•Call for a schedule of workshops on aromatherapy, nutrition and physical well-being.

•Credit cards: all major credit cards are accepted, as are personal checks with I.D.

di Pietro Todd

Spa #7
map page 196

250 Camino Alto
Mill Valley, CA 94941
(415) 397-0177

Spa #8
map page 196

177 Post Street
San Francisco, CA 94108
(415) 388-0250

$$ Cost
☐ Overnight
☐ Program
■ Day Use
☐ Hot Springs
☐ Hot Tubs
☐ Sauna
■ Massage
■ Skin Care/Salon
☐ Exercise
☐ Meals
■ Spa Products
☐ Workshops
☐ Children
☐ Pets
☐ Weddings

di Pietro Todd is a trip.

As an urban retreat, I put the Mill Valley facility first (although it is the baby sister of the two) because its spa services are more developed than those of the San Francisco shop. As is true of other urban retreats I have included in this book—Mister Lee's, for example—di Pietro Todd's focus is on hair. Unlike Mister Lee, however, who developed a stunning third-floor spa that now vies with his original hair salon for award-winning services, di Pietro Todd's massage, facials and pedicures seem like more of an add-on (in Mill Valley) and an afterthought (in San Francisco).

The Mill Valley facility is all high-tech blacks and corals with intriguing stainless steel window coverings that look like fabric. The reception desk, lobby, hair salon and juice bar take up the main area of this second-floor facility tucked behind the cluster of businesses and restaurants on busy East Blithedale. Its massage treatment rooms and charming pedicure cubicles are located in a quiet space in the back. Although I say that massage is secondary here, they do have two practitioners on staff, and I was impressed to learn that they will go to your home to do massage. (They have disabled clients who particularly appreciate that service.) I also enjoyed their practice of dressing clients in white robes if they are there for a massage and facial and in black robes if they are hair-salon customers. Color coding has always appealed to me; what can I say? (It didn't occur to me to ask what you wear if you're there for both.)

The San Francisco shop is wildly different. You take the elevator up to it from busy Post Street and walk into a "happening" place, with scruffy wood flooring, high warehouse-type ceilings and hair stylists in a variety of black-on-black outfits sporting jazzy hairstyles. Everyone—clients and staff alike—is in a buzz of activity. Of course, that scene might have been unique to the day I was there because they were in the midst of a benefit for local AIDS organizations. It is something di Pietro Todd has done every year since it moved into the San Francisco location. There was also a silent auction of work by local artists, something that has brought in considerable monies for them in the past. Walking around, I felt more as if I were in an art gallery than in a hair salon, and I saw some very appealing pieces.

I have to relate an anecdote here. A painting caught my eye because it looked very much like *di Pietro Todd*

one of my favorite Northern California country towns, Bodega, just inland from Bodega Bay where I used to take my children every summer. In the foreground of the bucolic vista with the old wood-framed church and steeple, the artist had painted a huge stone structure like a primitive, forbidding gateway. I remarked that it looked like the famous Stonehenge but in Bodega instead of England. When I got up close to see the title and the artist's name—well, guess what! It was called "Stonehenge at Bodega." And who says art is inaccessible? Thank you, Bill Morehouse.

The massage rooms here are way off to the side in a different world from the main hair salon. It's true that San Francisco workers can conveniently drop in here for a massage at lunch time or after a haircut, but this area needs a lot more "fluffing up" to compete as a place you would select for any extensive massage or spa services. A special area near the hair salon is reserved for makeup applications and makeup lessons.

HOURS
•Tuesday through Saturday, 9 a.m. to 6 p.m.

INCIDENTALS
•Credit cards accepted: MasterCard and Visa. Personal checks also accepted with I.D.

Espirit, Inc.

36 Tiburon Boulevard
Mill Valley, CA 94941
(415) 383-3534

Espirit has been around for nearly 20 years, the last decade in its present Marin County location, its sign quite visible from the Tiburon-East Blithedale exit off Highway 101 north. (And no, we have not misspelled "Esprit.")

Each of the body salons and urban retreats I am including in this revised edition, *California Spas & Urban Retreats,* has its own special style and ambience. At Espirit, I felt I was walking into the beauty parlor of my childhood, except that there was no line of ladies under plastic bubble dryers, absorbed in their movie magazines. All of the latest body-pampering developments are unveiled in the back, past the reception desk, the cases of wonderful skin-care products and the manicure tables that greet you as you enter the salon from the convenient parking lot.

Tucked into this area are four facial rooms, two wax rooms and two tiled steam rooms. A Japanese hot tub is in the massage therapy room. (Steam or hot tub is included with your massage.) Even here, the atmosphere is not ethereal. It is quiet without being hushed; it is pro-

Spa #9
map page 196

$$ Cost
☐ Overnight
☐ Program
■ Day Use
☐ Hot Springs
■ Hot Tubs
■ Sauna
■ Massage
■ Skin Care/Salon
☐ Exercise
☐ Meals
■ Spa Products
☐ Workshops
☐ Children
☐ Pets
☐ Weddings

fessional without being cold. It exudes a warm, friendly hospitality where services are provided without fanfare and pretense by skilled professionals who have been in the business for a good many years. On its menu are eight types of facials, including an acupressure anti-aging facial and a cryotherapy facial; a variety of makeup services including tints and makeup lessons; and hair removal, waxing/bleaching of body and face. Alpha hydroxy acids and cellular treatment products are also available.

Massage and body care includes a therapeutic herbal massage (for women and for men), a body peel and salt-glow treatment with massage, and a special body facial that adds a body mask to the treatment. Six of Espirit's 23 employees are massage practitioners; all are women.

In the spa world, if not in the world of pharmaceuticals, it happens to be true: If one hour is good, four are better; so, as elsewhere, Espirit invites you to indulge yourself in a "Spa Day" (four and a half hours) that gives you a European facial, a manicure, a pedicure, an herbal massage with steam treatment and lunch. (Incidentally, as is happening elsewhere, men are slowly beginning to use spa services.)

I had an interesting conversation with Espirit's owner-director, Genna Lewis, who told me that years ago estheticians had to get their training in Europe but that we have caught up and great training is now widely available in this country. Of course, all estheticians are constantly receiving training as new techniques come along (and/or old ones come back into public acceptance). Espirit's staff is board-certified and licensed by the state of California. Much of what Genna told me jibed with what I learned in my earlier days of working in a medical education program. She does not rely on marketing hype to make her points; she is solidly informed, well-trained, articulate and down to earth.

Genna's goal is to teach clients as much as possible about taking care of their skin so that if they cannot afford to buy services on a regular basis they can still maintain a good skin-care regimen. It seems obvious, but we do forget: The better care you take of your skin, the better it holds up for you over the years. She is proud of her staff, which operates as a team dedicated to serving the needs of each client, and she is happy with her product line, which includes imported and domestic products, some custom-blended, none involving animal testing.

If I were in the mood for a common-sense, family atmosphere for my spa experience, one that would leave me better informed than when I came, I would make Espirit my destination. With "world enough and time," of course, the best is to try them all, like Goldilocks, until you find the one that is "just right" for you.

HOURS
•Open every day. Tuesday through Friday, 8 a.m. to 8 p.m.; Saturday and Monday, 8 a.m. to 5 p.m.; Sunday, 9 a.m. to 3 p.m.

Espirit, Inc.

INCIDENTALS
•In-home/hospital service.
•Some insurance accepted.
•24-hour cancellation notice required.
•Credit cards accepted: MasterCard and Visa.
Personal checks accepted with I.D.

F. Joseph Smith's Massage Therapy Center

158 Almonte Boulevard
Mill Valley, CA 94941
(415) 383-8260

F. Joseph Smith's, a quiet neighborhood spa that carries on year after year without much fanfare, has been busily expanding and upgrading its facilities. Two major changes to date (more in the planning stages) are the addition of a "prayer garden" filled with plants, herbs, flowers, a lovely Japanese maple tree and a charming waterfall, and the expansion into the space next door for a wellness center. Called The Next Step, it offers chiropractic, acupuncture, Oriental medicine and specialty bodywork (Hellerwork, Trager®, Feldenkrais, Rosen Method, Lomi Lomi and more).

Small as it is, the facility houses three massage rooms (all with heaters), one at the front of the building with Japanese-style window shades that let in diffused light and the others toward the back, a public sauna (175 degrees but the client can control it), two changing rooms, two showers and two bathrooms. Al-

Spa #10
map page 196

$-$$ Cost
☐ Overnight
☐ Program
■ Day Use
☐ Hot Springs
■ Hot Tubs
■ Sauna
■ Massage
☐ Skin Care/Salon
☐ Exercise
☐ Meals
☐ Spa Products
■ Workshops
■ Children
☐ Pets
☐ Weddings

F. Joseph Smith's Massage Therapy Center

though it's a dry cedar sauna, there is a stove in the room and water can be drizzled over the rocks for steam.

Two redwood hot tubs, one very large and one medium size, both with whirlpool jets, are outside under the pines and are the most attractive feature of the spa. The temperature hovers between 104 and 106 degrees.

One massage practitioner is "on duty" at all times and some 30 others are available on call. In addition to the standards—Swedish-Esalen and shiatsu—some of the more esoteric forms of bodywork are available at the new wellness center. Pleasant, relaxing massage music (not necessarily the popular New Age tapes many spas use) is piped into the massage rooms.

Despite the aggressive entrepreneurial manner of F. Joseph Smith, this spa has a devoted following of men, women and children. In fact, it is one of the few spas where men constitute 50 percent of the clientele. So forget the hype about Marin County and try this no-frills spa.

HOURS
•Open daily 9 a.m. to 10 p.m.; Sundays noon to 10 p.m.
•Public hot tub and sauna, 9 a.m. to 6 p.m.

INCIDENTALS
•Advance registration is necessary for appointments at The Next Step. Call (415) 383-9779.
•House calls available by reservation.
•Credit cards accepted: MasterCard and Visa. Personal checks also accepted.

The Grand Central Sauna and Hot Tub Co.

15 Fell Street, San Francisco
(415) 431-1370

Spa #11
map page 196

17389 Hesperian Boulevard, San Lorenzo
(510) 278-TUBS

Spa #12
map page 196

376 Saratoga Avenue, San Jose
(408) 247-TUBS

Spa #13
map page 196

$-$$ Cost
☐ Overnight
☐ Program
■ Day Use
☐ Hot Springs
■ Hot Tubs
■ Sauna
☐ Massage
☐ Skin Care/Salon
☐ Exercise
☐ Meals
☐ Spa Products
☐ Workshops
■ Children
☐ Pets
☐ Weddings

Grand Central is another of the urban spas that pioneered the commercialization of the health and fitness movement that marked the 1970s.

Because it is the only so-called "chain" of city spas in this guidebook, let me speak to the romantics out there who might automatically conclude that "chains"—whether in the food, clothing or hot soak business—lack quality: What makes a chain work well is the owner's attention to which aspects of design, purchasing, policy, procedure and staffing need to be kept uniform throughout all branches, and which need to be kept flexible—allowed to evolve naturally out of the particular needs and style of the town in which it is located and the people it serves. I think Grand Central has done well in this respect. They seem to know who their customers are and what type of spa they are looking for, and to be sure they've got it right, each facility provides a "Tell us—we want to know" questionnaire for your comments.

The general design of the spa is essentially the same at each branch. The lobby/waiting room areas are all well designed in terms of space, furnishings and use of color; there is plenty of comfortable seating, conveniently placed coffee tables with reading materials, and a (surprising) video game machine or two. Plants, lighting and framed wall posters (for sale) add warmth.

All facilities sport a long spanking-white reception counter where you sign in, get your key (affixed to a colored shoe horn) and towel, and purchase a cold beverage to take into the room with you. (You might find an ashtray installed in the tub room but they are strict about no alcohol in your hand or noticeably on your breath and, as you will see below, they are scrupulous about their maintenance procedures.)

T-shirts with Grand Central's logo—an aerial view of a whirlpool tub—are for sale here and, if you wear your T-shirt into the place, you'll get a free drink.

All of the private suites, as they call them, wrap around the reception area in a U-shape with restrooms accessible to both sides. Besides being soundproof, each spacious suite contains the tub (usually circular in shape, constructed of redwood or fiberglass, and equipped with two Jacuzzi jets) set into a wooden deck area of high-gloss finish. Other features common to all suites are an open shower with ceramic tiling on the wall section behind it, a double-mattress (some single) resting area, a dry-heat cedar sauna with benches at two levels, a clock, a dimmer switch on the light, an intercom phone, an AM-FM radio and—a nice feature—a clothes rack with hangers.

Maintenance procedures are uniform for all spas, and Grand Central has taken great care to assure sanitary conditions, following practices more stringent, they say, than those of any health department under which they operate. Entitled "No Trouble in Our Bubbles," their handout sheet explains that tubs are drained, vacuumed and scrubbed once a week, that temperature and pH are tested three times a day, and that all tub water is filtered every fifteen minutes and automatically chlorinated. In addition, independent testing labs in each Grand Central location take water samples periodically and conduct microscopic tests on them. They also describe their use of a "closed system" that assures no "sharing" of the water in your tub with the water in any other tub.

Tub water ranges from comfortably warm to a high of about 108 degrees, depending on the tub room. Sauna temperatures also vary. If you have a temperature preference, say so when you sign in.

Now for the particulars at each location:

*The Grand
Central Sauna
and Hot Tub Co.*

SAN FRANCISCO

The Fell Street location is the most high-tech looking. Its lobby colors are a blue, green and white combination. This facility is also the only one to have suntanning equipment—Silver Solarium and Wolf for those who know. The manufacturers' literature on this equipment is available at the front desk, and I would suggest you read it before you use the machine. The desk attendant monitors your time, but there is a safety shut-off at the maximum of 29 minutes; it is wise to be aware of your own skin type and, in all cases, increase your exposure time gradually.

Fell Street has 20 private suites and is used to seeing after-work professionals, couples and even ballet dancers among their regulars. (Anywhere you go in San Francisco, be careful walking around after dark.)

SAN LORENZO

The San Lorenzo facility has attractive rust and beige furnishings in the lobby area. Unlike the other locations, at San Lorenzo half of their 16 private suites have saunas and half do not, some of their tubs are an attractive octagonal-shaped fiberglass instead of redwood, and—most inviting of all—a number of suites have high ceilings and skylights over the tub.

As you drive down Hesperian Boulevard looking for 17389, you may not catch Grand Central's distinctive logo until you're right on it. The next street sign you'll see is Quigley Road right in front of you. Turn in, but carefully; it is a two-way drive into the parking area and a car may well be coming right at you. Maybe the city will have done something about this by the time you go.

SAN JOSE

Tucked into the mall at Steven's Creek Boulevard and Saratoga Avenue, this facility has a very large attractive lobby, again in rusts and beiges, with video machines and comfortable built-in couches all around the perimeter of the room. Twenty-one private suites, all redwood, all with saunas, are available here. One nice feature of "chains" is that you know exactly what to expect when you arrive. If you like one, you'll like another.

Furthermore, if driving a lot is part of your working life, I can't think of anything more relaxing than the one-hour vacation of a hot soak or a sauna toward the end of the day. Regardless, these suburban spas seem to be well used by working people.

HOURS
•Open every day at 10 a.m. Closes at midnight Sunday through Thursday and 2 a.m. on Fridays and Saturdays.

INCIDENTALS
•Rates change after 5 p.m. and with the number of persons.
•First come, first served.
•Cash payment only.

Kabuki
Hot Spring

1750 Geary Boulevard
San Francisco, CA 94115
(415) 922-6002

Spa #14
map page 196

$-$$ Cost
☐ Overnight
☐ Program
■ Day Use
☐ Hot Springs
■ Hot Tubs
■ Sauna
■ Massage
☐ Skin Care/Salon
☐ Exercise
☐ Meals
■ Spa Products
☐ Workshops
■ Children
☐ Pets
☐ Weddings

Kabuki Hot Spring is the same as and different from other spas you'll find in California. It is the same in the services it offers—a good hot soak, a steam room or hot sauna, and a splendid massage—but it incorporates just enough Japanese ritual to be a one-of-a-kind experience.

The most striking feature at this 22-year-old facility is the very large, dramatically tiled communal bath area where you can capture (or recapture) the convivial social time that the baths have provided in Japan for centuries. On the perimeter of the room are Japanese-style showers and shower stalls, a spacious glass-enclosed steam room and a dry sauna. A circular cold-water pool (*mizuboro*) is in the center of the room next to the big hot-water soaking tub (*furo*).

Another difference from other spa facilities is that here, traditionally men have been the highest users. In recent years, however, Kabuki has responded to the increasing usage by women by adding one more day for women only. As of this writing, there are four days reserved exclusively for men and three days reserved exclusively for women.

While we're on the subject of differences, it is worth repeating the adage "Americans take a bath to get clean; the Japanese get clean to take a bath" because the Japanese way is assuredly what is now expected throughout the spa world and particularly so in the health-conscious '90s. At Kabuki, you can take your familiar western-style shower, or you can enjoy the difference of washing Japanese fashion—sitting on the low stools and settling down with the small bucket, soap, and wash cloth provided (and shampoo, if you want) in front of one of the several faucet/shower fixtures at the far end of the communal bath area.

After a hot, soapy scrubdown, you should rinse off thoroughly before moving on to the sauna, the steam room or the "big tub." The water temperature in the *furo* is regulated to stay at 104 degrees, in the cold pool, 55 degrees.

The sauna is larger than usual and is maintained at 180 degrees. The steam room temperature hovers around 110 degrees. Be prepared to perspire more in the steam room than in the sauna—such is the difference between wet and dry heat. At Kabuki, it is particularly important that you know your body's tolerance and respect what your body has to tell you. If you are not accustomed to these hot temperatures, ease into them slowly and shorten the duration of your stay until you and your body are more familiar with the whole process. Kabuki staff also recommend in their flyer that you shower or rest between each heat (cold) treatment and before your massage, especially if you are a newcomer.

People generally move around wrapped in their towels, and certainly so when leaving the communal room for the grooming room or the large, open "Satori Room" for a massage. Both men and women massage practitioners are in the massage room working on their clients. If you scheduled a massage at the desk, the receptionist will call out your key number on the public address system; if you did not, and decide spontaneously that you would like to follow up your tub or sauna with a massage, you can talk to the bath attendant in the massage area to see whether someone can accommodate you on short notice.

For those who prefer total privacy, Kabuki has 11 private rooms, each equipped with a steam cabinet, a massage table, a secure closet, a sink and such amenities as loofahs, shampoo, robes and mouthwash. The saunas are a few steps down the hall from the private rooms, but if you prefer sauna to steam, you can simply wrap yourself in a Kabuki Hot Spring kimono and step out, returning to your room when you are finished. Your massage practitioner will guide you through the process (starting with sauna or steam and followed by a loofah back scrub and a hot soak before the massage), and come in and out at appropriate intervals so that you don't have to watch the clock. Just let go and be taken care of. (Incidentally, another big difference worth mentioning is that there is no hourly limit on your stay at Kabuki. Old-timers make a long relaxing time of it.)

The massage practitioners (all certified massage therapists) are used to doing shiatsu—meaning simply "finger pressure" at key points on the body. Many are trained by the nearby Amma Institute in the ancient system called Amma, of which shiatsu is but one technique. The story of shiatsu and Amma is intriguing—see pages 37 to 45 for more about these and other types of massage.

Over the years, Kabuki Hot Spring has become multicultural in its staffing as well as in its clientele. Despite the ethnicity reflected in the name of this spa and in the plans it offers (Shogun, Kabuki, Kiku, Fuji and Sakura Plans), as well as in its rituals and ambience, the traditional Japanese *massaji-shi* is now commonly referred to as a massage practitioner and may have Europe, Africa or Asia as his or her national origin. There are about 25 licensed massage practitioners on Kabuki's staff.

The San Francisco Police Department requires that "client cards" be issued to each patron. Their interest is to maintain the legitimacy of the spa facilities, but Kabuki makes its own use of these cards to note particular pains, injuries, likes and dislikes of its regular clients, as well as to send guest passes for a free massage to those who have 10 visits recorded.

Kabuki has completed its major renovation—new carpeting throughout, re-tiling of the communal room and private rooms, installation of specialized plumbing and equipment to make everything wheelchair-accessible. In the lobby is a beautiful 60-gallon aquarium and a changing display of local artwork.

The substantial dollar investment represented by these changes is testimony that Kabuki intends to retain its place in San Francisco's places-to-go/things-to-do recommendations for years to come. A major advantage it has as a local and tourist attraction is that the AMC Kabuki 8 Theaters on the upper level of the building are home to the San Francisco Film Festival and to many competitions and events related to Japantown's Cherry Blossom Festival in May. If you're from out of town or out of state, you might want to plan your visit around one or more of these events.

HOURS
•Open seven days a week, Monday through Friday, 10 a.m. to 10 p.m.; Saturday and Sunday, 9 a.m. to 10 p.m.

INCIDENTALS
•Fully wheelchair accessible.
•Children under 18 must be accompanied by an adult; children under 10 free with parents.
•Gift certificates are available.
•Bridal, bachelor and corporate parties can be arranged.
•Check hours for massage when making reservation.

•Three-hour validated parking at Japan Center Garage after 5 p.m. and all day Saturday and Sunday.

•Miyako Hotel is next door for overnight or extended stays and several good restaurants are close by.

•Kabuki Hot Spring T-shirts and other spa products for sale at counter.

•Credit cards accepted: MasterCard, Visa and American Express. No personal checks.

La Clinique

333 Miller Avenue, Suite 1
Mill Valley, CA 94941
(415) 383-7224

Spa #15
map page 196

$$ Cost
☐ Overnight
☐ Program
■ Day Use
☐ Hot Springs
■ Hot Tubs
☐ Sauna
■ Massage
■ Skin Care/Salon
☐ Exercise
☐ Meals
■ Spa Products
☐ Workshops
☐ Children
☐ Pets
☐ Weddings

Even though La Clinique was not quite altogether there when I visited, I must include it because it promises to be quite a special place—and its doors will have opened wide by the time you read this. La Clinique specializes in women's health, offering standard spa services (Jacuzzi, massage, facials, and so on) but, in addition, colonics and lymphatic drainage (about which I know nothing, so don't ask).

Owner Nancy Gardner, who has been in the business for 20 years, explained to me the five-point (head-to-toe) program she has developed for women. It consists of (1) deep tissue massage of neck, back and shoulders; (2) cellulite treatment for hips, thighs and buttocks; (3) lymphatic drainage for breasts, abdomen and groin; (4) antistress massage for neck, head and face; and (5) foot reflexology. And, of course, you can also select your own treatments *à la carte* from her extensive menu.

I was intrigued by Gardner's down-the-road vision for La Clinique. She plans to establish a women's health library, similar to Planetree, the health resources library in San Francisco where, for a nominal donation, a person can drop in and find information on a multitude of medical procedures, conditions, illnesses and the like.

Planetree came into being with the health revolution of the '70s which, among other things, focused on patients' being informed and taking charge of their own health. Resisted by the medical profession at first (physicians are concerned about laypeople trying to doctor themselves), patient self-reliance in the area of health and well-being is now the physicians' ally. Informed individuals are likely to be more responsible as patients and less likely to demand that the MD "fix it or be sued." Gardner has associations with local physicians who, like her, are committed to holistic health care, natural healing forces and non-invasive, non-chemical procedures, and she intends to use them as referrals for her clients who want consultation beyond the level of services she provides.

When you arrive at La Clinique, you will see what I could only visualize as Nancy walked me through. (The only aromatherapy going on was the pungent smell emanating from buckets of peach paint.) The front lobby will be furnished in pale green wicker, the walls will be sponged with peach-colored paint, and there will be "lots and lots of big, beautiful plants." Walls were slated to be torn down when I was there to open up a big space for a juice bar and comfy pillow-cushion seating. Paintings on the wall will be those elegant bare-skinned or barely clothed ladies from days gone by and classical flute and similarly "mellow" music will waft throughout the spa.

Behind the lobby and juice area are six treatment rooms, dressing rooms, baths and showers, two steam cabinets and two Jacuzzis. Cotton robes and towels are provided. The tub room is totally private and Nancy has assured people that they do not need to bring a swimsuit with them.

The trend toward accommodating couples, or twosomes, is not confined to Calistoga. Nancy intends to have the Jacuzzis side by side with a massage table in between where one partner can massage the other. After your special two-hour instruction at the Calistoga Massage Center (see page 149), you'll be ready to practice what you've learned.

Brochures should be ready by the time you read this. Check it out and let me know what you think.

HOURS
•Tuesday through Saturday, 9 a.m. to 5 p.m. Earlier and later appointments are available on request.

INCIDENTALS
•Ample parking in back, where the entrance is located.
•No credit cards accepted. Personal checks are accepted with I.D.

Mister Lee's Beauty, Hair and Health Spa

834 Jones Street
San Francisco, CA 94109
(415) 474-6002

Mister Lee (Lee Bledsoe), an award-winning hair stylist whose salon has occupied this old San Francisco building since 1968, decided to move into the spa world following a bout of illness that took him to France to recover, mostly from the sense of having been overmedicated. Introduced to the wonders of hydrotherapy and aromatherapy there, he came back charged with new purpose.

With his already highly successful hair salon occupying the first two floors of the building (Mister Lee was the official hair stylist for the Mondale-Ferraro campaign and recently worked on the tresses of Miss California and Miss Hawaii), in 1988 he turned the third floor into one of the most elegant and unusual spas you are likely to find anywhere. An "urban retreat" it is indeed.

On the first two floors, you will see busy, bright, gleaming hair-care stations with their

Spa #16
map page 196

$$ Cost
☐ Overnight
☐ Program
■ Day Use
☐ Hot Springs
■ Hot Tubs
☐ Sauna
■ Massage
■ Skin Care/Salon
☐ Exercise
☐ Meals
■ Spa Products
■ Workshops
☐ Children
☐ Pets
☐ Weddings

large, rope-framed mirrors, display cases of beautifying products, exposed brick walls and glass used to bring the outdoors in, dark tile pavers on the floors, Klimt prints, wonderful posters and other art on the walls, including interesting memorabilia, a charming Guillaume depicting four ladies under elongated egg-shaped hair dryers and framed testimonials to Mister Lee. A narrow mezzanine level has been given over to makeup application.

The *pièce de résistance* is when you continue up the carpeted marble steps to the upper reaches. Turn a corner in the stairwell to glance at a charming bronze sculpture of a young girl in a slip dress, her hair plaited in front and pony-tailed in back, seated casually on a pedestal with one leg folded under her, and know that the best is yet to come.

When you reach the third floor, the dim lights and the atmosphere of near-complete still-ness that envelops you on the landing signals that you are about to enter a special place. You will open the door to a visual treat immedi-ately in front of you—a wall of stone from which a young goddess is emerging, some limbs completely extricated from the stone, others only partially. (As I stood there, I immediately remembered being taught that Michelangelo saw himself simply as a workman whose job it was to release the sculpture hidden within the stone.)

In the context of the spa, and judging from the words of Vivi Mandel, Mister Lee's effu-sive, French-accented spa director who was my guide, this stunning wall art might be regarded as symbolizing the promise of Mister Lee's spa to release the god and goddess within. (Mister Lee's is a "gender-friendly" place, I was told.) Egyptian motifs are everywhere here, reminding us that the use of body perfumes, oils, sea water and scents have an ancient and venerable tradition.

Our voices now hushed, Vivi opened the door to a perfectly splendid massage therapy room—again, dimly lit, the walls paneled with Egyptian-style art, and billowy silken curtains forming a picture-perfect backdrop. Functional as well as beautiful, they can be drawn around the table for total privacy. A private bath is nearby. Mister Lee's staff of massage practitioners (all women) are skilled in most forms of massage clients request, including reflexology.

Even in the body-treatment room next door, with its gleaming white tile, sink with brass fixtures, and generally more "clinical" look (in stark contrast to the ambience of the massage room, for example), elements of ancient Egyptian times are cleverly used to evoke the mystique and mythology of another world and another time. Besides Egyptian-style wall panels covering the tall windows that would otherwise look out to Jones Street (three stories and many centuries away from where we stood), each of the three treatment tables were made of stone with bas-relief designs along the sides and were supported by cylindrical legs of stone.

It is in this room that you receive body scrubs; full and partial body wraps that use natural sea algae, plant products and essential oils; back facials; and other exfoliating, toning and polishing treatments with and without aromatherapy. Needless to say, cellulite treatments, a series of six plus one complimentary treatment, are also among Mister Lee's popular offerings. This room is also used for waxing, which is usually followed by an application of soothing body milk enhanced by essential oils.

The next exciting area Vivi led me to, one that has been well photographed and publicized in such magazines as *W* and *Self*, among others, is the hydrotherapy tub room. Once again, the atmosphere is one of hushed, cool, gray stone where planters bulging with exotic plants protrude from the walls and Egyptian ladies are profiled in long, narrow wall panels behind two stunning hydrotherapy tubs placed at angles to each other to form an apex. Each porcelain tub is embedded in a heavily ornamented stone casing that magically transforms the twentieth-century look of its elaborate controls, water jets (72 of them), and chrome safety bars.

Hydrotherapy, well known and used in all parts of Europe, requires highly trained therapists. Once the jet streams are perfectly adjusted so that the bubbling aromatic waters reach different parts of your body—legs, hips, back—at the appropriate force (at a body-neutral temperature, by the way), the attendant will finish by using the underwater massage hose to promote lymph drainage and thereby rid the body of the toxic waste material we accumulate in the course of daily living. As elsewhere, billowy curtains can be drawn around each tub so that two strangers can take their hydrotherapy treatments at the same time.

Toward the back of the building are the facial rooms, which, based on personalized skincare consultation, range from deep pore cleansing to "rejuvenating" face and throat treatments. All include the use of selected aromatherapy products.

Before we left this magical third floor, Vivi showed me the small room where Mister Lee's product line is enticingly displayed. She is obviously quite proud of their line, which uses no animal products or mineral oils. Unlike commercial, over-the-counter products, their packaging is deliberately kept simple; they want the value to remain where it belongs—in the product itself. It seems that their products are in such high demand, nationally and internationally, that an 800 number was recently set up for ordering Mister Lee products. All you have to do is dial 1-800-MY DAY SPA.

We proceeded to open bottles and jars, to smell and "ooh" and "aah" for some time before I drifted back downstairs, enveloped in the illusion that I had actually experienced every one of these body-beautiful regimes instead of having enjoyed them vicariously.

It is easy to see why Mister Lee's has a local, national and international following among women and men alike. For all of the exotica its elegant third-floor spa offers, the prices, as others have reported, are not astronomical.

Mister Lee's

HOURS
•Open six days a week, 8:30 a.m. to 5:30 p.m. (Thursday until 7:30 p.m.). Closed Sunday.

INCIDENTALS
•Gift certificates are available.
•Men's "Relaxation Day," "Corporate Packages" and half-day and full-day spa packages are available.
•25% deposit required (non-refundable) on all spa packages.
•24-hour cancellation notice on half- and full-day packages.
•Mister Lee available for lectures, seminars and make-overs.
•Parking garages nearby.
•Credit cards accepted: all major credit cards. Personal checks also accepted with I.D.

Norma Jean's
The Beauty Studio

1013 Larkspur Landing Circle
Larkspur, CA 94939
(415) 461-8820

Attracted by an ad I saw for a *three-hour* massage special at Norma Jean's The Beauty Studio in Larkspur Landing, and intrigued by the fact that despite its location in my back yard, I had never heard of this place, I immediately called. Although I was not looking for the "great pre-wedding stress relief" promised by this massage ad, I *was* in the market for post-wedding stress relief. My youngest daughter had just married, and while she and her husband-to-be had spared me all the work that traditionally falls to the mother of the bride, they did not keep me from dancing up a hurricane, an experience my body didn't let me forget for weeks after.

Once at Norma Jean's, I ended up having an all-day sampler that included a facial, makeup application, a manicure, a pedicure and one hour of massage by a young, fresh-faced, healthy blonde woman named Tania. It was one of the most terrific massages I have ever had. So right off the bat, I can tell you that Norma Jean is

Spa #17
map page 196

$$ Cost
☐ Overnight
☐ Program
■ Day Use
☐ Hot Springs
☐ Hot Tubs
☐ Sauna
■ Massage
■ Skin Care/Salon
☐ Exercise
☐ Meals
■ Spa Products
☐ Workshops
☐ Children
☐ Pets
☐ Weddings

very shrewd about the people she hires. Don't expect to see a Marilyn Monroe look-alike in Norma Jean, despite her name, although you will see on display some of the Marilyn memorabilia people have contributed to her shop. Being of mixed ethnic origin, Norma Jean is particularly alert to and knowledgeable about differences in skin type and what these differences mean in terms of the care and feeding of your skin.

Before elaborating on her services, let me first tell you about Larkspur Landing. It is that area where Highways 580 and 101 and Sir Francis Drake Boulevard all meet at the landmark trestle bridge and force you to recall whether you're en route to Samuel P. Taylor Park and Point Reyes, or south to Sausalito, or north to San Rafael. It is where the latest-model Golden Gate ferries arrive and depart, but in the eyes of locals, "Larkspur Landing" is shorthand for the Larkspur Landing Shopping Center, a large, well-designed complex that has been in place since 1978.

Among its specialty shops, its supermart, its popular movie house, its attractive clusters of rental units and its many restaurants and businesses (including Weight Watchers, a 24-hour Nautilus and Norma Jean's) is also the six-year-old hotel, Courtyard by Marriott. In talking with Norma Jean, I learned that many of her clients are referred by the hotel or find her in the course of exploring the well-used shopping center.

Having worked in hospital administration

for years, Norma Jean, at the urging of her daughter, turned her career around in 1986 to one centered on pleasure and well-being. For all of her studio's attention to the beauty that can be achieved from skillful topical applications, whether it is nail polish, tweezing and tinting of eyebrows, waxing or makeup, her philosophic commitment is to her clients' health and well-being. She is also very results-oriented. She knows what can be achieved when a sound skin-care regimen is followed—and she is a convincing model of her own philosophy. She is also a wealth of information for anyone skeptical about the difference between over-the-counter products and product lines sold at salons and spas or about the benefits of glycolic acid treatment of the skin.

When you walk into Norma Jean's studio, you think you're in a typical beauty parlor. There is the small appointment table, the manicure stations and the makeup center. What doesn't immediately show are the quiet spaces where the magical body treatments take place—upstairs for massages and in a back room for facials.

On her list of body treatments are: three-hour massages (includes body scrub, combined Swedish and acupressure massage and foot reflexology), at a discount for first-time clients; two-hour and one-hour massages; European facials (75 minutes), mini-facials (45 minutes) and back facials; as well as cellulite treatments in a single session or series of six.

Two perfectly wonderful items on her menu are limited massage treatments, one focusing on hands and arms and the other on feet and lower legs. I think that's a particularly smart service to offer. For one thing, it allows someone who is still timid about full-body massage to ease into it and, for older people, athletes, runners and those who, fit or unfit, have pushed themselves too hard (like a woman who danced too strenuously and too long at her daughter's wedding), it offers welcome relief.

As already mentioned, you can pick and choose from a number of different facials (including acne treatment) and beauty services—nails, tinting and tweezing, waxing (many of her waxing clients are men), and makeup—a single application for a special event or a lesson so that, armed with information about your own skin and face, you can perfect your at-home routines.

Norma Jean's is a small and unpretentious urban retreat that, like others in this category, allows you to spend an hour or a day enjoying one or several of its spa services. Because of its location, it is attractive to couples and twosomes where one wants to see a movie, shop or hang out at the bookstore and the other wants to spend some quality time at a spa.

Whatever your choices at the spa itself, whether to be nurtured, to be informed, to prepare for (or recover from) a special event, or simply to take care of your beauty and skincare needs, what Norma Jean wants, always, is that her clients leave her studio "smiling and feeling completely taken care of."

HOURS

•Monday through Saturday, 9 a.m. to 5 p.m.
•Early morning or later evening appointments
by arrangement.

INCIDENTALS

•Gift certificates are available.
•Credit cards accepted: MasterCard and Visa.

The Physical Therapy Center

125 Throckmorton Avenue
Mill Valley, CA 94941
(415) 383-8770

Spa #18
map page 196

$-$$ Cost
☐ Overnight
☐ Program
■ Day Use
☐ Hot Springs
■ Hot Tubs
■ Sauna
■ Massage
☐ Skin Care/Salon
☐ Exercise
☐ Meals
☐ Spa Products
☐ Workshops
☐ Children
☐ Pets
☐ Weddings

I learned about The Physical Therapy Center through an Italian friend from Milan who knew nothing of my explorations into the spa world. She simply volunteered in passing that she always schedules a massage appointment at PTC whenever she is in this country. With that recommendation, I set out for downtown Mill Valley.

Still tucked between the corner Coffee Roastery and Sweetwater, where people come from far and wide to hear top R&B and rock groups, The Physical Therapy Center's nondescript doorway opens to a bare public lobby area carpeted in well-worn—now *very* well-worn—gray floor covering. To get to PTC, you let the gray carpet lead you around to a surprising, circular stairway. Look up, as I did, and imagine a 1940's vintage Hollywood star poised at the top, hand on banister, about to descend. Once you reach the top of the stairs, you'll be greeted with one of several batiks painted by the Center's in-house artist whose inspiration comes from the changing colors she sees on the mountains and beaches of Marin. At the head of the stairs, simple lattice panels are used very effectively to separate the reception area from the public hot tub that occupies much of the expansive, airy, second-floor space.

Although the Stutzman family has owned and operated The Physical Therapy Center since 1976, primary management responsibility is now with Christopher and Kathleen, both massage therapists themselves, as is Mark Stutzman who continues to work at the Center.

As I mentioned, the large, hexagonal, public hot tub is obscured on three sides by judicious use of tall latticework panels. When you come around to the fourth, open side, you'll be as impressed as I was at the view of the hot tub, decked out with huge tropical plants brought in from Hawaii and graced above with "naked" sky—at least in nice weather. At night and during colder weather, the roll-back roof is closed, but because it is of glass, you can still look up and see the stars as you soak with the friends you came with, friends you arrange to meet there or friends you're about to make. (Incidentally, you are asked to wear a swimsuit, so you either bring your own or they will provide one.) The spacious sauna area, which faces the hot tub just across a walkway, runs horizontally, and has a shower at midpoint that you can pop into intermittently to avoid overheating. All the cedar in the sauna has recently been replaced.

Although the tub occupies center stage and

can be rented by the hour, the hot tub and sauna are regarded as adjuncts to the Center's primary reason for being, which is massage and body therapy. The Center employs 30 massage therapists, part-time and full-time, all highly experienced. Most massage practitioners in the area continually update their skills and knowledge by participating in the many workshops and trainings available in this state, regarded as a "mecca" for massage and bodywork.

Given that massage and bodywork is PTC's central concern, and that an increasing number of physicians are recommending it to patients as part of a rehabilitation process, it's not surprising that The Physical Therapy Center offers all of the standard massage practices and then some, as its name suggests.

Treatment rooms are situated all along the periphery of the large square area that houses the reception desk, open lounge (primarily for staff to take a break), public hot tub, sauna, changing rooms, showers and laundry area for staff use. Each treatment room has its own space heater (more economical to heat individual rooms when a client arrives). Although they play soft instrumental or New Age music, you can bring your own music tapes.

Locals use the Center as a place to meet and relax together in a tub or sauna before dinner at La Ginestra or O'Leary's, or a rockin' night at Sweetwater. Except for your massage, which will be in one of the private treatment rooms, the PTC is not for those who want total seclusion. Both the tub and the sauna hold many bodies at one time, so depending on the day and the hour, you may be alone or one among many.

HOURS
•Open year round, Monday through Saturday, 10 a.m. to 10 p.m.; Sunday, 11 a.m. to 10 p.m.

INCIDENTALS
•Free half-hour use of tub and sauna *before* one-hour or one-and-a-half-hour massage.
•Bring swimsuit. Towels and lockers provided.
•Some insurance accepted with a doctor's prescription.
•Gift certificates available.
•Reservations preferred.
•Credit cards accepted: MasterCard and Visa. Personal checks also accepted with I.D.

Piedmont Springs

3939 Piedmont Avenue
Oakland, CA 94611
(510) 652-9191

Located on Piedmont Avenue, a street filled with good things from produce markets to bookstores to restaurants to flower stands, Piedmont Springs is an easy walk from a nearby public parking lot, and in the evening, street parking is a definite possibility. The spa has created a black-and-white brochure that should receive a graphics award. It effectively reflects a facility that "is serious about sanitation and your health," that exudes serenity, and that wants to keep its clients coming back time after time.

After you register at the counter and pick up your towel and a cold drink (Crystal Geyser mineral waters and various juices), you'll walk down a corridor to the back of the facility. Here, you abruptly leave the polished look of the interior and come upon an enclosed gravel pathway and the natural brick and redwood and lush greenery that grace the four open-air tub rooms in front of you.

A fifth room provides a tub and indoor sauna and is called "the combination room." The temperature of the tub water is between 104 and 106 degrees; every tub is equipped with a constant filtering system and is flushed and cleaned daily and thoroughly scrubbed weekly.

For general use, there is a spacious, dry (Finnish) cedar-lined sauna; for a wet sauna, you can pour water over the rocks and send some welcome vapor into the room.

Piedmont Springs has approximately 30 massage therapists on call—two to four are present during the day and another two to four in the evening. In addition to the standard favorites—Esalen, Swedish and shiatsu—Piedmont has practitioners on call who do deep tissue work, Rosen Method or polarity therapy. (If one of those is what you're looking for, be sure to give them advance notice.) Four massage rooms are available and so simultaneous massages can be given as long as you have reserved ahead.

Piedmont now offers "the European Facial," which includes skin analysis, cleansing, massage, non-chemical peel, deep pore cleansing and moisturizing. Allow one hour. They also offer the "Ultra Moisturizing Facial," an "Herbal Facial" and a "Mini-Aromatherapy Facial." Two added treatments you can request with your facial are a special "Eye Treatment" or a "Hand Treatment."

I have to confide that my sister was recently given a gift certificate to Piedmont Springs. Because she was a complete newcomer who would not have elected to go on her own, I felt very protective of her and eager that she enjoy the experience. She opted to have a facial. I told her everything I could think of—the positive, the potentially negative (I don't like steam in my face, for example), where to park, how to tip. I was like a mother sending her child off on the first day of school. Well! She reported back that she loved every minute, that her Belgian facialist was superb, that the steam, the foot-and-hand massage, everything was—well, as she put it, "I thought I had died and gone to heaven." (Thanks, Piedmont!)

HOURS
•Open year round, every day, from 11 a.m. to 11 p.m.

INCIDENTALS
•Two-person minimum charge on Fridays and Saturdays after 5 p.m.
•Discount cards and 10-use passes available—good any time of day or night.
•Gift certificates are available.
•Children 10 and under are free (limit two children per adult).
•Senior discounts.
•No alcohol and no smoking rules enforced.
•The spa provides towels, robe, soap and hair dryers. Bring your own towel and get a $1 discount—$1.50 on Mondays.
•Massage oils, soaps and hair-care products are for sale at the front desk.
•Monday-Tuesday discounts on massage, plus any massage scheduled before 5 p.m. gives you a free half-hour tub or sauna. Prices go up after 4 p.m.
•Credit cards accepted: MasterCard and Visa.

Shibui Gardens

19 Tamalpais Avenue
San Anselmo, CA 94960
(415) 457-0283

Shibui Gardens has not changed since I wrote about it last. It remains where it has been for nearly 20 years now, just off San Anselmo Avenue in one of Marin County's nicest towns. It is also still true that a person could spend hours feasting and shopping in this antique-rich community that puts on a stunning street fair every year.

As printed in the tiniest brochure of all the spas in this book—5¹/₂" long by 2¹/₄" wide— Shibui means "a quality of beauty...that might be associated with humility, unpretentious virtue and unassuming tastefulness." Small, unpretentious and tasteful as it is, Shibui is not particularly Japanese in style.

It is sandwiched in at the back of a parking lot serving the spa, a skin-care salon and a delightful family-owned Russian restaurant. You reach the spa via a charming brick walkway lined with shrubs and brimming with flowers (at least in the spring). On a busy weekend evening, you'll hear happy voices filtering through the trees from the outdoor tubs on the other side of the path.

*Spa #20
map page 196*

$-$$ Cost

☐ Overnight
☐ Program
■ Day Use
☐ Hot Springs
■ Hot Tubs
■ Sauna
■ Massage
☐ Skin Care/Salon
☐ Exercise
☐ Meals
☐ Spa Products
☐ Workshops
■ Children
☐ Pets
☐ Weddings

Shibui Gardens   Its small waiting room boasts an old "Detroit Jewel" stove converted into the reception desk, a large photograph of San Francisco's famed Sutro Baths, a Venus statuette, a lovely, faded blue velvet armchair, and an upholstered wooden loveseat.

Its four tub rooms, three private and one a communal cold plunge, are open to the sky with wisteria-draped fencing hiding them from public view.

The decking around the tubs is decorated with large plants or flowers, and open showers are nestled into the corner of the room so that if you want to cool down and then pop back into the hot water (which ranges from 104 to 106 degrees), you can do so without having to scurry back and forth to the cold plunge.

The one sauna is adjacent to a tub room and if a party wants both a sauna and a hot tub, the otherwise locked connecting door can be opened. Several dressing rooms, showers and restrooms are packed into a relatively small space inside the building.

There are two massage rooms, one inside and one located at the end of the outdoor walkway next to a large corner tub area. At Shibui, two people can book simultaneous massages so that one doesn't have to wait for the other. Massage practitioners offer largely Swedish massage, although, as in other facilities, you'll find that many massage therapists are trained in shiatsu and other forms of bodywork. At any given time, two massage practitioners will be available, but if you want a massage appointment at an off-day or time, be sure to reserve ahead. Your hot soak is free when you have a one-hour or hour-and-a-half massage.

As in other city spas, Shibui uses a constant filtering system and attendants take daily readings, adding bromine as necessary to maintain the right pH. Tubs are thoroughly cleaned and scrubbed once a week.

There is a tiny kitchen area behind the reception desk where cold beverages are kept in the refrigerator. Buy your drink before you go into the tub. (More and more spas have signs such as Shibui's: "Alcohol and hot tubs do not mix.") They encourage you to bring your own towels, although if you forget or drop in on the spur of the moment, they have towels to rent.

HOURS
•Monday through Thursday, 2 p.m. to 11 p.m.; Friday and Saturday, noon to midnight; Sunday, noon to 11 p.m.

INCIDENTALS
•Discounts for children (under 7 are free) and for groups of more than three in a tub.
•Seniors can tub at half price.
•Gift certificates are available.
•A variety of good restaurants at moderate prices are within walking distance.
•No credit cards accepted; local checks accepted with I.D.

Skylonda Retreat

16350 Skyline Boulevard
Woodside, CA 94062
(800) 851-2222
(415) 851-4500
(415) 851-5504 fax

Spa #21
map page 196

$$$$ Cost
■ Overnight
■ Program
☐ Day Use
■ Hot Springs
■ Hot Tubs
■ Sauna
■ Massage
■ Skin Care/Salon
■ Exercise
■ Meals
■ Spa Products
■ Workshops
☐ Children
☐ Pets
■ Weddings

Each edition of my guidebook to California spas announces a "find," and each find has been entirely different from the one before. The first was Two Bunch Palms, the second, Willow, and this time around, it has to be Skylonda Retreat.

Just opened in April 1993, its avalanche of descriptive PR material, elegant and informative as it is, cannot hope to capture the feel of this stunning retreat. Words will fail me, too, but I'll try to give you my impressions.

For natural splendor (its beautifully crafted log lodge is set into a lush redwood forest between Highway 280 and Half Moon Bay), interior design (every inch has been planned and decorated by someone with a keen eye for color, fabric, furnishings, art work and comfort), fitness regime (designed by experts, reviewed by exercise physiologists and individualized according to your goals and level of fitness), and fine meals (nutritious "fuel" foods elegantly prepared and presented—1,300 to 1,600 calories a day, 10 percent fat), Skylonda has few equals.

The lodge is constructed of Ponderosa logs and river rock and, I was told, every effort was made throughout its construction to assure the very least disturbance to the environment. In fact, Dixon Collins, president of the Skylonda Retreat, apparently was able to avoid some of the tree cutting that was to have taken place had he not bought the property when he did. As it was, no redwoods were cut, and of the 30-some trees above 18 inches in diameter that had to be removed, most were tan oaks.

In its construction, he took care to see that non-toxic building and interior finish materials were used and that ecologically safe systems were installed throughout the lodge, pool and spa. The pool, for example, uses an ozone filtration system (no chlorine, minimal Muratic acid) that allows the water to flow from the interior pool to the spa on the outside deck and back in a self-cleaning action.

In the end, Skylonda qualified for PG&E's highest energy-conservation award for building insulation, double windows, soundproofing and safe lighting. A final environmental note, if Al and Tipper Gore aren't already rushing to register, is that Skylonda is located at an altitude of nearly 2,000 feet. As noted in its literature, being at this altitude and in a forest region accomplishes two things: The altitude means you are above pollution levels; the forest yields higher than average levels of oxygen.

The main dining room in the lodge takes "lodgeness" to a new level with its huge rock fireplace, nine glorious chandeliers, and massive refectory table decked with fresh fruit and flowers. Round tables are placed throughout the room for guests to sit in small groupings. From this room, everywhere you look gives you a view of the tall redwoods that quietly and continually remind you of your place in the universe. A coffee/juice bar is along the wall separating the dining room from the equally massive kitchen.

I found the guest rooms especially appealing. First of all, instead of the austere, angled bed with flat-finish fabric spreads, these beds (queen and two to a room—if alone, you'll be buddied up) are covered in poofy peach comforters with forest green pillows (or vice versa). Even for someone who is not just returning from the daily two-hour hike, they beckon you to sink down into their warm embrace. Carpets are all wool, closet area is ample, and each room has writing tables and a private bath. A final thoughtful detail is a curtain that can be drawn between the beds, should one want to read and the other sleep. Incidentally, there are 15 rooms so the maximum number of guests at any one time will be 30.

The "Great Room" above the main dining room is really a work of art from its 23-foot-high trussed ceiling to its 14-foot-high stained glass panels and its collection of one-of-a-kind rugs on the floor. (All of the details of color and fabric and furnishings, incidentally, were selected by Kathy Collins, whose title at Skylonda is Special Events Manager but whose professional background is in interior design.) It is this large, wonderfully comfortable sitting room that houses a library, large television set, and game tables and welcomes the resident group to the various activities and lectures that take place in the evening.

In planning the decor of this room, Kathy told me she started with the rugs. Certain that she didn't want a "theme" (e.g. Oriental or Southwestern), Kathy selected several different colors and designs, each complementing the others. The chairs and couches are covered in burgundies and greens that pick up the tones in the rugs, as do the delicate stained-glass panels that grace this room.

Outside the Great Room is a wraparound deck where we stood for a few minutes listening to what Kathy described as "tree rain," the only sound breaking that incredible stillness that permeates the forest. She also told me that the logs used for the deck fencing at this level were painted a deep burnished red to match the madrones just beyond.

I can't resist telling you all of these features of Skylonda. Let me "show you" the downstairs pool and spa area, and then get on to the kind of structured program you can expect to enjoy here.

Each area of this 18,000-square-foot lodge opens up a new architectural and design wonderland. Having marveled at the upstairs areas, I should have known that the pool and spa area would be equally magnificent. A wall of river rock takes up the length of the swimming pool, which is enclosed in beveled glass and looks out to a beautiful outdoor spa and the trees beyond. The water here pumps into the outdoor spa (105 degrees) and back into the inside pool (86 to 90 degrees.) Aquatics offered in this pool are usually reserved as a cool-down activity after more strenuous workouts.

The rest of this floor is taken up with a large exercise studio that looks out to a lovely grassy area. Wall mirrors, standard features in most exercise studios, are purposely kept to a minimum here to encourage you to focus less on how your body looks and more on how your body feels.

On the same floor, below the main dining room, are the various areas reserved for saunas and steam baths, massages, manicures, pedicures and facials. (Skin-care services were developed by a woman trained in France and the product line used is Decleor.) Among the many details that catch your eye as you wander through Skylonda—the fetish of the salamander signifying growth and renewal appears quietly throughout the property, for example—you'll find wonderful prints by local artists in this section of the building. They are there on consignment and the office staff can give you a list of titles and prices.

Okay. Here is what a typical day looks like. (And did I tell you that all of the essential clothing you'll need is supplied? Even rain gear? But forget your toothbrush before you forget to pack well-broken-in hiking shoes or boots.)

Depending on the arrangements you have made when you register, you will be picked up at the airport or at another location at noon on Sunday (no need to drive the long, often fogged-in road I traveled) and arrive at the lodge to be registered and get your spa clothing by about 1 p.m. For the next three hours, everyone goes through the initial interview, weigh-in and fitness-testing process, which includes a reading of your blood pressure and body measurements. At 4 p.m., you get to take your first one-hour hike, followed by stretch, yoga and meditation. At 6:30 the fabulous gong on the upstairs deck outside of the Great Room will call you to dinner. After dinner, you will gather in the Great Room and be formally introduced to the group of people with whom, until now, you've only gotten to chat a bit. These are the people you'll be with for the week and who, for some, will become fast friends.

From Monday through Friday, your wake-up call is at 6 a.m. Stretch, yoga and meditation follow at 6:30 and breakfast at 7:30. Your morning hike starts at 8 and you'll be back about 10:30. For the next hour or so, you will be in a circuit training or movement class with a cool-down aquatics session just before lunch at 1:15. The after-lunch hour is reserved for rest or body treatments with circuit training and movement classes starting again at 2:45. Having recovered from your morning hike (?), you're ready to hike again—from 4 p.m. to 6 p.m. From 6 to 7 p.m., you get a well-earned hour of silence or a hot sauna or a dip in the pool. Dinner is at 7 p.m. The evening program starts at 7:30 and ends at 9 p.m. I'm not entirely sure, but I think you get to go to bed then!

Saturday, because you don't return to the airport or local pickup location until noon, starts with the same 6 a.m. wake-up call followed by stretch, yoga and meditation. But then you stop for a "weighing-out" and a recheck of your measurements. After that, you have time to browse through the gift shop, drink a smoothie and join the others for a group photo. But it's only 9:15 a.m. (they really know how to pack it in) and you won't be leaving without a final hike before your late breakfast at 10:45 a.m. You'll have a half-hour to pack and, at noon, you're heading back home to a distinctly altered reality.

I can't possibly cover everything, but I do want to add just a bit about the hikes. Those who designed the program regard its hikes through meandering trails covered with 3,000-year-old redwoods that suddenly open up to breathtaking vistas as "core to every guest's experience at Skylonda." You can see from their prominence in the schedule that these hikes, perhaps all by themselves, constitute a major force in renewing you, physically, emotionally, intellectually and spiritually. You will have hiked an average of 60 to 70 miles during the course of your stay, with the promise that no one will hike the same trail twice.

If you're concerned about your ability to manage these hikes, don't worry. Not only is your fitness level assessed at the beginning of your stay but on your arrival you will be assigned to the hiking group that suits your level. Vans take you to and from the various trailheads, some of which lead to the ocean.

Skylonda guests, I was told, occasionally ask to have a less than one-week stay. Except for accommodating corporate groups, the staff wants to maintain a commitment to its one-week program. As the Scriptures say, "There is a time for every season..." and in spas that offer total programs, it seems to take four days to reach a certain "aha" level: the point where you recognize that something has shifted. It is in the next few days that the experience is solidified—where it becomes something less likely to dissipate after you leave.

Skylonda is a place designed for those who want to be challenged. As Kathy pointed out, that challenge will be physical for some, but for others it might be social, emotional or spiritual. And I suspect that you might not know what the challenge will be for you until you experience it. If you're looking for something more than a week of pampering, or a week of beautification, or a week of restful quiet, then I would say there arc few places in the state that offer a more inspiring, supportive and visually stunning environment in which to take that existential journey. And although in the four-star price range, Skylonda costs less than other fitness resorts in its league.

HOURS
•The office is open from 9 a.m. to 5:30 p.m. daily.

INCIDENTALS

•A nonrefundable deposit of $1,000 is required to confirm your reservation. Full refund is possible if your reservation is cancelled 30 days prior to arrival. If it is cancelled closer to your reserved time (no less than 48 hours) the deposit may be applied to a future stay within one year. No refunds or transfers will be made when cancellations are received with less than 48 hours' notice.

•No smoking; no alcohol served or permitted.

•Call for schedule of specialized programs.

•Except for family or other specialized programs, no one under 16 years of age is allowed.

•Corporate packages for 20 or more are available for 3-day, 4-day and 6-day sessions; all others are 7 days/6 nights.

•Credit cards accepted: MasterCard and Visa. Personal and business checks are also accepted.

Spa Nordstrom

San Francisco Shopping Centre
865 Market Street
San Francisco, CA 94103
(415) 978-5102

Spa Nordstrom (or Nordstrom Spa, as I find myself saying) is an example of the best among the urban retreats included in this book. New to this guidebook but not new to San Francisco, the spa has been in place since this wonderful department store first opened its doors in the city several years ago. This is the largest of Nordstrom's three branches; the two others are located in Paramus, New Jersey and Oak Brook, Illinois.

I like many features of this spa and will tell you about them in detail, but the first thing I appreciate is its location on the fifth (top) floor of the San Francisco Centre building in which the Nordstrom department store is housed. (Not "Nordstrom's," by the way, although you'll hear that said frequently.) In other words, except for surrounding offices, the spa is serenely and appropriately situated "far from the madding crowd"—the hustle-bustle of the shop-till-you-drop set. It is also easily reached by foot from one of several parking garages. I use the one at Sutter and Stockton streets and walk

Spa #22
map page 196

$$-$$$ Cost
☐ Overnight
☐ Program
■ Day Use
☐ Hot Springs
☐ Hot Tubs
■ Sauna
■ Massage
■ Skin Care/Salon
☐ Exercise
☐ Meals
■ Spa Products
☐ Workshops
☐ Children
☐ Pets
☐ Weddings

straight down Stockton.

I was immediately charmed when I walked into the spa. It exudes a stately elegance in its Italianate design that is softened by the comfortable and unpretentious atmosphere created by the spa's warm, friendly staff. (Incidentally, behind-the-counter staff and spa attendants were all dressed in delightful "easy-wear"—pale gray cotton-jersey overalls with white T-shirts. That alone brought a smile to my face.)

The lobby area has immediate visual appeal with its gleaming marble floors, tall columnar structures, miniature poplars, carved stone receptacles filled with dried chrysanthemums in muted colors, and black-and-gray prints of architectural details—cornices, pediments, gables and the like—that are echoed by the grays, whites and blacks of the marble floor. On display and for sale at the counter are lovely terra cotta-colored pumice stones in different shapes and sizes—quite unlike the conventional gray ovals we have all bought at the local drugstore since time began. The clay color alone brought me back to the days of Pompeii—or maybe to the day I spent in the beautiful Trastevere section of Rome.

For all of its understated splendor, I was pleased to find that Spa Nordstrom's focus is not on face-and-body-beautiful as much as on health and well-being. Yes, you will be wonderfully attended to while you are here, but you will also be quietly educated about what it takes to feel beautiful from the inside out, to treat your body kindly and well, and to maintain health, energy, and—I would add—a graceful disposition.

As for the particulars, Spa Nordstrom has a staff of about 28, comprising facialists, massage practitioners, spa assistants, nail therapists and front desk receptionists. Its staff is multi–cultural, as is its clientele. In the inner sanctum, once you pass through the lobby, you will be shown a dressing area (with everything you might conceivably need to take yourself apart and put yourself together again). After changing into one of their natural-colored terry robes (also for sale) and slipping on paper scuffs, you'll be escorted to an inner waiting area where all guests receive a complimentary foot bath. Then, depending on the treatment or treatments you registered for, you'll move to the appropriate room. Each service is one hour long, but if you have the time and inclination, try the five-hour day spa which gives you six delectable treatments plus a spa cuisine meal!

Their three manicure/pedicure rooms are lovely. Instead of sitting at the conventional manicurist's table in a large, open area, soaking one hand in Palmolive and chatting it up while the manicurist works on your nails, you will be taken to a quiet, private space where you can lean back in a large reclining chair and close your eyes while your hands and feet are meticulously cared for. (The "sports manicure" includes a therapeutic massage and paraffin dip and the "sports pedicure" is followed by an exfoliating foot and leg polish and a customized aromatherapy conditioning treatment. Now do you understand why the spa refers to these staffers as "nail therapists"?)

In another treatment area is the thalassotherapy tub. Popular for years in Europe, this otherwise normal-looking porcelain tub is equipped with strategically placed jet faucets that allow the water to gently pummel your body, increasing circulation and accelerating the detoxification of your skin. Whatever else this treatment accomplishes, like other body treatments spas offer, it surely succeeds in "melting away stress." If you choose, aromatherapy oils can be used in your thalassotherapy session as well as in massages and facials. Your spa attendant will talk with you to arrive at the particular "flavor" that is right for your mood and need of the moment.

In addition to its facials and its inviting list of body treatments (thalassotherapy, massage, algae or marine mud wraps and spearmint body polishing), all of which can be enhanced by aromatherapy oils, Spa Nordstrom does waxing and sells a marvelous array of skin-care and aromatherapy products. Hair care is not done at the spa but if that is a must on your agenda, they will direct you to a salon downstairs in the San Francisco Centre mall.

Next time you are in San Francisco, plan to visit Spa Nordstrom. If you haven't time to indulge yourself, at least take a peek at this hallmark of an urban retreat and schedule an advance appointment. (Men are also welcome clients at Spa Nordstrom.)

HOURS

•First and last appointments are scheduled Monday through Friday, 9 a.m. to 7 p.m.; Saturday, 9:45 a.m. to 5:15 p.m.; Sunday, 10:15 a.m. to 4:30 p.m.

INCIDENTALS

•Gift certificates are available.
•24-hour cancellation notice is required.
•Credit cards accepted: MasterCard, Visa, American Express and Nordstrom.

Central California
Spas

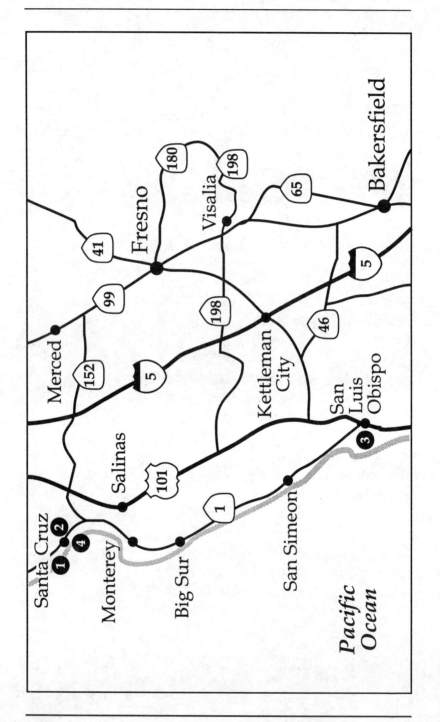

Heartwood Spa

3150-A Mission Drive
Santa Cruz, CA 95065
(408) 462-2192

Heartwood, nestled in a residential community at the southerly end of Santa Cruz as you drive down Soquel Drive toward Capitola, is housed in a small stucco building done in pale pink with purple trim. It has its own convenient parking lot.

The focal point at Heartwood is the lovely outdoor area with its expansive lawn and garden of "never-ending blooms." Walk toward the back to reach the large community hot pool, sauna, cold plunge and shower area or wander off on another pathway to find a totally fenced area with a private tub and its own changing area and shower. (In its brochure is the statement: "Community areas are clothing-optional and a safe, problem-free environment is carefully maintained.") I sat a spell "under the old apple tree" and listened to the wind chimes punctuate the quiet conversation of a woman immersed in the pool talking to an older man in the altogether, sunning himself on one of the deckside benches.

Heartwood was recently voted "Best Wholistic Massage and Treatment" according to a

Spa #1
map page 280

$-$$ Cost
☐ Overnight
☐ Program
■ Day Use
☐ Hot Springs
☐ Hot Tubs
■ Sauna
■ Massage
☐ Skin Care/Salon
☐ Exercise
☐ Meals
☐ Spa Products
☐ Workshops
☐ Children
☐ Pets
■ Weddings

reader survey conducted by the widely read Santa Cruz *Good Times*. In hushed tones, I was told by a staffer: "We really do have the best massage people here." Two or three massage practitioners are always immediately available, and others come on an as-needed basis. Inside are five unpretentious massage rooms and a sitting area where you can sip a cup of tea as you browse through their album of pictures and testimonials.

Owner Ethel Herring is clearly proud of her "baby" and the warm attention it continues to get from the community.

HOURS
•Daily, noon to 11 p.m. by appointment or on a drop-in basis. Sundays are reserved for women only from 6:30 p.m. to 11 p.m.

INCIDENTALS
•In addition to general admission day-use of facilities, there are special discounted packages —one offering one month unlimited use; another, ten visits in two months.
•The private tub, charged by the hour, also offers a special: five hours in three months for two.
•Discounts are offered to Santa Cruz Community Credit Union members, seniors (65 and over), and students with I.D.
•Children up to 16 are free.
•Gift certificates are available.
•The facility is available to private parties.
•No credit cards accepted: personal checks or cash only.

Kiva Retreat House

702 Water Street
Santa Cruz, California
(408) 429-1142

I am indebted to my readers for leading me to the terrific day-use spas in Santa Cruz. I have long been fond of this town which has somehow managed to retain the best of the '60s.

It was not difficult to find the Kiva Retreat House. Not only is it on a main Santa Cruz street, but it is a strikingly sweet 110-year-old Victorian beauty, all dressed in pale blues with darker blue and deep red "accessories" (read "trim"). The lobby area is equally inviting. As I waited, I read the bulletin board that let me know I could have a membership (one month, three months, six months or a year) or a 10-visit pass in addition to just dropping in for a soak, a sauna, and/or a massage.

To reach the front parlor, you walk through a very plain co-ed dressing room area equipped with lockers, the least inviting area of this otherwise fabulous place. Guests use the parlor to lounge about and talk quietly after or between soaks and treatments. (Incidentally, Kiva offers a hot herb tea that is consumed in great quan-

Spa #2
map page 280

$-$$ Cost
☐ Overnight
☐ Program
■ Day Use
☐ Hot Springs
■ Hot Tubs
■ Sauna
■ Massage
☐ Skin Care/Salon
☐ Exercise
☐ Meals
■ Spa Products
☐ Workshops
■ Children
☐ Pets
☐ Weddings

tity. Restore those electrolytes!) The massage rooms, three of them, are upstairs and Kiva has massage practitioners who offer a Thai form of massage as well as Rolfing, reflexology and prenatal massage. (Speaking of prenatal massage, let me say right here that Kiva is strongly family-oriented. Mothers and fathers, alone and together, routinely bring their children to take the waters with them.)

My impression was that this is like a second home to folks in the community. Of all the clothing-optional places I have seen, Kiva and its clientele seemed most comfortable with nudity. As the manager told me, Santa Cruz has been at ease with nakedness for a very long time; it is far less an issue here than in many other supposedly progressive areas. Like Kabuki in San Francisco, Kiva offers a women's morning on Sundays from 9 a.m. to noon, for women who prefer to be with their own gender.

Walking down the pathway into the large open-air area behind the house (fully fenced, by the way, with no visible neighbors) was what we used to call an "eye trip." It is beautifully landscaped, for one thing—gardeners come two to three times a week, and it shows. There are two large community tubs, one redwood and one fiberglass, for those who want to be social and two private tubs as well as cold-plunges. A large redwood sauna (maintained at about 180 degrees) and outside showers are located across from the community tubs. Guests stroll back and forth from sauna to shower to tub. The Santa Cruz Health Department, I was told, permits only chlorine to be used as its water disinfectant. In answer to my question, I was told that the Health Department comes around monthly to inspect. It seems that Kiva has received top rating for its water quality.

At the very back of the yard is a wide, covered deck with five massage tables for those who prefer to have their treatments outdoors or to exchange massages with each other. Despite the number of people there the day I visited, and the presence of children, guests keep their voices low. Make no mistake: This is a serious, health-oriented facility, not a Disney waterworld.

HOURS
•Open year round. Sunday to Thursday, from noon to 11 p.m.; Friday and Saturday, noon to midnight. Women's morning on Sundays, 9 a.m. to noon.

INCIDENTALS
•Towels and lockers rented.
•Reservations recommended for private tubs and massage.
•Children (allowed during daytime hours only) admitted free under 8 years old.
•Memberships and 10-visit passes available.
•Lotions and potions for sale.
•Credit cards accepted: MasterCard and Visa. Checks are preferred to credit cards.

Sycamore Mineral Springs Resort

1215 Avila Beach Drive
San Luis Obispo, CA 93401
(805) 595-7302
(800) 234-5831

Spa #3
map page 280

$$$ Cost
■ Overnight
☐ Program
■ Day Use
■ Hot Springs
■ Hot Tubs
☐ Sauna
■ Massage
☐ Skin Care/Salon
☐ Exercise
■ Meals
☐ Spa Products
☐ Workshops
■ Children
☐ Pets
■ Weddings

Sycamore Mineral Springs joins that group of Southern California spas that hark back to 1897. At that time, it was not Native Americans settling near the healing waters but men drilling for oil who—alas(?)—struck hot water instead. In the 1920s, it was used as a pleasure spot by celebrities en route from Hearst Castle down the coast. By the '30s, however, it was touted as a therapeutic center where people came for the "cure." The one remaining building to boast of historicity is the beautiful stucco-and-curved-tile-roof bath house, vintage 1935, nestled in the center of the property and the focal point of the resort.

The 120-acre parcel, or what I saw of it, sprawls up hills and over dales, first giving out one impression, then another. A country spa? No, it overlooks a well-trafficked road to Avila Beach. Well, a very Northern California place? Yeeeees, but it is surrounded by such Southern California coastal landmarks as Hearst Castle,

Solvang and the outrageous splash of pink gingerbread on Highway 101, the Madonna Inn. This mineral springs resort is a strange hybrid.

Sycamore Mineral Springs Resort

If you climb the steep stairs that jog their way up through the oaks and sycamores on one side of the bath house, you come upon small wooden signs—"Harmony," "Xanadu," "Enchantment" and "Paradise" for example—each one pointing toward its own enclosed area where individual redwood tubs hide behind simple lattice fencing. (Once you are a "regular," you can ask for the area you want by name.) These whimsically named hillside tubs—there are 23 nestled inconspicuously about—are used mostly by the drop-in clientele, the greatest number of whom come to this 24-hour facility between noon and midnight, many for an under-the-stars hot soak.

Open-air showers are right next to the tubs, and each tub area is protected enough from the main pathways that you can relax in the nude, if you choose—and most do. I especially enjoyed being able to watch civilization carry on below me as I soaked away the strains of freeway driving, but you can also book an even more secluded area where people and traffic are neither visible nor audible. Whatever location you choose in this hot tub wonderland, when the old-fashioned lamplights come on at dusk, you'll have just enough light to find your way to the tub area assigned, and not a smidgeon more.

The redwood tubs are drained and scrubbed down on a daily basis. An elaborate pH-monitoring system senses when the balance is off and corrects it every two minutes. The temperature is set at approximately 102 degrees.

Down the long stairway, past the large heated swimming pool next to the old bath house and up into the opposite side of this lush wooded area, an entirely different scene awaits. Here you will come upon a cluster of rooms—27 of them lined up in a row, each with its private spa on a screened-in porch facing only the trees and God's creatures great and small. That your private tub is of acrylic and not weather-beaten redwood is compensated by the convenience of having it right there, all the time, away from the main spa traffic.

Except for the nicety of providing lotions and shampoos in the room, Sycamore's accommodations are relatively plain and serviceable—just give-me-a-good-night's-sleep rooms that don't mind if you pop out of bed at 3 a.m. and take a tub. Other citified amenities here are color cable television sets and telephones.

Way up in the hills—I stopped counting the stairs—is "El Grande"—a tub that purportedly holds 4,000 gallons of water and 50 people (to look at it, you wouldn't imagine 50 bodies could do anything but stand up like asparagus stalks in a cauldron). It goes without saying that El Grande is not filled until there is a confirmed reservation. It is situated in a long rectangular clearing that has a picnic table and fire pit to one side and the tub on the other.

All of that would really be enough to make this a wonderful stopover or short vacation—

but there is more. In addition to its large heated swimming pool and two sand volleyball courts is an outdoor courtyard with a theater stage available for banquets, receptions and company parties. A snack bar is located adjacent to the courtyard and catering can be arranged for large groups. And in the old bath house is a "body care center" which, by appointment during the day, offers massage, foot reflexology, energy balancing and back/neck/shoulder massages, each of which comes with a half-hour hot mineral water tub.

In short, Sycamore is a comfortable-feeling place whether you are single, coupled or a family. It is just removed enough to let you know you're in the country, but close enough so that any time you want to jump in the car and spend an hour or two in the city, you can. This area features some of the most scenic country in the state—taking you in short succession from rolling green hills to rocky outcroppings along the ocean, through sudden interludes of lush woodsy areas, and in and out of such towns as East Cambria Village, which manages to be cosmopolitan (many specialty shops stay open late) without losing its small country flavor. Try it for an ice cream cone, an evening stroll, a late-night supper or a sudden urge to shop 'til you drop.

Sycamore's plan to build a restaurant and bar was realized in the winter of 1992 when they opened The Gardens of Avila restaurant and its adjacent mahogany-paneled bar. In its lush floral setting, patrons feast their eyes as well as

Sycamore Mineral Springs Resort

their palates. An eclectic mix of European, Asian and traditional American dishes are on the menu. Portions are generous and prices reasonable. A banquet room is available for weddings, receptions and meetings and—a touch I always like to see—local artwork is on display.

The next goal is to add more units and cottages. Stay tuned.

HOURS
•Open 24 hours a day, year round.
•The office is open 8 a.m. to 8 p.m.

INCIDENTALS
•All spa services include a half-hour hot mineral water tub.
•Discounts available on all one-hour spa services for resort guests.
•Banquet and catering services available in outdoor courtyard.
•Day-use and monthly passes for pool and recreational facilities with special rates for children 10 and under.
•Call for "getaway specials" that include golf privileges at the San Luis Bay Course.
•Color cable TV and telephones in rooms.
•All reservations must be guaranteed with advance deposit or credit cards.
•Credit cards accepted: MasterCard, Visa and American Express.

Well Within

112 Elm Street
Santa Cruz, CA
(408) 458-WELL

In its own words, "Well Within was created to provide individuals, families and friends with a quiet environment where they can relax and benefit from hot tubs, saunas and massage."

Do not be put off by the slightly scruffy buildings on each side; once inside its wide wooden gateway, this small, beautifully cared for facility is a delight. The reception area, with its Japanese prints on the wall, cut flowers, light oak floors and sun streaming in from a skylight above, has a super-clean, airy feeling. Stacks of purple, green and cranberry-colored towels are shelved here and add warm color. Tea pots and cups in the lobby and soft, piped-in music drop subliminal messages that Well Within will keep the promise embodied in its name.

Well Within has been around for almost a decade. Its owner, who previously occupied a restaurant on Pacific Avenue that backs up to the spa, was pleased not to lose the 40-year-old bamboo garden where her café customers used to take their afternoon tea. Now, the same garden is accessible from each suite of her Japanese-style spa. After your tub or sauna, just step

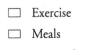

Spa #4
map page 280

$-$$	Cost
☐	Overnight
☐	Program
■	Day Use
☐	Hot Springs
■	Hot Tubs
■	Sauna
■	Massage
☐	Skin Care/Salon
☐	Exercise
☐	Meals
■	Spa Products
☐	Workshops
■	Children
☐	Pets
☐	Weddings

outside the sliding door to a place of peace and beauty encapsulated in the middle of Santa Cruz's daily buzz.

Two of Well Within's rooms have fiberglass tubs and saunas, and two others have tubs only. (There is a slight price difference between the two.) All rooms are done in unobtrusive neutral tones and warm, dark wood. Down a long Mexican-tiled passageway, at right angles to the tub area, are two massage rooms. As in most spas now, massage practitioners on staff or on call to the facility practice a variety of massage styles and, with advance telephone registration, those who want something other than the standard Swedish-Esalen and shiatsu can pretty much expect to be accommodated without much fanfare. Incidentally, for all its serenity, Well Within encourages family use.

HOURS
•Summer: 2 p.m. to midnight, Monday through Thursday; noon to midnight Friday through Sunday.
•Winter: Noon to midnight, Sunday through Thursday; noon to 1:30 a.m. Friday and Saturday.

INCIDENTALS
•Children under 11 are free.
•Telephone reservations suggested.
•Gift certificates available.
•Towels and complimentary tea provided.
•No credit cards: personal check or cash only.

Southern
California
Spas

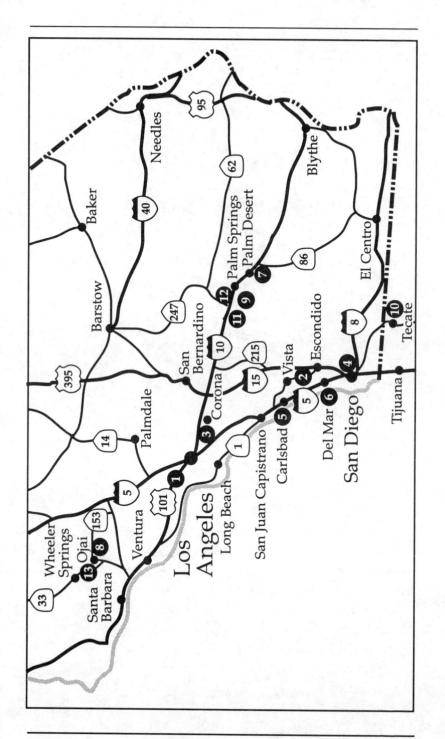

The Ashram

Post Office Box 8009
Calabasas, CA 91372
(818) 222-6900

The Ashram is far and away the toughest spa in this guidebook. It is where the fit go to get fitter, to be in the pure mountain air, to enjoy the rigors of peak physical conditioning. When you write for information about its fitness program, however, you will still receive its single, heavyweight, fold-out flyer with cartoons of pink cherubic cartoon characters and the deceptively lighthearted verses that start: "When your body's gone to flab/And your emotions jingle-jangle/You're bursting in the seams/And your fat goes dingle-dangle…" It goes on. Do not be deceived.

Swedish born owner-chiropractor, Dr. Anne Marie Bennstrom, and manager Catharina Hedberg, graduate of the University of Stockholm in Physical Medicine and Physical Education, searched for some time to find the right location for an ashram. Dr. Bennstrom was familiar with the Santa Monica Mountains, having hiked its ranges for some time. She knew that the place she envisioned had to be there. The site finally located was perfect: Houses were very few and far between and the upper ranges

Spa #1
map page 294

$$$$ Cost
■ Overnight
■ Program
☐ Day Use
☐ Hot Springs
☐ Hot Tubs
☐ Sauna
■ Massage
☐ Skin Care/Salon
■ Exercise
■ Meals
☐ Spa Products
☐ Workshops
☐ Children
☐ Pets
☐ Weddings

were protected as a nature conservancy. She did not build a "facility" here—she built a house. Indeed, it is home for the 10 guests who come to know each other well in their strenuous seven-day pilgrimage of body, mind and spirit. What gets them through, besides their own inner resources, is Catharina's indomitable spirit. She is "Mama Bear" to her captive cubs, and to know her for 15 minutes is to trust and admire her.

Although the program is strenuous, you won't walk into it by mistake. Once you've decided this is the time in your life when you want a real challenge—and don't think for a minute that only your body will be called to task—you will have a lengthy telephone conversation with Catharina so that you will understand the demands this program will place on you.

Your week at The Ashram is to be regarded as a retreat. As such, once here, you will be protected from the kinds of interruptions most of us accept as normal and unavoidable in our daily lives. To that end, you will be asked to agree not to receive telephone calls during the time of your stay. As Catharina emphasizes, physical fitness is the foundation for self-awareness, and to get all you can from a one-week program demands total concentration and total participation.

Depending on your fitness level, you will be asked to start working out harder before you are scheduled to come. (You'll have time to do that since reservations must be made four months in advance.)

Ahhhhh, but once here. The house is relatively small and quintessentially "homey." I know it must sound incongruous at this point, but when you walk into the bedroom you'll be sharing with another, it's easy to feel that you've come for a college reunion or even a pajama party. In other words, the program may be Spartan but your home for a week is as warm and inviting as that of your best friend.

Just outside the comfortable living room-dining room is an enclosed patio that looks out onto the mountainside panorama and reminds you of how big the world is, and how peaceful your seclusion. Outside is a small swimming pool where you'll participate in water calisthenics everyday before lunch. Speaking of food, most of what you will be eating will be fruits and raw vegetables, and, for beverages, herbal teas and water.

Your day is scheduled from 6:30 a.m. yoga and meditation (which you can do in a lovely geodesic dome structure up on the hillside) to 10 p.m. which is "bedtime." Somewhere in your day you will have a massage, which most guests enjoy having in the dome. When we asked what type of massage, what we got from Catharina was "superb massage" followed by laughter all around. Although your day is strictly scheduled from a two-and-a-half-hour morning hike, to aerobic exercises, to use of free weights, to pool workouts, Catharina does not hustle anyone out of one activity and into the next.

Things quiet down after your evening walk, yoga and meditation, and dinner is fashionably late—8:30 p.m. (You can leave your watch at home—Catharina and staff will take care of orchestrating you through your paces.)

As the flyer will tell you, most of the clothing you will need is provided: sweatsuit, T-shirt, robe and kaftan. You will want to bring toilet articles, good walking shoes, socks, a bathing suit and shorts. Maybe a book. You are discouraged from bringing much else. There is a television set in the living room, but the group will negotiate its own rules about TV watching.

Beyond what I have told you, the only other intriguing bits of information I want to pass on are two comments from Catharina: One, that in her experience, withdrawal from sugar is by far the most difficult for most people, and two, that each ashram constitutes itself differently and she never knows exactly how any one group will evolve. Mentally, she sits back and watches and waits. She has a keen eye and finely tuned sensibilities. When it is evident what the group consciousness is, she will "ride the horse in the direction it is going."

HOURS
•Open year round.

INCIDENTALS
•No one under 18 years of age is admitted.
•Medical examination is conducted on arrival, including cardiovascular ergometer stress test.
•No automobiles ("closed campus").
•Airport service is available at specific hours from three locations (Marriott Airport Hotel, Bel Air Summit and the Valley Hilton) or on a

will-call basis.
•No credit cards accepted.

Cal-a-Vie

2249 Somerset Road
Vista, CA 92084
(619) 945-2055

Spa #2
map page 294

$$$$ Cost
■ Overnight
■ Program
☐ Day Use
☐ Hot Springs
■ Hot Tubs
■ Sauna
■ Massage
■ Skin Care/Salon
■ Exercise
■ Meals
■ Spa Products
■ Workshops
☐ Children
☐ Pets
☐ Weddings

Inspiring people to change their lifestyle from an unhealthy one to a healthy one is the underlying goal for most of the spas described in this guidebook—and certainly for the ones that offer week-long programs of one kind or another. At Cal-a-Vie, it is one of the clearly expressed wishes of owner William F. Power, a longtime developer of health-care institutions throughout the state.

Power regards stress as a major health problem in this country, and, in spite of his own total commitment to fitness, he knows that most people need to be externally motivated to take care of themselves. Power's interest in opening Cal-a-Vie is to keep people out of the medical institutions he's been instrumental in building.

Cal-a-Vie offers American attention to fitness and nutrition with European expertise in body and skin care—that combination is the major inducement that attracts people to this pricey Southern California spa. Besides providing a stunning setting and facility for his guests, Power sets a limit of 24 guests at any one time, and insists on a plenteous supply of home-grown, fresh vegetables and fruits.

Cal-a-Vie is dedicated to educating, or re-educating, its guests about what a healthy lifestyle means. In an array of classes, top people in the fitness and nutritional arenas will show you how to achieve and maintain your proper weight, strength and flexibility, and how to feed and care for your body so that you can look forward to optimal health and vitality in the years to come.

As for geographical inspiration, there is no question that this "secluded valley on 125 acres of rolling hillside north of San Diego" with its splashes of bougainvillea, roses, jasmine and lavender is stunning, but it is not simply the natural setting that is so attractive. The build-ings—clusters of cottages in pale salmon-col-ored stucco with terra-cotta tile roofs—encircle the swimming pool and are indeed, as the lit-erature tells you, nestled into the countryside. The aerial views of the spa complex confirm this most clearly, and Cal-a-Vie rightly shows itself off this way in its postcards and other pro-motional materials.

Inside the cottages (each one different in decor) and throughout the facility, the furnish-ings are drawn from the tastes and styles that are distinctive to different European countries, primarily England, France and Ireland. Each cottage has its own deck, and each looks out to the panorama of flowers, hills and oak trees that go a long way toward restoring peace to the soul after a day of workouts for the body.

Much of what I am telling you here can be gleaned from Cal-a-Vie's brochures (works of art in themselves) rather than from my own experience of the spa. Although I did tour the facility and sample one of the chef's aesthetically lovely and nutritionally perfect luncheons, my hostesses took extreme care to respect the privacy of their guests—a consideration that is particularly important in smaller spas where people expect to be out of public view for the period of time they are there.

The dining room is very nicely located at the top of what appears to be a cascade of buildings overlooking the grounds. In good weather (pretty much year round), you can eat outside on the patio. From here, you'll hear the gentle sounds of a brook that runs along the terrace and be able to look out on the panorama of foothills and valleys that make Cal-a-Vie so special. Cal-a-Vie's nutritional philosophy, I was told, is one of *balance* and *moderation*. It goes without saying that the spa serves only fresh, whole foods, low in fat and high in nutrients. Every Friday evening, a cooking class is held in the spa's wonderful kitchen. Once you learn the nuances of their spa cuisine—the preparation and the presentation—you can re-create those dining experiences at home.

As for your fitness program, it starts with an early morning hike through the trails that weave in and out of the hillsides. Your day proceeds depending upon the results of your personal fitness evaluation, which is conducted first thing Monday morning. A computer printout lets you know important information about your percentage of body fat, your lean body mass and your basal metabolic rate, and from that, your personal program is set up for the week.

Because it is an individual program based on your needs, it is obvious that some might be working harder than others or on different things—flexibility or body contouring, for example. Similarly, some might be eating at the level of 1,000 calories a day and others up to 2,000. But all will have a chance to get in the three important types of conditioning exercise: stretching for flexibility, aerobics for cardiovascular conditioning and weight training for strengthening muscles. (When you do aerobics at Cal-a-Vie, you'll be working on a state-of-the-art floor designed for maximum resilience, which is kind to your skeletal system.)

A "Body Awareness" class serves to do just what the name suggests—make you aware of your own body's strengths and weaknesses; it is in this early morning class that you will also work on body alignment, posture and movement. When you've completed whatever exercise classes have been recommended, you'll take what is listed as "The Plunge"—a pool workout that has a way of making it all seem like fun after all.

The afternoons are generally your time to be pampered. In addition to a daily massage, Cal-a-Vie is proud of its European body treatments administered by practitioners who have been described as "virtuosos" by one of the many writers who have described a day in the life of this celebrity spa. Advocates of these treatments, some of which are more exotic than others, make convincing claims about the use of natural plant derivatives and sea extracts to cleanse and "re-balance" the body. Whatever such delights as aromatherapy, thalassotherapy and the more familiar hydrotherapy do for body chemistry and skin tone, they certainly work magic on the psyche and satisfy one of our most basic and often unmet needs—to be touched, nurtured and cared for. Take it—you will have earned it.

Yoga and t'ai chi classes are also available as part of the fitness program, and for those who want to continue their favorite sports while they're here, tennis courts (and pro instructors) are available, and an 18-hole golf course is adjacent to the spa. Jogging courses also abound for the inveterate jogger. A recent addition to Cal-a-Vie's sports offerings—one that is apparently popular with both men and women guests—is its "Boxercise" class. It is conducted by a former Olympic boxing champ who knows how to get the blood pumping (jumprope) and the stress out (target punching).

Evenings offer a chance to socialize, watch movies, play games or read after a day scheduled from dawn to dusk with classes, lectures and treatments. (By the way, you are encouraged to dress very casually throughout your stay, and that includes the way you come to meals. Warm-up jackets, warm-up suits, T-shirts, shorts, robes, bath shoes, visor and rain gear are all provided by Cal-a-Vie.)

Most of the year, Cal-a-Vie caters to a co-ed population, although the spa does provide some women-only and men-only weeks at intervals during the year. Check with them if those special weeks interest you. Beyond that, Cal-a-Vie now offers different plans for you to choose from: the European Plan includes all classes in addition to 18 treatment sessions; the American Plan includes all classes, one private fitness session and six massages—at a substantial savings. (If you opt for the American Plan, you can still purchase selected European skin treatments *à la carte*.)

Finally, Cal-a-Vie has launched a campaign to entice corporate America to vacation here and experience the value of letting go and recharging. There's no disputing that this kind of "health insurance" works.

HOURS
•Open year round except for Christmas holidays.

INCIDENTALS
•Tennis lessons, golf at the adjacent country club golf course, and private fitness and nutritional counseling all are available as extras.
•Reservations must be secured with a nonrefundable deposit.
•Complimentary transportation is provided to and from San Diego Airport.
•Write for a descriptive brochure.

Glen Ivy
Hot Springs

25000 Glen Ivy Road
Corona, CA 91719
(909) 277-3529

Spa #3
map page 294

$$ Cost
☐ Overnight
☐ Program
■ Day Use
■ Hot Springs
■ Hot Tubs
■ Sauna
■ Massage
■ Skin Care/Salon
☐ Exercise
■ Meals
■ Spa Products
☐ Workshops
■ Children
☐ Pets
☐ Weddings

Glen Ivy calls itself "the ultimate day spa."
And it surely is. It's a place where you can spend
time in many different ways—hanging out and
having fun snacking and swimming, relaxing
in hot mineral water pools, and/or enjoying its
newly expanded menu of body- and skin-care
services. Whether you're here for conviviality
and fun (its weekend look) or for a deeply re-
laxing massage or body treatment and a healthy,
satisfying time-out (its weekday look), or for a
conference (whenever), Glen Ivy has some ter-
rific features you won't find anywhere else in
the state.

The most striking is its outdoor red clay mud
pool ("Club Mud"), the size of a large swim-
ming pool, where you can sit, stand or roll
around like a crocodile until you're covered with
this gorgeous goop. (Wear an old swimsuit; the
mud can stain some fabrics.) A "mud hut" with
showers is close by. No enclosure, no tub, no
attendant to hover over you, this pool is do-it-
yourself sheer fun—although this elegant mud

does its magic on your body while you're not looking. And it's fine for your hair, too. (Incidentally, the pool is chlorinated, drained and refilled every day.)

Here is what you can expect to find once you have driven into the parking lot and walked past bougainvillea-draped walls and other gorgeous flora that continues into the spa area:

Mineral Water Pools: Water, water everywhere. The largest and coolest outdoor swimming pool is kept at approximately 85 degrees (free half-hour "aquaerobics" daily at 2 p.m.); a row of seven sunken tile whirlpool tubs that take up the width of the main pool (97 to 104 degrees); a large covered hot therapy pool where water temperature is approximately 104 degrees; a pool within the main pool where the water is hotter; twin pools on the "upper deck" where water is heated to 100 and 104 degrees (and reserved for adult use only); a children's pool; an 18-inch-deep sun-warmed floating pool for drifting, dozing and people-watching; a cold plunge; and, the latest additions, two champagne-glass-shaped pools in a newly landscaped area at the south end of the spa. In the winter months these pools are kept at 102 degrees but in warm weather one is left unheated. These pools are equipped with more than the usual number of jets and give you more than the usual neck and back relief.

Massage: Swedish, shiatsu, hydro-massage; others by request. (Glen Ivy has 16 massage rooms and spiffy well-equipped separate dressing areas for men and women.) They ask that you call ahead for reservations: (909) 277-3529, extension 522.

Sauna (Co-ed): Dry heat saunas lined with redwood. (The co-ed sauna idea is not just for the fun of it—it is also smart not to be alone in any heat treatment where you can and do lose sense of time.)

Spa Salon: Glen Ivy now provides a luxurious variety of manicures (including a men's manicure), pedicures, and five styles of European facials as well as waxing, body polishing, deep cleansing back facials, aromatherapy massage and an aromatherapy cellulite body treatment. Reservations are strongly recommended.

Spa Café: Also new is the spa café, located near the entrance to the facility. Here, you can get sandwiches, salads and drinks (beer and wine as well as soft drinks) and Haagen Dazs ice cream! A children's menu is available. A mini-bar serving snacks and beverages is located at the south end of the spa.

Spa Shop: The spa shop sells its own line of skin-care products (including its special red clay facial mask), as well as T-shirts, a good assortment of spa clothing and playwear, and sundries.

Conference Areas: The Spa Pavilion can be reserved for conferences. A group of 200 or more can rent the entire facility for all types of parties. Glen Ivy will provide catering and entertainment.

In some of the spa resorts that have been around as long as this one (since 1882), you can sense a historical presence, or see it in some of the refurbished but still-standing structures.

It's harder to believe Glen Ivy's age. It has gone through many, many evolutions in the past 100 years, and the changes and improvements just keep on coming. This is not a place to miss if you are traveling up or down the state.

As for accommodations, Glen Ivy now has arrangements with three local inns. Two of them, Kings Inn and Country Side Inn, are 15 minutes away, and the third, Mission Inn, is 30 minutes away. All of them provide you with a continental breakfast at the inn and paid admission and a spa lunch at Glen Ivy. I am told that Mission Inn is a luxurious four-star hotel in Riverside in what was once one of California's missions. For families with RVs, there is an RV park right at the base of the glen within shouting distance of the resort.

For those who like to wander off and do other things, you can go down the road apiece and shop at Tom's Farms produce market or the wine and cheese shop.

HOURS
•March through October, open daily 10 a.m. to 6 p.m.; November through February, open weekdays 10 a.m. to 5 p.m.; weekends, 10 a.m. to 6 p.m.
•Closes at 4 p.m. on Christmas eve and New Year's eve, and closed all day on Christmas and Thanksgiving.

INCIDENTALS
•No reservations required. (Advance reservations recommended for spa services.)

Glen Ivy
Hot Springs

•Discounts for groups; 15% discount to military personnel; senior discount (60 and over).
•Occasional half-price admission specials—call for details.
•Annual passes available.
•Picnic area.
•Conference facilities available.
•Accommodations: Kings Inn (800) 892-5464; Country Side Inn (909) 734-2140; Mission Inn (800) 843-7755.
•Write for a copy of the *Glen Ivy Sun Times* and ask about workshops scheduled.
•Credit cards accepted: MasterCard, Visa. ATM cards also accepted.

The Golden Door

Post Office Box 46377
Escondido, CA 92046-3077
(619) 744-5777
(800) 424-0777

The famed Golden Door continues to exude an air of timelessness. Perhaps it is the more than 200-year-old bell that once hung in a Japanese temple and now hangs in the center courtyard, or the rain chains quietly suspended at each corner of the pitched roof that covers the rectangular sand garden, or the *honjin*-inn-style housing that give this spa its serene and historic presence.

These are the words I used in the last edition of *California Spas,* and there is nothing—or very little—that has changed in the years since I last visited. Accordingly, what I wrote then I present to you again.

On my first visit to the Golden Door, I glanced around at the Japanese-inspired design that dominates its architecture, its interior furnishing and its landscaping, and found myself recalling the words of famed architect Mies Van der Rohe: "God is in the details." That attentiveness to detail is also reflected in the services provided by the staff, who accept as their task to anticipate what any individual guest might

Spa #4
map page 294

$$$$ Cost
■ Overnight
■ Program
☐ Day Use
■ Hot Springs
■ Hot Tubs
■ Sauna
■ Massage
■ Skin Care/Salon
■ Exercise
■ Meals
■ Spa Products
■ Workshops
☐ Children
☐ Pets
☐ Weddings

need. I still maintain that it is perhaps all of this and none of this at the same time that gives "The Door" its mystique and its renown the world over.

Within that atmosphere of another world, another place that dominates the 177-acre property is a thoroughly modern health and fitness program overseen by Alex Szekely, the son of Deborah Szekely, who opened Rancho La Puerta in Tecate, Mexico in 1940 and The Golden Door in 1959. (The Golden Door moved to its present location in 1975.) At the time we visited, Deborah Szekely, to celebrate a significant birthday, had just climbed one of the Kuchumaa mountains that surround Rancho La Puerta.

The life story of the Szekely family is intriguing, and their early contribution to the "health and fitness industry" is profound. Edmond Szekely, in his lifetime, wrote 140 books on a wide variety of subjects. Deborah is founder and president of the Eureka Foundation and spends much time in Washington, D.C. and traveling around the world, leaving the executive management of the two facilities to Alex. When my daughter and I first heard these stories, we smiled knowingly when told that a brilliant orange koi we were marveling at in The Golden Door's pond was named "Deborah."

As for its being thoroughly up-to-date, Alex Szekely writes in his welcoming letter: "Being number one means daily proving our worth." It is still true that women who used to come here simply for weight reduction now come for stress reduction. Men's weeks, couples' weeks and co-ed weeks are scheduled at frequent intervals throughout the year.

Happily, along with spa managers and inveterate spa-goers, most of us are learning to replace the concept of "diet" with "good nutrition" and "exercise" with "fitness"—in other words, we have learned that feeling good and looking good involve far more than what the scale and the tape measure have to say.

Not only has the Szekely family played an important role in bringing about this attitudinal change, but they also have been forerunners in the day-to-day business of operating a first-class facility—buying the best equipment and staying in touch with the best minds in exercise physiology.

With the increase in staff-to-guest ratio from three to one to its present four to one, the attention to individual needs is fastidious in the best sense of the word. It translates to your being assigned a personal fitness guide at the moment you begin your stay, having your dietary plan discussed and written out for you (with any allergies or even simple food antipathies noted), having each workout supervised and your target heart rate regularly monitored, having your daily massage (usually Swedish but shiatsu and sports massage are also available) in your own room and, for those who have scheduled beauty appointments, seeing your personal esthetician standing quietly outside the salon like a western-style *geisha*, waiting for your arrival.

Guests are encouraged—and this we heard

The Golden Door from most of the other "celebrity" spas—to let go of daily makeup routines, and without neglecting basic skin care, to use their time at the spa to give their faces a rest, too. The advice given to you as soon as you unpack is to save all the city primping and hair styling for the end of your stay—just before returning to the life you left outside the massive golden doors.

Those who know The Golden Door know that the emphasis here is not on pampering. You will be pampered and you will be scrupulously attended to, yes, but the week-long program is a vigorous one, designed to set you on a clear path to health and well-being. To that end, you will eat a high-fiber, low-sodium, low-cholesterol menu artfully prepared by Michel Stroot, who is back as chef. Michel fetches all of the vegetables and herbs he needs—not one moment before he needs them—right out of The Golden Door's elaborately planted, four-acre organic garden. Eighty percent of the food you will be eating comes from the garden and the orchards maintained on the property.

Your day will be structured—flexibly, but structured, nevertheless; and you will be sent home with a complimentary and individually customized videotape to keep the fitness program alive and well in your daily at-home routine. In short, if this spa is not for those in moderate income brackets, neither is it for those who just want to get away, occasionally have their feet massaged and float around in a pool of hot water. The closest activity to what you are used to at home is tennis. Guests have access to two courts, and, for a slight fee, a tennis pro can be called in to help you perfect your game.

For those of you who are not among the 65 percent of guests who return annually and semi-annually, the informational material you will receive on request is itself a splendid introduction to this very special place. Not only do the lush color photographs speak the truth about The Golden Door, but the sample schedule of "one day of a glorious Golden Door week" shows you, from your wake-up call and mountain walk in the early morning, to your Japanese hot tub and mini-massage at night, just what is in store if you decide to spend a week or more at this jewel of a spa.

For many, The Golden Door will be too precious whether in terms of its small size, its high rates or its elaborate attention to each person. On the other hand, even if you never go as a guest, reading about this celebrity spa and seeing it reproduced in color photographs and other beautifully crafted publicity materials provides a delightful experience for the night-table traveler who is content to sojourn in the mind.

This spa may not be the one for you now, but may well suit you to perfection in another time, another place.

HOURS
•Open year round. Closed for two weeks in December.

The Golden Door

INCIDENTALS

•Men's weeks held eight times a year, couples' weeks held two times a year (limited to 20 couples).

•Special-events programs such as a New Year's Retreat for Women (December 27 to January 3) are also available. Check for other special programs.

•Credit cards accepted: MasterCard, Visa and American Express. Personal checks accepted.

La Costa Resort and Spa

2100 Costa del Mar Road
Carlsbad, CA 92009
(619) 438-9111 (hotel)
(800) 729-4772 (spa)

Those who know La Costa know it to be the showiest of all the spas in the state. To describe the extravaganza of services and programs offered means coming up with descriptive materials that weigh in pounds what these resorts are worth in dollars.

I sense that it is La Costa's delight to overwhelm. La Costa does not know the meaning of "excess," and, as was confirmed for us by its staff, people who go to La Costa go to be seen. It is a celebrity spa, where money is thrown around exuberantly and unabashedly—and if you are looking for a hideaway, this ain't it! I will, then, not describe the enormous hotel-resort complex but, instead, will go right to the spa.

The spa at La Costa maintains physiologists and nutritionists on its staff, and your fitness program (assuming you can stay for more than a day or two) begins with various tests, evaluations, measurements and personal consultation.

Spa #5
map page 294

$$$$ Cost
■ Overnight
■ Program
■ Day Use
☐ Hot Springs
■ Hot Tubs
■ Sauna
■ Massage
■ Skin Care/Salon
■ Exercise
■ Meals
■ Spa Products
■ Workshops
■ Children
☐ Pets
■ Weddings

La Costa Resort and Spa

Conducted by La Costa staff working closely with the Scripps Memorial Executive Health Center, its primo program, "La Costa Healthy Lifestyles," is for folks who are serious about wanting to turn their lives around. A full eight days and seven nights, it is structured to take a thorough look at: your present level of fitness, what you would like to achieve, and how you can accomplish the most in the least amount of time. Then, an individualized program is designed for you that truly fits into your life and can be taken home—meaning that if you're always on the road, it will have to be made easily portable.

Not only that, they get down to the nitty-gritty details of how to handle your grocery shopping once you're back in your own kitchen, and, more useful to some, how to continue to eat wisely in places that do not have your best nutritional interests in mind. La Costa also sends you home with your own "Lifestyle Management Reference Book."

Having seen a great many people through this program, the staff is very sensitive to the importance of the attitudes people bring to eating, exercising and being fit and to the attitudinal and mood changes you can expect to go through during the course of your program. In addition, they know that putting your body through its paces for a week means nothing if your mind does not digest the information you need to sustain a strong desire to be fit and stay fit. And so part of the program is to have you participate in various lectures designed to give you the latest information you need to have and to answer your personal questions.

A five-day, less intensive, program, "La Costa Indulgence," is also available for those who want a packaged program that omits the lifestyle consultations and trainings. And, of course, guests can always select at will from a long inviting list of spa services.

Whether you use the spa on an *à la carte* basis or in an individually tailored program, you will have luxurious choices to make among its pavilion of whirlpool baths, Roman pools, rock steam rooms, saunas, exercise pools, steam cabinets and an exercise gym. In addition, your menu of special services includes such selections as a complete body massage, reflexology, aromatherapy massage, shiatsu and Reike (which they describe as a hands-on body treatment originating in Japan). When you book your massage, you can indicate your preference for a man or woman as your massage therapist.

For body treatments, you can take a simple whirlpool bath with aromatherapy, sea algae or Kur crystals as the only enhancement, or you can go for an herbal wrap, a vigorous loofah body scrub, a thermal sea wrap, total body exfoliation or a skin-smoothing treatment using the rare Moor mud.

Seven different types of facials are available, including a deep-cleansing back facial (men love this one) and a special "sun lovers' facial" that soothes and calms the skin. Obviously, La Costa also maintains a full-service beauty salon that can be accessed directly from the spa as well as from outside the building.

Couples walk in hand in hand into the spa facility and, after checking in at the reception desk, wait together in the spacious lobby to discreetly people-watch until called in to their separate areas. Among all of its other fitness and spa services contained in a mere 70,000 square feet of space, the men's spa offers complete salon services as well. At La Costa, facials became very popular among the men years ago, and they are now easygoing clients who know how to "take it like a man."

Once you are ushered into your gender's quarters, you'll go to the scheduling desk where an attendant will give you a menu card of activity choices. When you have worked out what you want to do, she will check to see what appointments need to be made ahead and whether the order of activities needs to be adjusted. Fitting in massage appointments, for example, is a tricky scheduling task everywhere we went. (Speaking of massage, your massage practitioner will give you the choice of being in an interior massage room or out in the sunny Roman pool area.)

When the attendant, with typical La Costa proficiency and good humor, has worked out the finer scheduling details for you, she will send you on your way into the huge inner sanctum of the spa where your first sight is the lovely glassed-in, open-to-the-sky Roman pools that dominate the center space and serve as an orienting marker as you proceed through the day's activities.

Your first stop is the locker room where you will be given a terry wrap and footwear to move around in from station to station. If you get confused or lost (we're talking BIG spa), an attendant is also seated at a desk in this area to speed you on your way, and the guests themselves are often old hands at the routine here. An area is reserved for coffee, cold juice and water just across from the easily remembered Roman pool, and you can stop here between appointments to sit and relax.

Daily exercise classes are listed and permit you a wide range of choices. All aerobics classes are low-impact. Although La Costa takes care of almost every need you could dream of having while you are there, if you're going to take aerobics or other exercise classes, instructors make a strong point to the women of wearing a good sports bra.

Finally, you should also know that despite the strong desire of the staff at La Costa that you make fitness a key part of your life, they have no illusions that La Costa is an ashram. Indeed, if you can resist the temptations that surround you at La Costa—one being its eight eating places from simple café fare to elegant (jackets requested) dinner—you can probably resist anything you'll encounter in real life. You can select your meals from the spa menu only (I found it very useful and informative to see how many fat calories are lurking in which foods) or, if you want, you can test out La Costa's system for eating wisely wherever you go.

If you know you'll be eating with others not

La Costa Resort and Spa

on the spa plan, you may want to mention that on your first day of consultations with the medical staff. At any rate, the point is that you are essentially on your own—you can sample what they offer, get a little information and advice, use golf and tennis as part of your exercise regime, or totally immerse yourself in learning what it means and feels like to be as healthy a human being as you can be: It's up to you.

HOURS
•Open year round, 7 a.m. to 7 p.m.

INCIDENTALS
•Children under 16 are not allowed in the spas, but check out Camp La Costa's supervised activities for children aged 5 to 13. (Children of hotel guests can enjoy all this for $25 a day, which includes lunch.)
•Transportation to and from San Diego Airport via La Costa vehicles is available, as are private limousines.
•It is imperative that you send for information and prices on the many changing programs, guest activities and special services provided by this first-class hotel resort—not just for making rational plans but also because their literature is a treat to read.
•All La Costa products are displayed in a sumptuous catalog and are available for purchase.
•Credit cards accepted: MasterCard, Visa, American Express, Carte Blanche, Diners' Club, Discover.

L'Auberge Del Mar

1540 Camino Del Mar
Del Mar, CA 92014
(619) 259-1515
(800) 553-1336
(619) 259-1919 (spa)

Those who know the southland probably know the small town of Del Mar, described in the thick publicity packet developed by L'Auberge as "a charming seaside village." I know Del Mar as one of those over-in-a-minute coastal towns oozing with charm.

L'Auberge is more than the "inn" conveyed by the name and more than a spa. Akin to the Marriott in Palm Desert, it is a major hotel resort that features a full-service health and beauty spa. Furthermore, those who know the Bel Air Hotel Company and the various resorts it manages, from L.A. to Cap-Ferrat to Puerta Vallarta to the British Virgin Islands, among other locations, probably know what to expect in any hotel they operate.

The hotel itself has 123 guest rooms and suites and uses red oak, marble and natural stone to re-create what they describe as the "informal but elegant tradition" of the French country inn. When Bel Air came in to manage the inn in 1992, part of its refurbishment was to re-

Spa #6
map page 294

$$$ Cost
■ Overnight
☐ Program
■ Day Use
☐ Hot Springs
☐ Hot Tubs
☐ Sauna
■ Massage
■ Skin Care/Salon
■ Exercise
■ Meals
■ Spa Products
☐ Workshops
■ Children
☐ Pets
■ Weddings

L'Auberge Del Mar   create the double-sided stone fireplace and hearth that was a distinctive feature of the original hotel, built in 1912. Like so many tucked-away resorts and spas south of Ojai, L'Auberge has had its share of Hollywood celebrities in the 1920s and 1930s. Their guest suites and meeting rooms have been named after the many legendary stars who have stayed there (my childhood idol, Rita Hayworth, among them).

It goes without saying that this is a place offering small groups and large corporations ample meeting space. They have seven versatile meeting rooms (4,000 square feet total) and most have French windows and ocean views. It should be no surprise at this point to learn that their grounds are beautifully landscaped and graced with lush foliage, waterfalls and streams, and that their restaurant offers a mouth-watering menu of American and Southwest foods (which you can enjoy, in fact, out on the terrace next to the waterfalls and herb gardens). I was surprised, however, to find they also have an amphitheater for art exhibits and other cultural events.

But the spa is the thing. Like most major spas in the state these days, European skin care has become a *sine qua non* among spa services. Here as elsewhere, the philosophy, whether expressed or tacit, is that the two cannot be extricated. To be healthy is to be beautiful, and to care about the fitness and tone of your body, using exercise and massage, is less than complete unless you also care about your skin—all of it but particularly your face.

For its spa consultant, L'Auberge brought in Toni Beck, a woman with outstanding credentials and significant experience developing programs for leading spas across the country. I appreciate her lofty goals: She wants the spa program to assist individuals in focusing their physical and mental energy in productive and positive ways aimed at achieving their highest state of well-being. For her, well-being "begins with the recognition of our uniqueness and the reality upon which we attempt to build a more expanded self." Now managed by Iceland-born Gudrun Kaneen, the fitness and skin-care services sound just wonderful.

In addition to organized walks on the beach (for hotel guests) the spa facility provides a good variety of massage therapies: Swedish, shiatsu, sports, neck and shoulder, reflexology and hydrotherapy. Its "supreme massage" gives you hydrotherapy followed by a Swedish massage. And, of course, you will be able to get an aromatherapy facial or a mini-facial—men have their own "rejuvenating" facial—and an herbal wrap. As a full-service spa, you can also use their hair salon and nail-care treatments as well as waxing services.

The spa has put together four special packages as well, from "The Spa Sampler" (at under $100) to a "Day of Glamour" for just over $200. The "Day" gives you quite a lot, I would say. It includes hair conditioning and styling, a makeover and a light lunch in addition to a facial, massage, herbal wrap and use of the spa facility and sports pavilion. (Use of spa facilities means

L'Auberge Del Mar   you can take advantage of the sauna, steam bath, Swiss shower, pools and outdoor Jacuzzi. The sports pavilion is equipped with Stairmasters, Lifecycles and a treadmill, from which you can gaze out to the Pacific Ocean.)

An extended stay or a day at L'Auberge sounds very inviting to me. In the immediate area, you will also find tennis courts, championship golf, hot-air ballooning, polo fields and the Del Mar Racetrack.

HOURS
•The spa is open Tuesday through Sunday, 9 a.m. to 7 p.m.

INCIDENTALS
•Available for day use, "overnighters" and extended hotel stays.
•Full conference facilities available.
•Tourlas Restaurant and Terrace, Durante Pub available.
•Inn has cable TV, telephones in baths, afternoon tea, on-site travel agency, same-day laundry/dry cleaning.
•Amtrak station nearby.
•Credit cards accepted: all major credit cards.

Marriott's Desert Springs Resort & Spa

74855 Country Club Drive
Palm Desert, CA 92260
(619) 341-1856
(800) 255-0848

Spa #7
map page 294

$-$$$ Cost
■ Overnight
■ Program
■ Day Use
☐ Hot Springs
■ Hot Tubs
■ Sauna
■ Massage
■ Skin Care/Salon
■ Exercise
■ Meals
■ Spa Products
☐ Workshops
■ Children
☐ Pets
■ Weddings

This $200-million world-class resort continues to flourish in Palm Desert. Clusters of flamingos perched on small islands in the many waterways and ponds greet you as you drive on to the grounds of this 892-room hotel. (Can Alice in Wonderland, seeking a rousing game of croquet, be far behind?).

This "sprawling, horizontal structure," as the hotel has been described, harbors in its lobby a stunning 100-foot-high atrium in which palm trees, two stone-tiered waterfalls and an interior lake create a sight not to be believed.

Whether you walk in at street level and look up to the ceiling high above and down the circular stairway to the lake below, or come in from the lower level entrance and look up and up and up, it is not difficult to appreciate interior designer Jane Dillon's intention "to create the impression of an unlimited horizon." In selecting the desert colors of lavender, sage green and bleached driftwood to carry out her concept, Dillon drew on the paintings of Georgia O'Keeffe for inspiration.

I remain awestruck by the interior lobby of this stunning establishment—where gondolas sweep you quietly away through magical open-sesame glass doors to more watery splendor outside. It seems that pumps capable of moving 8,000 gallons of water a minute circulate the water throughout the resort's lakes and over a waterfall, from which it tumbles into the interior lake in the main lobby.

Marriott's Desert Springs regards itself as a hotel-resort-spa complex specifically designed for people who want to combine vacation and business. It is a place where executives enjoy the benefits of a full-service health and fitness spa at their hotel (not just a tub and massage tacked on as an amenity), and also a place where mates, partners or families can lose themselves for hours while significant others are involved in high-level meetings.

If you have any question about the hotel's focus on serving business groups, you might be interested to know that 650 of its 1,400-member staff are "devoted exclusively to serving and coordinating meetings." I would guess that there is no amenity that the new Marriott, sitting pretty in the beautiful Coachella Valley Mountains, does not or cannot provide; be sure to write for more information about its lavish facilities.

Now to the "elegant, bright, uncluttered

spa...surrounded by 23 acres of lakes, a Ted Robinson-designed golf course, and the towering Santa Rosa Mountains."

The spa's 27,000-square-foot one-story building was efficiently designed for ease of use by both guests and staff, and is situated so that you can look out to their marvelous grounds at frequent intervals as you move from one activity to another. A branch of Jose Eber's hair-design center (not *HOsay* by the way; he is French) is at the entrance to the building, and skin care is under the guidance of Stockholm-born Kerstin Florian whose natural products are designed particularly for skin showing signs of aging. Her products are designed to "maintain youthful and well-balanced skin."

They offer everything you would expect in a first-class spa where the focus on fitness is reflected in the latest equipment, a 22-station gym, an aerobics room with state-of-the-art resilient flooring and a superb sound system, an exercise lawn and walking and jogging paths. One-on-one fitness consultations, cholesterol testing and nutritional consultations also are available.

The spa's body and beauty center provides all the goodies that an inveterate spa-goer has come to expect, and it does so in particularly lovely surroundings and soft desert colors. In addition to herbal wraps, salt-glow loofah scrubs and massage (Swedish and shiatsu), the Marriott invites you to try its underwater massage where you can stretch out in a specially designed pool and, not touched by human hand, feel the percussive gentle pounding of the water against your body. Allowing the water to hold on to you is extraordinary, for it relieves you of the last scrap of effort you are obliged to put out, and it takes away any concern about the practitioner pressing too hard or not hard enough. For some people, this treatment is a godsend.

The spa also has an outdoor exercise pool, sauna and steam rooms, a calorie-controlled snack bar and fitness apparel shops.

If you are staying at the Marriott, you can, at very low cost, sample a number of spa activities without committing yourself to a four-day or longer program. For example, a low daily membership fee entitles you to use their saunas, steam rooms, lap pool, plunge pool, Jacuzzi and weight room—and gives you a personal locker and your spa wardrobe. Exercise classes are less than $10 a class. Start out in the morning with a brisk "wellness walk and stretch" at no charge. (Sure you can do those things alone, but will you?)

The present menu of classes includes: "Intro to Step," "Step Right Up," "Body Sculpture," "Aqua Fit," "Relaxation in Movement," "Low-Impact Aerobics" and "Super Step." All classes are co-ed and taught to all levels of ability.

Because it is designed as an adjunct to the hotel, the spa has come up with very flexible ways for you to make use of their services during your stay. The choices are a day-use menu that allows you total pick-and-choose freedom; an *à la carte* menu that includes massages, facials and body treatments on a fee-for-service basis; and a special called "The Renewal" in which you are dressed in spa clothes and moved through a delightful program of activities that combines working out (in unlimited exercise classes), a facial, a salt-glow loofah rub, a massage and use of all spa facilities.

If you're tied up in conferences during the day, you can arrange early morning and evening activities at the spa. (Try the Superspace Relaxer for an end-of-the-day float at body-neutral temperature. It is touted as "ideal for relieving jet lag.") You can also opt to listen to relaxing music, watch a Sybervision video to improve your game of tennis, or life, or remain in total silence.

Alternatively, if you are with someone who's tied up during the day and leaves you to "make the most of it," you've got a lot of "most" to work with here. In short, if someone said to me, "I've got a conference to attend at Marriott's Desert Springs—want to come along?" I'd jump—truly I would.

HOURS
•Open year round, 6:30 a.m. to 7:30 p.m.

INCIDENTALS
•Day use of spa for a nominal fee (includes use of a spa wardrobe).
•*A la carte* services: fitness classes, personal training or fitness session, computerized body composition analysis and fitness consultation, nutritional counseling, Swedish and shiatsu massage, skin care by Kerstin, facials, biologi-

Marriott's
Desert Springs
Resort & Spa

cal peels, herbal wraps, mud therapy, thalasso bath, loofah scrubs, private whirlpools, underwater massage and Superspace Relaxer.

•Call or write for information on packaged spa programs and conference facilities.

•Limousine or shuttle from Palm Springs airport. By car, Country Club Drive intersects Interstate Highway 10 between Los Angeles and Indio.

•Credit cards accepted: all major credit cards.

The Oaks at Ojai

122 East Ojai Avenue
Ojai, CA 93023
(805) 646-5573
(805) 640-1504 fax

Spa #8
map page 294

The Palms at Palm Springs

572 North Indian Canyon Drive
Palm Springs, CA 92262
(619) 325-1111
(619) 327-0867 fax

Spa #9
map page 294

$$$ Cost
■ Overnight
■ Program
■ Day Use
☐ Hot Springs
■ Hot Tubs
■ Sauna
■ Massage
■ Skin Care/Salon
■ Exercise
■ Meals
■ Spa Products
■ Workshops
☐ Children
☐ Pets
☐ Weddings

Sheila Cluff remains at the "top of her game" with her two well-established spas, The Oaks at Ojai and The Palms at Palm Springs—and she continues her countless other health-and-fitness-related activities. Sheila continues to be a stunning example of what it looks like to stay fit, trim and active. Her "bio" would take up too much space here, but when you send for spa brochures, you'll see in one of the descriptive insert sheets her illustrious credits as physical fitness specialist and entrepreneur.

One of her recent ventures, in fact, is an entrepreneurial camp for teen girls. Called "An

The Oaks at Ojai

The Palms
at Palm Springs

Income of Her Own," the idea for this program came from Joline Godfrey, author of *Our Wildest Dreams*. Given at The Palms, this special camp educates teenage participants about writing business plans and developing marketing strategies—all in the context of its fitness program. (Call 800-350-2978 for information about this program.)

Also check Sheila's books: *The Ultimate Recipe for Fitness*, written with Eleanor Brown, one of the originators of the famous spa cuisine at The Oaks and The Palms, *Aerobic Body Contouring* (a low-impact exercise routine for "the ageless body," and *Recipes for Very Busy People*. To top it all off, Sheila finds time not only to teach classes at each spa (8 to 10 a week between them) but to talk with guests and encourage them personally in whatever goals they hope to achieve.

Both The Oaks and The Palms are the places of choice for people who are serious (but not grim) about getting the most mileage out of themselves and the time they've set aside for a health and fitness vacation. Guests (75 percent are repeat clients) know that the fitness program is a solid one that works if they work. They also know they'll get the support they need from other guests and from a capable staff.

What's more, both facilities prefer to keep accommodations basic so that fitness vacations can be offered at an affordable price. Both spas are on the American Plan, serving low-calorie, low-sodium, nutritionally balanced meals and snacks, so you don't have to include meal dollars in your budget, and you don't have to worry about being tempted by the food on other people's plates.

For those who have limited time, you can sign up for a "Spa Day" where fitness and body toning activities are packed in to give you a sampler of what a full program might do for you.

What I particularly like about both spas is that they are right in town, and if I feel like some diversion, I can walk down the street and look at shops or go to the pharmacy or the post office. In fact, Sheila encourages and promotes contact with the community, inviting the public in in various ways: At The Oaks, residents can come in the early morning hours and use the spa facility as a health and fitness club; spa guests can participate in tennis tournament finals held in Ojai; and local experts frequently give lectures on topics of interest. At The Palms, spa guests can enjoy the desert art galleries and museums close by.

If you don't venture out to see the town on your own, you'll see it on the early morning walk, which you shouldn't miss. Besides the long mountain hikes offered in both facilities at dawn's early light, in Ojai you can take a short walk through the back streets where you get to see the town's charming neighborhoods, and at The Palms you get to take a five-mile "Celebrity Walk" where you can enjoy seeing how more than 70 luminaries live the good life.

Before you start out on your walk, you'll do warm-ups—at The Oaks, in the lobby or right outside the main entrance. Motorists passing

The Oaks at Ojai

The Palms at Palm Springs

by early in the morning are probably used to seeing a group of women and men in sweats bending, twisting, stretching and laughing. In fact, the camaraderie guests develop over the course of their stay starts with the morning warm-up, which is one reason not to sleep in.

What really makes The Oaks and The Palms special among spas is the competence of the staff that directs their fitness programs and the sound theory that stands behind what they do. (The fitness program is, of course, Sheila Cluff's design.)

The importance of including three major components in your fitness regimen—stretching, aerobics and muscle strengthening—is made beautifully clear in an Introduction to Fitness talk given to new guests at The Palms. When you plan your program activities with one of the staff, you can trust that selections will be made to assure you're getting a complete workout. (Incidentally, both facilities now have new single-station weight-training equipment.)

In addition, Sheila puts out excellent printed materials that give simple information on a variety of topics: what a massage and a facial are and do for you, a "ten-pack" of recipes, a good newsy newsletter and a monthly *Fitness, Fun & Travel Guide*. Sheila also puts out audiotapes for pool exercises and tons of other printed matter. Being informed is clearly a value in Sheila's book.

Another feature here is that programs often are developed around specific themes or issues—some are sheer fun, such as Mother/ Daughter Days and others, the Spa Cuisine Cooking Week, features famous chefs and authors of cookbooks.

Finally, not to be outdone by the more lavish resort spas (and by the way you don't need your Gucci-wear here), both The Oaks and The Palms give you access to tennis courts, horseback riding, biking, golf and—depending on which spa you choose—special recreations associated with the town, from hot-air balloon rides, the famous aerial tramway, and shops, shops, shops in Palm Springs, to boating and fishing at Lake Casitas, the Ojai Music Festival, or various sports events and annual festivals held in and around Ojai.

It is not so much what they do at these spas, it's the way that they do it. Each spa has a slightly different program of activities, but whether you opt for a 5-, 7-, or 12-night package (which pushes it into a $$$$ price category), you can expect to have on your fitness schedule: a morning walk (vigorous mountain hike or more leisurely city walk); a stretching class; a choice of low-impact aerobics or, for the very fit, a challenging traditional aerobics class; weight training; some form of water exercise, either "Aquatoning" that uses water resistance to improve muscle strength or "Aquaerobics" that gives you a vigorous cardiovascular workout; body contouring; and, at day's end, quiet, relaxing Hatha yoga.

These activities are broken up, of course, by meals, broth or juice breaks and orientation lec-

The Oaks at Ojai

The Palms at Palm Springs

tures. In the evening over "happy hour" and a juice cocktail, you can talk to other guests and make friends. (After all, friends are people who've seen you sweat, right?) Both places offer various evening programs, generally listed on an activities board in the main lobby.

Billed as "special services" are massages (including a scalp massage), body composition analysis, facials, waxing, a hair salon with a complete range of beauty treatments for women and men, and a boutique. The Palms adds hypnotherapy to its special services as well as movies, which are shown several times a week in their Winner's Circle Lounge.

There it is! All you have to do now is decide whether you prefer being in the "sunny vacation atmosphere of Palm Springs" or the "picturesque Ojai Valley."

HOURS
•Both facilities are open year round.

INCIDENTALS
•"Spa Day" available for under $100.
•Group discounts are available.
•On-site evening programs.
•Gift certificates are available.
•On request, roommates will be located for singles wanting to share.
•Call for a schedule of special program packages as well as seasonal rates, a calendar of events, and a list of "Health Holiday" cruises. (Bring a group and you go free.)
•Sheila Cluff's audiocassette series of six tapes,

her "Aerobic Walking Workout" and Shirley
Jones' videotapes featuring Sheila Cluff are all
available for purchase along with many health
and skin-care products.
•Credit cards accepted: MasterCard, Visa and
Discover. Personal checks are also accepted.

The Oaks at Ojai

*The Palms
at Palm Springs*

Rancho La Puerta

Tecate, Baja California, Mexico
Post Office Box 463057
Escondido, CA 92046-3057
(619) 744-4222
(800) 443-7565

Spa #10
map page 294

$$$$ Cost
■ Overnight
■ Program
□ Day Use
□ Hot Springs
■ Hot Tubs
■ Sauna
■ Massage
■ Skin Care/Salon
■ Exercise
■ Meals
■ Spa Products
■ Workshops
■ Children
□ Pets
□ Weddings

As with The Golden Door, the second-born of the Szekely family's world-renowned spas, little has changed at Rancho La Puerta.

It remains true that simple numerical statistics go a long way in revealing Rancho La Puerta to someone who has never been there: It accommodates a maximum of 150 guests on 300 acres; its staff size is 200; its elevation is 2,000 feet; it has 341 days of sunshine a year; and, of course, it has been in the spa/fitness business since 1940.

The experience of staying at this granddaddy of spas has been charmingly captured in an article entitled "How I Spent My Aerobic Vacation" by William F. Buckley, Jr., writing in his inimitable erudite style for *The New York Times Magazine*. Whatever else one thinks of the man, he does know how to turn a phrase. (Evidently the Ranch's public relations staff were also taken with Buckley's prose—they quoted him in their colorful promotional literature.) Apparently, fearing "biological atrophy," he and his wife, on the recommendation of a friend, started going to "the Ranch" in 1981.

Besides serving as the forerunner of the latest and best in spa facilities, and thereby the authority for many newcomer spas that also emphasize fitness, the Ranch is physically stunning from the moment you pull into the parking lot and look around you at the profusion of flowers, cacti and indigenous trees that encircle the property. Actually, as proprietor Alex Szekely notes in the letter you will receive when you request information about the spa, all of their public facilities were leveled to the ground several years ago and replaced with classic Mexican colonial-style buildings.

The Ranch displays an extensive collection of paintings and sculpture throughout. Many of the Mexican village scenes by Pescina were commissioned by managing partner José Manuel Jasso, the former mayor of Tecate who was deeply involved, as were his parents, in the health and fitness world of Rancho La Puerta.

It is the main administration building that will take your breath away. Beyond its massive doors and into the lobby, you will encounter an enormous, semicircular stained-glass window that serves as a backdrop to the registration desk, and then marvel at the high beamed ceiling, red tiled-floor, finely crafted wicker furnishings, native arts and crafts on display, and bright splashes of color everywhere you look. The lobby conveys a sense of grandness and intimacy at the same time. In fact, this was my overall impression of Rancho La Puerta—a sense of grandeur in the architecture and in the physical country and a sense of intimacy in the way its 150-person accommodations are nestled into the landscape.

As you walk along the trails to the villas and haciendas where you will spend well-earned nights of rest, you could almost walk by them if they were not pointed out to you. The desert terrain and the mountains in the distance are allowed to dominate, and whether or not the Ranch's architect and the Szekelys intended to send a silent message about mankind's place in the universe, it is that message I received.

The dining hall, reconstructed several years ago, is another Mexican colonial beauty with high raftered ceilings, a circular staircase and a splendid assemblage of wood, tile, glass and wrought iron. It is no wonder that 80 percent of Rancho La Puerta's guests return year after year, and many even more frequently.

As for the food, it is all nutritionally-complete vegetarian except for fish two nights a week. We were there at lunchtime and walked back through the dining room to a large kitchen area where we served ourselves, cafeteria-style, and then returned to find a place at a large round table with other guests. Caloric values and fat grams are labeled to inform you, but the choices you make and the amounts you take are up to you. I found the selections ample, the taste of everything delicious, and I had no feeling of gnawing deprivation when I finished. (More than 50 percent of the fruits and vegetables served at The Ranch are grown right there—

free of insecticides and chemical fertilizers.)

As for the fitness part of your life at the Ranch, the week-long program starts on a Saturday with a hike. Between 6 and 7 a.m., you can take a "meditation hike," a mountain hike or a meadow hike before breakfast, which is at 7:30 a.m. For the rest of the day, you will be introduced to a few important classes (stretching, aerobics and body toning) and you will tour the grounds and set up your program for the week. "Cocktail" hour is at 5:30 p.m., dinner at 6 p.m., and at 7:30 p.m. you meet the staff and get a preview of the events scheduled for the week.

You will be able to pick from a feast of classes and activities that range from what you would expect to have at a world-renowned spa and fitness resort—stretch, aerobics, circuit training, yoga, body toning and contouring, swimming, tennis and the like, and a few you might not have expected: a "better breathing" picnic hike, a back care workshop, a class in painting on silk, and running and walking clinics. You also can sign up for a fitness evaluation.

Unlike most spas we visited, the Ranch has a library (the elder Szekely wrote some 140 books on a variety of subjects), separate women's and men's health centers, and a craft and lecture hall. And if their beauty salon is prosaically called a beauty salon, their boutique is appropriately called "El Mercado."

Rancho La Puerta is a spa that is loved and used by celebrities as much as by just plain folk. The price for the week-long program—given that it includes all meals, use of tennis courts, gyms, pools, saunas, hiking trails, exercise classes, evening programs and films—is about what you would spend at a major hotel for room and meals alone. The luxuries of massage and beauty treatments are extra, of course, and El Mercado is there to tempt you if you let it. Overall, I would put the Ranch up there in the top three for my own spa vacation—and the randomly picked number of three would depend on what social atmosphere I wanted at the time, what geographical region I felt like being in, and how long I wanted to stay.

As with other celebrity spas, the literature, by itself, is a feast for eyes, mind and spirit. To celebrate its 50th anniversary, The Ranch published a coffee-table-size folio, *Siempre Mejor*, featuring informal portraits and lively sketches of some of its many notable guests over the years. Write for a copy and you will see what makes this spa so very special. Whether or not you make The Ranch your spa vacation this year, you must buy a copy of *The Rancho La Puerta Cookbook*. The artfully conceived, nourishing low-fat meals may be enough to lure you to the spa itself.

HOURS
•Open year round.

INCIDENTALS
•Children age 7 and under are not allowed.
•You will need one of the following for identification: a birth certificate, naturalization pa-

pers, passport or certificate of voter registration. •Credit cards accepted: MasterCard and Visa.

Rancho La Puerta

Spa de Jour

Gold's Gym Airport Complex
4050-B Airport Centre Drive
Palm Springs, CA 92264
(619) 864-4150
(800) 659-4391

Spa #11
map page 294

$-$$ Cost
☐ Overnight
☐ Program
■ Day Use
☐ Hot Springs
☐ Hot Tubs
☐ Sauna
■ Massage
■ Skin Care/Salon
☐ Exercise
☐ Meals
■ Spa Products
☐ Workshops
☐ Children
☐ Pets
☐ Weddings

Spa de Jour (literally "day spa") recently had its grand opening. Its "labor of love," as owners Marci and Philip Lacy refer to it, fittingly came to fruition on Labor Day, 1993.

This "urban retreat" in the resort area of Palm Springs is located in a complex entirely given over to health, fitness and beauty establishments. Starting with the state-of-the-art Gold's Gym (24,000 square feet), the complex at this moment consists of Spa de Jour, a health food restaurant, a hair salon, a tanning salon and a nutrition counseling service. The next tenant is slated to be a physician or health practitioner committed to holistic practices.

The 2,000-square-foot Spa de Jour is situated in the corner of an L-shaped configuration with a 30-foot tower in the apex. When you enter the spa, your first vision is up and away to the top of the tower. The treatment rooms are all large with high ceilings.

What struck me among its dazzling array of massage, facials, hydrotherapy, body treatment and manicure and pedicure services were the following:

- Massage treatments (Swedish, sports, integrated massage therapy and aromatherapy) can be done in your home or office.
- Spa services include: an enzyme body smoothing, therapeutic mud bath, cellulite treatments (six in a series with home regimen) "Executive Recovery" back treatment, aloe vera body wrap for after-sun.
- Facials include "Coup d'Eclat Face Lifting," eye lifting, neck lifting and two special facials for men.
- Hydrotherapy tubs (recommended before all facials and body treatments) include underwater massage and the optional use of aromatherapy oils, French seaweed or mud. (Their mud is Moor mud—no peat or clay—and is considered to be the most therapeutic.)
- Pedicures (performed in a European pedicure Jacuzzi) include a "basic" treatment with aromatherapy salt scrub or oils, or a more elaborate treatment with mud or with a French seaweed foot bath and reflexology.

Spa de Jour also offers extensive makeup assistance, including complete wedding services. Waxing is also on the list, and all services use cold wax products.

On top of all that, the Lacys have put together four special packages, most calling for

Spa de Jour

two hours of your time but one, "The Glamour Package," asks you to reserve five hours. In addition, you are invited to put together your own package and receive a 10% discount on any group of three services and a 12% discount on any group of four or more services. If you let them know in advance, you can order a "Spa Cuisine Luncheon" for $10!

HOURS
•Open every day, 8 a.m. to 8 p.m.

INCIDENTALS
•Credit cards accepted: MasterCard, Visa and American Express. ATM cards also accepted.

Spa Hotel and Mineral Springs

100 North Indian Canyon Drive
Post Office Box 1787
Palm Springs, CA 92263
(619) 325-1461 (hotel)
(619) 778-1SPA (spa)
(800) 854-1279

Spa #12
map page 294

This architecturally distinctive 230-room hotel-spa, with its landmark columnar structure (highly visible) and its 50,000-gallon holding tanks of hot mineral water (submerged and not visible) has undergone major changes in recent months. As of this writing, many details are still being completed for its grand opening.

First, it is now under the ownership of the Agua Caliente Development Authority, an agency of the Agua Caliente Band of Cahuilla Indians, according to a report in *The Desert Sun*. And that seems fitting. Not only does the facility rest on the site of the original mineral springs from which the Agua Calientes took their name but a plaque outside the hotel has long commemorated the Native Americans who first gathered there to enjoy the healing waters and to share them with travelers passing through this desert region.

$$\text{\$\$-\$\$\$}\quad \text{Cost}$$

■ Overnight
■ Program
■ Day Use
■ Hot Springs
■ Hot Tubs
■ Sauna
■ Massage
■ Skin Care/Salon
■ Exercise
■ Meals
■ Spa Products
☐ Workshops
☐ Children
☐ Pets
■ Weddings

Spa Hotel and
Mineral Springs

Agua Caliente Tribal Council Chairman Richard Milanovich called attention to the importance of this transfer of ownership when he said:

"This land and its hot mineral springs has special significance for the tribe as owners. The springs are the historical focal point of our cultural activities. Our Spanish and Cahuilla tribal names were, in fact, derived from these revered mineral springs. For these reasons, and because of the large investment of tribal resources, we are committed to making the Spa Hotel and Mineral Springs a showcase facility of which we and the community will be proud."

In the heart of Palm Springs, the Spa Hotel has always been a major convention and meeting site, and with its renovation by Frank Urrutia of Urrutia-Prest, an award-winning architectural firm, it is bound to attract more of this business. In Urrutia's design, the exterior will retain its basic structure. The outside has been repainted in salmon tones with teal trim, the interior is in earth tones and features other design elements that reflect the culture of the Agua Calientes, and awnings and tinted glass are being installed over glass areas that have been unshaded. The hotel will have eight meeting rooms ranging in size from a boardroom for 15 to the 7,900-square-foot Agua ballroom with a seating capacity of 650.

Without dwelling on the upgrading of the hotel proper—which encompassed all rooms (20 suites), the café and bistro as well as another all-day restaurant with indoor and outdoor patio dining, the bar, and the pool areas, as well as the installation of a new roof, an improved air-conditioning system, wheelchair accessibility and numerous other renovations that pushed the price tag to nearly $9 million—let's get to the spa.

Although housed in this splendid hotel, the spa is open for day use as well as for hotel guests, and you can still take advantage of special weekend programs. Spa facilities are designed so that men and women can be together and apart in their spa activities, meeting from time to time in the fully equipped co-ed gym, at the Caliente Café, or in the roof solarium. The clothing-optional solarium on the roof remains a magical place where you can lounge under a cloudless sky and look out to the majestic mountains that make this desert area so awesome. A special elevator will zoom you directly to the roof so you can just put on your robe, your scuffs and a smile and reach for the stars.

The women's spa, a sea of light gray marble, is quite spacious, with glass-enclosed saunas and rooms devoted to special treatments, such as the eucalyptus inhalation room, private mineral water tub rooms (with lovely body-contoured tubs), and a cooling room where you are swaddled in linens and your eyes covered with herbal-scented eye pads as you rest quietly, enveloped in the sound of soft classical music. (The men's facility has sunken tubs in off-white marble.)

One of the luxurious amenities in the spa is a thick robe that you will be given to wear while you are moving from one treatment to another.

Stretching and toning exercises are provided in the aerobics room, but exercise is also offered in the beautiful covered mineral water pool outside. Working out in water is great, not only for fitness purposes—water supplies heavy but gentle resistance for the body to work against—but also for social reasons: water games are a good way to get acquainted with others.

When I was there, Ilona of Hungary had her own facial salon on the lobby level near the pool. I understand that her salon is no longer there, but in its place will be a first-rate facial salon operated by the spa.

As I indicated, spa services, delivered by a staff of over 50 (including 20 massage practitioners, men and women), can be used by "day-trippers" as well as guests. The spa services offered in what they call "The Spa Experience" include use of the infra-red heat/eucalyptus inhalation rooms, sauna, hot mineral water bath, cooling room, fitness center and solarium. As of this writing, The Spa Experience is only $25 for day-use visitors and only $10 for hotel guests.

Obviously, other treatments are available to both day users and hotel guests on an *à la carte* basis. I was pleased to find out that all of its three pools (one with city water at 78 degrees and the other two natural mineral water pools at 90 degrees and 104 degrees, respectively) are open 24 hours a day, and that poolside luncheons will be available from 11 a.m. to 3 p.m. daily.

If you have only 24 hours in Palm Springs, or if you're with someone who has business to do during the day, look into Spa Hotel's personalized "Day of Pampering." It is available from Monday through Friday, 9 a.m. to 5 p.m. (with 11 to 1 on your own to shop or sightsee around town). All service charges and taxes are included in the moderate price, which is discounted 15% for hotel guests.

For those who have time and high purpose, however, I would suggest you register for one of their two packaged programs. These programs have been orchestrated by people who know about fitness, and, as at other top-notch facilities, they have been designed to give you the experience of what it feels like to live the fit life. Knowing that we often go home and gradually forget what we've experienced and learned in our week's program, the spa staff will give you some take-home reminders in print.

The two-night, three-day "Sampler" is meant for people who simply can't take a lot of time out of their lives to test the longer programs. The week-long program "Discover the Springs" with its five nights and six days of spa activities, gives you a solid footing for starting a lifelong fitness program. Healthy meals are included in both programs. By the way, the spa has added six "wet tables" for salt glow rubs, loofah scrubs and herbal wraps.

Whichever you select, you will be scooped up at the airport, housed, fed, taken for morning walks, exercised, tubbed and scrubbed, massaged, facialed, pedicured and otherwise invited to partake of a menu of services that are as pleasureful as they are healthful. (I spent a wonderful day here, so I know whereof I speak.)

Finally, Spa Hotel still houses an elegant full-service beauty salon, which is open to the public as well as to spa guests.

I suggest you write for the spa's latest brochure to get a full description of all of its programs, activities and services. Any time you are in Palm Springs, I strongly suggest you drop by and treat yourself to one or more of its small splendors. (I need not remind you that Palm Springs offers many attractions: the Desert Museum, the aerial tramway, jeep tours, balloon rides, wonderful restaurants and shops, and of course, golf, golf, golf.)

HOURS
•Open year round.
•Spa hours: 9 a.m. to 7 p.m.
•Gym hours: 7 a.m. to 7 p.m.

INCIDENTALS
•Minimum age is 16 years old.
•As in all desert towns, check for off-season discounts.
•All guest rooms and suites (230 units, some with kitchenettes) are equipped with air conditioning, cable color TV and direct-dial telephones.
•Conference facilities available: 17,000 square feet of meeting space serving groups of 15 to 650 persons. Complete audiovisual equipment provided; banquet food and service available.

•Credit cards accepted: MasterCard, Visa, American Express, Carte Blanche, Diners' Club, Discover.

Wheeler
Hot Springs

Post Office Box 250
16825 Maricopa Highway
Ojai, CA 93023
(805) 646-8131
(800) 227-9292

Spa #13
map page 294

$-$$ Cost
☐ Overnight
☐ Program
■ Day Use
■ Hot Springs
■ Hot Tubs
☐ Sauna
■ Massage
☐ Skin Care/Salon
☐ Exercise
■ Meals
☐ Spa Products
☐ Workshops
■ Children
☐ Pets
■ Weddings

Wheeler Hot Springs is another one of those resorts that has been around since before the turn of the century when health seekers from the East Coast headed west to enjoy the mountain air and to take the healing waters. In those early days, visitors braved a long stagecoach ride to get to the site. In 1891, the original lodge was built by Wheeler Blumberg, but it was in the 1920s and beyond that Wheeler was sought out by Hollywood celebrities as well as famous boxers, bankers and bootleggers. Many fires and rebuildings later (a common occurrence among these century-old resorts), people again flock to the Ojai valley and "motor on up" to Wheeler. Recently, Mrs. Frances Hurst of Ojai was invited to celebrate her 90th birthday at the hot springs she had first visited as a girl in 1910.

With the reawakening of interest in health and fitness that came in the late '60s and '70s, and the continuing advice of health practitioners in the '90s that we reduce the stress in our lives, it is no wonder that these historic hot springs, with their time-honored promise of waters that heal, are reinventing themselves against all odds.

It is obvious that the Landucci-Kaufer family (owners of the property since 1969) enjoy the history of the land and of the Chumash Indians who were native to the area and discovered these healing mineral waters long before any of us arrived. Their respect for the history of Wheeler and its earliest inhabitants shows in the simple details they have either retained or incorporated to keep a historical presence alive. Look around the lounge and bar and you'll see what I mean.

Driving to Wheeler from Ojai is in itself worth the trip. Maricopa Highway out of Ojai takes you on a winding journey with striking cliffs on one side and sheer drops on the other. If you don't spot Wheeler's sign by the wooden bridge on the left side of the road, you will know you have arrived when you see a small bar-café on the right and a bridge on the left. Just drive over the bridge and into its large parking lot.

Wheeler is unusual in its combination of rustic and historic (the structure housing its tubs, sauna and massage rooms) and elegant and contemporary (its first-class creekside restaurant, presided over by a French-Italian chef and featuring a full bar). And while it has for years brought in top performers in jazz, folk, rock and classical music on the weekends, it has only recently constructed a stage in the main dining room to accommodate the likes of such entertainers as the Manhattan Transfer, Kenny Burrell, Joe Pass and more. So while the family has made a few changes and looks forward to enlarging its spa facilities and building its own accommodations on site (right now, staff will refer you to one of Ojai's many good motels and B&Bs with whom they have made special arrangements), as spelled out in its new bimonthly newsletter, "Project Facelift" is intended to make Wheeler even more what it already is. In other words, *"Plusque ça change, plusque c'est la même chose."*

The bath house and restaurant face each other. Obviously, you made your reservations in advance, so, when you arrive, just go right up the stairs of the bath house past a wayward lizard or friendly frog and into what has to be the tiniest waiting room in the West. You'll spy a person sitting in an enclosure behind a desk ready to check you in and an attendant will show you to your tub room and ask that you shower first—showers are down a short hallway. (Wrap yourself in a towel or robe for this trip; even though your tub room is private, both genders use this passageway to the showers.)

There are four tub rooms, each one having two redwood tubs, one filled with hot spring-fed water (heated from its natural 102 degrees to approximately 105 degrees) and the other with cold spring-fed water from a separate source. (All pool and drinking water, by the way, comes from their natural springs.) Two of the tub rooms accommodate only two at a time;

the other two can hold up to six. The tubs are up a few stairs from a tiny dressing (and undressing) area where light filters in from skylights above and glasses of cold lemon water await you. Folded bath towels are hung over the railing that separates the tub area from the entry and dressing area. In the evening, the room is softly lit and conducive to quiet relaxation. (Even more romantic is their vision of having private hot and cold tubs scattered along the mountainside in the open air.)

Once you have showered and come back into your private space, you can forget time; the attendant will come by and knock on your door when it's time to leave or to continue on to your massage. Twenty massage practitioners are on call at Wheeler and although, as at other spas, Swedish is the most popular technique used and asked for, shiatsu and other forms are available. If you have a preference, state it when you call for an appointment.

Depending on what time of day you are there and how you want to spend your time, you can take a quick swim in the near-Olympic-size swimming pool next door, or get out of your wet look entirely and prepare for dinner. In walking across the few yards that separate the bath house from the restaurant, you will be leaving the rustic world of softly worn redwood and gently proffered but spartan amenities and enter the elegant simplicity of the restaurant-bar with its gleaming hardwood floors, its spacious, airy feeling, its massive fireplace whose size alone reminds you of another era, and the smiling *maître d'* who looks genuinely pleased to be there and doing what he's doing. (By the way, the dining room is a no-smoking area but smokers are welcome in the 100-year-old tavern. Both areas are air conditioned.)

Perfectionists and gourmands, the Kaufers labor over the menus, the wine selections and the ambience—continually working out new ways to bring together the two nurturing experiences of immersion in hot water and immersion in good food. They are pleased to have kept the same chef, Gael Lecolley, formerly of Remi and Beaurivage, and pastry chef Guy Leclerot, for many years. (Did I tell you that they bake their own breads and desserts and smoke their own chicken and fish?)

The entrées on the (*à la carte*) menu range from warm lobster salad to duck *à l'orange* and lamb *à la fleur de thym.* Also available are appetizers, soups and salads as well as pastas and vegetarian dishes. Prices are what you would expect in any good restaurant; the quality of the food is beyond that.

If I have not made it clear, Wheeler sparkles in the evening. I still say that a hot soak, a massage and dinner are perfect ingredients for a very special time-out from the busy lives most of us lead. And even in the evening hours, you will see families at Wheeler. When I was last there, I showered next to a young mother and her little girl (children are allowed as long as they are strictly watched over by their parents and those under 14 are advised not to use the hot tubs) and I later met a single woman in the restaurant lounge who had been a Wheeler regular for some time. Most of the spas we visited, perhaps all, rely on a high percentage of repeat customers, and Wheeler obviously attracts such a clientele.

If evening hours don't work for you, Wheeler offers a brunch-and-soak special on Saturdays and Sundays, with such tantalizers as Mayan Omelette, Crab Cakes Benedict and a "Down East Waffle with a cloud of whipped cream." Children's portions are available. Champagne goes with the brunch, needless to say, but if champagne isn't your cup of tea, try fresh-squeezed (Ojai) orange juice and/or cappuccino, espresso or another beverage. (For hardier drinkers, the bartenders are quite proud of their special recipe for Bloody Marys.)

Their monthly concerts—jazz, blues or folk music—have attracted a devoted following over the years. In 1991, for Wheeler's centennial, Lanny Kaufer rounded up some of the jazz and blues greats (Clarence Brown, Charles Brown, Mose Allison, among others) who have been appearing intermittently throughout the years. Needless to say, Wheeler is happy to host special events and weddings.

Although it is a day-use-only spa at this moment, do keep checking to see when they will have put in their own cabins on the property. If nothing else, write to Wheeler to get on its mailing list; that way, you will also find out what is going on locally in the Ojai area (such as its annual music festival) so that you can plan your trip accordingly.

Wheeler
Hot Springs

HOURS
•Open year-round.
•Spa: Monday through Thursday, 9 a.m. to 9 p.m.; Friday, Saturday and Sunday, 9 a.m. to 10 p.m.
•Restaurant: dinner Thursday through Sunday, 5 p.m. to 9:30 p.m.; brunch Saturday 11 a.m. to 2 p.m. and Sunday 10 a.m. to 2:30 p.m.

INCIDENTALS
•Reservations must be made in advance for all spa services and restaurant. Minimum 24-hour cancellation notice requested.
•Towels, gowns and hairdryers are provided.
•Call or write for news about concerts, special events, and hot tub-dinner packages.
•Saturday-Sunday *Hot Tub and Brunch for Two* special and Thursday-Friday-Sunday *Hot Tub and Dinner for Two* special.
•Live entertainment and full bar.
•Restaurant and lawns available for weddings and events on weekdays, early Saturdays, or late Sundays.
•Credit cards accepted: MasterCard, Visa and American Express.

Desert Hot Springs Spas

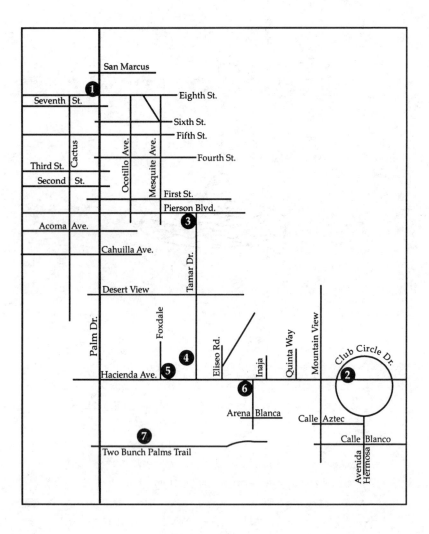

Introduction to Desert Hot Springs

When *California Spas* first came out in 1992, I noted that the mineral-rich healing waters of Desert Hot Springs had obviously done the job: According to the city's statisticians, the mean age had dropped to a young 47. Where it stands now, I don't know, but the last time I visited, the town seemed perfectly satisfied with itself.

Despite the presence of a couple of major hotels among the many, many Mom-and-Pop operations and mobile home parks that distinguish Desert Hot Springs, I saw no signs of its yearning to compete with its Palm Springs neighbor or to uproot its retiree population with any ambitious public relations campaigns that would usher in change. In other words, Desert Hot Springs still lives in an "if-it-ain't-broke-don't-fix-it" state of mind. (I say this in spite of the presence of Two Bunch Palms, which continues to inhabit its own world, as you'll see when you get to page 392.)

Although I still see Desert Hot Springs as a sister to Northern California's Calistoga—both towns possessing an unlimited outpouring of natural hot mineral spring waters that spawned the development of wall-to-wall spas, they have little else in common. As rapidly as Calistoga grows and develops, as firmly does Desert Hot Springs dig in its heels—at least from the eyes of this stranger.

Unlike Palm Springs, which tricked Mother Nature and turned itself into a lush tropical oasis, Desert Hot Springs, with or without intention, has kept its desert identity. For my taste, I have to look beyond a scattering of plastic flowers here and there, cutesy bric-a-brac, an occasional lawn and other inappropriate imports and just gaze out at the mountains and the expanse of desert to focus on the natural beauty of the region.

Whatever harsh demands the desert places on you with its lack of cover, its winds and its soaring heat in the peak summer months, it gives back much more: magnificent skies, dawns and sunsets of dazzling and subtly changing colors, sparkling clear air, low humidity, mountainous vistas everywhere you look, relentless sunshine and the silkiest, soothingest, soaking waters around. And make no mistake—immersing your body in mineral water that has been cooled down to tolerable temperatures is quite a different thing from sitting in city water that has been heated up.

For man-made recreations, the work is also largely done: There are tennis courts, golf courses, hiking and bridle trails through craggy canyons and up distant mountain slopes, historic Native American reservations, wildlife preserves, RV parks for the family, desert museums and more. And if you want some of Palm Springs' glitz or food fare, it's only a sandstorm away.

Architecturally, an intriguing sight in Desert Hot Springs itself is Cabot's Old Indian Pueblo, a 35-room adobe built and rebuilt by the eccentric Cabot Yerxa from 1939 to 1965. It is four stories high and has 65 doors and 150 windows, no two of which are alike. An unusual landmark, this museum/house filled with artifacts offers a field day for California history buffs and anyone with an attraction for the quixotic.

But it is the spas, of course, that are the lifeblood of the town, just as they are in Calistoga. Most individual spa owners are old-timers with a clientele that doesn't change much from one year to the next. For the most part, spa owners know that what they have to offer "sells itself," and they seem to see their job as just being smart enough not to get in the way.

With few exceptions, the spas in Desert Hot Springs are configured in the same way: The basic design you'll see throughout the area is motel units, single or double story, encircling a courtyard pool area with minimal spa services (sauna and massage) carried out in small rooms just off the poolside walkways.

In addition to the characteristic design of the facilities, you'll find wall-to-wall astroturf that most spa owners install to deal with the constant wet-foot traffic that goes with the territory. (Whoever comes up with a highly water-resistant floor covering that has elegance as well as durability will be a prince among princes to those beleaguered owners and managers of watery wonderlands.)

Some places offer desert hikes or special programs, but most desert rats lounge around the mineral water pools and occasionally soak tired legs and feet in the Jacuzzi and call it a day. In other words, to describe every one of its forty-some spas would be folly. They are listed on the next pages along with other "stats" about climate, dress and sights to see in and around Desert Hot Springs.

The spas described in this chapter constitute a rather random selection. I tried to give you a sampling of the old and new and the same-as and different-from places available. I did intentionally leave out a couple of the major hotels in Desert Hot Springs because, for my taste, they are conventional resort complexes that could be plunked down anywhere; that is, they have little or no "desert personality." For the traveler who wants a predictably reliable Best Western accommodation, however, it exists.

Generally speaking, neither the omission nor inclusion of a Desert Hot Springs spa carries any hidden message of "don't go" or "go." If you want a simple do-nothing vacation where you can luxuriate in the waters all day long, Desert Hot Springs offers you many choices, from the large, convivial, eight-pooled Desert Hot Springs Spa Hotel to the tiny, serene Lido Palms to the many others where quietude reigns. Or hie yourself to Two Bunch Palms, still the pricey outlaw spa on the outskirts of town where the roaring twenties live on.

ABOUT DESERT HOT SPRINGS

The following information was adapted from material sent to me by the Desert Hot Springs Chamber of Commerce, 13-560 Palm Drive, Desert Hot Springs, CA 92240; (619) 329-6403; (800) FIND-DHS.

Location: Desert Hot Springs is located 112 miles from Los Angeles in the foothills of the San Bernardino Mountains overlooking Palm Springs and the Coachella Valley.

It is approximately two hours from Los Angeles by car via Interstate 10 or from San Diego via Interstate 15 and Interstate 10. It is 509 miles from San Francisco. The Palm Springs Airport is 12 miles away. Several commuter lines serve other hub cities.

Sunline buses provide service between Desert Hot Springs and other valley attractions. Amtrak offers service from Indio, and Greyhound Bus Lines and Desert Stage Lines are based in Palm Springs. Taxis, limousines, car rentals and Dial-a-Ride are also available.

Climate: There are approximately 337 days of sunshine a year. Although summer months are warm, the low humidity and elevation keeps them from being uncomfortably so.

Average Temperatures:

Month	High/Low
January	69/40
February	72/43
March	79/46
April	83/50
May	87/55

June	92/65
July	98/75
August	97/74
September	92/66
October	85/57
November	74/50
December	68/41

Dress: The desert calls for casual dress. Lightweight cottons and natural fabrics that "wash and wear" are the best to bring. Light wraps and knits are sufficient for evening wear or for cooler winter months.

Activities: Besides the therapeutic mineral waters that are the main attraction in Desert Hot Springs, the area offers golf, tennis, swimming, shopping, sightseeing, horseback riding, bicycle rentals, ballooning and hiking. Also accessible are museums, concerts and other cultural events.

Spas in Desert Hot Springs: The spas in the following list are only those belonging to the Chamber of Commerce. Almost all have such amenities as air conditioning, kitchenettes, TV, and airport transportation, and accept major credit cards; many, however, do not have in-room telephones. Those marked with an asterisk (*) accept small pets. Desert Hot Springs is one of the few spa areas to allow pets.

Ambassador Health Spa
12-921 Tamar Drive
(619) 329-1909
(800) 569-0541   20 units

Atlas Hi Lodge
13-336 Avenida Hermosa
(619) 329-5446   6 units*

Broadview Lodge
12-672 Eliseo Road
(619) 329-8006   12 units*

Cactus Springs Lodge
68-075 Club Circle Drive
(619) 329-5776   11 units

Caravan Spa
66-810 East Fourth Street
(619) 329-7124   15 units*

David's Spa Motel
11-220 Palm Drive
(619) 329-6202   18 units

Desert Hot Springs Hotel and Spa
10-805 Palm Drive
(619) 329-6495
(800) 843-6053   50 units*

Desert Palms Spa Hotel
67-485 Hacienda Avenue
(619) 329-4443   40 units

Desert Springs Inn
12-697 Eliseo Road
(619) 251-1668   7 units

denotes spas/hotels that allow pets

El Reposo
66-334 West Fifth Street
(619) 329-6632   22 units*

Emerald Springs Resort
68-055 Club Circle Drive
(619) 329-1151   17 units

Flamingo Resort Hotel & Spa
67-221 Pierson Boulevard
(619) 251-1455
(800) 438-4379   33 units

Hillview Motel
11-740 Mesquite Avenue
(619) 329-5317   16 units

Karson's Katering at the Oasis Inn
12-561 Palm Drive
(619) 329-5258   6 units*

Kismet Lodge
13-340 Mountain View Road
(619) 329-5461   10 units*

Las Primaveras Resort Spa
66-659 Sixth Street
(619) 251-1677   9 units*

Lido Palms Spa
12-801 Tamar Drive
(619) 329-6033
(800) THE-LIDO   11 units

Linda Vista Lodge
67-200 Hacienda Avenue
(619) 329-6401
(800) 334-7200   42 units

Lorane Manor
67-751 Hacienda Avenue
(619) 329-9090   10 units

Ma Ha Ya Lodge & Health Spa
68-111 Calle Las Tiendas
(619) 329-5420   23 units

Miracle Manor
12-589 Reposo Way
(619) 329-6641   6 units*

Mission Lakes Country Club
8484 Clubhouse Drive
(619) 329-6481   8 units

The Moors Resort Spa Motel
12-673 Reposo Way
(619) 329-7121   9 units

Ponce de Leon
11-000 Palm Drive
(619) 329-6484
(800) 922-6484   107 units*

Pyramid Motel
66-563 East Fifth Street
(619) 329-5652   15 units

denotes spas/hotels that allow pets

Royal Fox Inn
14-500 Palm Drive
(619) 329-4481
(800) 423-8109   115 units

Royal Palms Inn B&B
12-885 Eliseo Road
(619) 329-7975
(800) 755-9538   7 units*

Sahara Spa Motel
66-666 East Fifth Street
(619) 329-6666   23 units

Sandpiper Inn
12-800 Foxdale Drive
(619) 329-6455   26 units

San Marcus Inn
66-540 San Marcus Road
(619) 329-5304   15 units*

Skyliner Spa
12-840 Inaja
(619) 251-0933   6 units

Spa Town House
66-540 East Sixth Street
(619) 329-6014   10 units*

Stardust Spa Motel
66-634 Fifth Street
(619) 329-5443   19 units*

Sunset Inn
67-585 Hacienda Avenue
(619) 329-4488   20 units

Swiss Health Spa
66-729 Eighth Street
(619) 329-6912   11 units

Tamarix Spa
66-185 Acoma
(619) 329-6615   9 units*

Tramview Lodge
11-149 Sunset Avenue
(619) 329-6751   7 units*

Travellers' Repose B&B
66-920 First Street
(619) 329-9584   3 units

Tropical Motel & Spa
12-962 Palm Drive
(619) 329-6610   31 units

The largest and most expensive on the list are the full-service hotels, Ponce de Leon and Royal Fox Inn, where prices range from $60 to $160 per night. Many others are in the $30 to $60 per night range. Most spas lower their prices in the summer months; all add an 8% to 10% occupancy tax.

denotes spas/hotels that allow pets

Desert Hot Springs Spa Hotel

10805 Palm Drive
Desert Hot Springs, CA 92240
(619) 329-6495
(800) 843-6053

Spa #1
map page 364

$$ Cost
■ Overnight
☐ Program
■ Day Use
■ Hot Springs
■ Hot Tubs
■ Sauna
■ Massage
■ Skin Care/Salon
☐ Exercise
■ Meals
■ Spa Products
☐ Workshops
■ Children
■ Pets
☐ Weddings

Different from the typical motel-pool design is Desert Hot Springs Spa Hotel sitting at the head of Palm Drive. Its uniqueness is not just in the huge elephant head bursting out of the wall of the cocktail lounge (still there last time I checked) nor in George, the roadrunner bird, who comes to the door of the coffee shop for his morning handout, with two little runners beside him.

Even though, like other spas in the area, its 50 (double-decker) rooms are wrapped around a central courtyard, the comparison ends there. Not only is the courtyard studded with tall palm trees but, instead of the usual swimming pool and indoor/outdoor whirlpools, this spa has EIGHT pools—one Olympic-size in conventional rectangular shape at a comfortable 85 degrees and seven other large circular tubs at temperatures that range from 94 to 108 degrees. You have the luxury of moving from one pool to the next, from hot to cool (which is the way 98 and 85 degrees feel after you've been soaking in higher temperatures), and from one group of soakers to another.

Another feature that makes people come from far and wide to this particular spa is that its doors are open to anyone who wants to just make a day of it. Sun worshippers come from Riverside, Los Angeles and San Diego counties on the weekends, arriving first thing in the morning and not leaving until nightfall. It's no wonder when you have immediate access to food and beverages (served to you at poolside), a bar and restaurant serving everything from sandwiches to steaks, and piped-in music by day, and a guitarist or pianist in the evening.

As for spa services, their massage business is going strong. They offer Swedish-Esalen, deep tissue, foot reflexology, and more, as well as facials and body wraps. Desert Hot Springs Spa Hotel has 10 cabanas they use for massage. Years ago, these little 10' by 10' cabanas were rented out for the day and, in fact, were all that stood on an open, chain-link fenced property.

In its retail store, swimwear and T-shirts for women and men are among the popular items sold.

This spa is always jumping, so if you're a convivial sort wanting to mix it up with like-minded others, this spa hotel should be your choice. Stop by during daytime hours and check it out. If you decide to stay overnight, you have the choice of a lower- or upper-level room. All rooms look out to the inner courtyard pools.

For guests, golf privileges are extended at the

nearby Mission Lakes Country Club and the Fields Golf Club.

P.S. An attraction that has not changed is the appearance in the spring of a skydiver soaring over the spa hotel complex and landing in the courtyard!

HOURS
•Open year round.
•Restaurant open from 7 a.m. to 11 p.m.

INCIDENTALS
•Eight outdoor hot mineral-water pools at varying (85- to 108-degree) temperatures.
•Makeup instruction by appointment.
•As with all desert spas, check off-season rates.
•Pets allowed with a deposit.
•Credit cards accepted: MasterCard, Visa and American Express.

Emerald Springs Resort

68-055 Club Circle Drive
Desert Hot Springs, CA 92240
(619) 329-1151

Canadian-born Meg and Londoner John Hilton are still the owners of Emerald Springs Resort. Nothing has changed, they tell me, and so here is my story about them and their "rare jewel of the desert" just as I wrote it in the previous edition of this book.

The Hiltons lived for many years in Britain where they stoutheartedly suffered all the body aches and pains associated with London's unforgiving climate. Through a series of twists and turns, they ended up in Desert Hot Springs listening to their son, Robert, extol the healing waters and the superb desert air he had discovered here. Skeptical at first ("whot d'ya take me for, mate?") John and Meg agreed to "give it a go" and slowly found their aching bodies responding to the mineral water heat therapy and the dry, bone-warming climate.

Not only have the Hiltons turned their own lives around since owning, operating and taking the waters of Emerald Springs, they've seen others hobble in and walk out, pain-free.

Spa #2
map page 364

$$ Cost
■ Overnight
☐ Program
☐ Day Use
■ Hot Springs
■ Hot Tubs
☐ Sauna
■ Massage
☐ Skin Care/Salon
☐ Exercise
☐ Meals
☐ Spa Products
☐ Workshops
■ Children
☐ Pets
■ Weddings

John, who spent 40 years in construction, and his son Robert, a jack-of-all-trades according to Dad, are very proud of the pumping system they built to take the well water from the ground to the pools. The set-up allows him to change the water in his three pools every four hours.

John took us out back to inspect the mechanical splendors of his well and pump, and scooped up a glassful of the magical water, which he raised to the sunlight to show us how clear it was. (Desert Hot Springers, especially those in the coveted hillside area where Emerald Springs is located, seem delighted that the water has none of the sulphur odor associated with hot springs in the north, and that it is crystal clear. I found on my last foray into the Calistoga area in Northern California that they, too, want to play down the familiar odor associated with sulphurous waters. Shucks! Just when I had learned to accept it as the country version of aromatherapy.)

I have not done any comparisons of the mineral content of either Desert Hot Springs water or Calistoga water, but that might be interesting to analyze in terms of your experience of the water and its perceived beneficial effects. It's the high sodium content that imparts the softer-than-soft quality you feel in some natural mineral water pools. Spas in both towns are generally eager to show you these data.

Down to the spa itself, Meg and John's 17 rooms surround the large, rectangular pool area. The rooms are airy, clean and spacious. Most have fully equipped kitchens. Suites are also available.

The large outdoor pool is kept at a comfortable 90 degrees, the outdoor hot pool at 102, and the charming indoor spa at 106. If you want a massage, the Hiltons call on Judy deBoer, a Dutch massage practitioner in Desert Hot Springs who will come to the spa to pick you up. John told us that several massage practitioners in the area like to use his pools for their personal soaking respites.

Meg and John do most of the work around the place ("It never ends" they say in unison), and there is something very pleasant about seeing Meg standing poolside, folding the day's towel supply, or John hustling around to check a leak here, a lock there. It brought me back to my stay at a pension in Florence where the concierge and her daughter folded laundry out in the roof garden, chatting up an Italian storm the whole time, and always ready to respond to a question: *"Le mi dica, senora?"*

HOURS
•Open year round.

INCIDENTALS
•Weekly, monthly and off-season rates.
•Cable color TV.
•No telephones in rooms.
•Airport pickup and delivery.
•Credit cards accepted: MasterCard and Visa.

Flamingo Resort Hotel and Spa

67221 Pierson Boulevard
Desert Hot Springs, CA 92240
(619) 251-1455
(800) 438-4379

Spa #3
map page 364

$$ Cost
■ Overnight
☐ Program
☐ Day Use
■ Hot Springs
■ Hot Tubs
■ Sauna
■ Massage
☐ Skin Care/Salon
■ Exercise
☐ Meals
☐ Spa Products
☐ Workshops
■ Children
☐ Pets
■ Weddings

With a new name and new manager, what was once Desert Holiday Motel and Spa has seen extensive improvements. Nothing can take away from Flamingo Resort's great location, which features a long, unobstructed view down Pierson Boulevard into an expanse of desert. The architectural plan of the spa remains unchanged from the old days. The whole facility has a wide-open spacious feel—particularly when you walk out to the large asymmetrical courtyard and look down the three-tiered cement patio area to the inviting mineral water swimming pool on the lowest level.

The Flamingo invites small groups to enjoy unwinding, relaxing and conferencing here, and even encourages celebrations and weddings. Besides its attractive 32 rooms (18 with kitchens and 12 that connect two separate one-bedroom suites) all with cable TV, guests can now step outside to enjoy *six* hot water pools. (The Flamingo has its own hot springs.) In addition to adding hot pools, there is now a small café-restaurant, a poolside cabana-bar, a barbecue and a garden gazebo. Unusual in Desert Hot Springs are any kind of exercise programs, so it was a pleasure to learn that aerobics and, even better, water aerobics, are now offered on a regular basis. The indoor spa and sauna remains for those who want privacy or simply to be out of the bright sun.

Children are still welcome here and no age restrictions apply.

HOURS
•Open year round.

INCIDENTALS
•Conference facilities available.
•Weekly and monthly rates available.
•Credit cards accepted: MasterCard and Visa.

Lido Palms Spa

12801 Tamar Drive
Desert Hot Springs, CA 92240
(619) 329-6033

Spa #4
map page 364

$$ Cost

■ Overnight

☐ Program

☐ Day Use

■ Hot Springs

■ Hot Tubs

■ Sauna

■ Massage

■ Skin Care/Salon

☐ Exercise

☐ Meals

☐ Spa Products

☐ Workshops

☐ Children

☐ Pets

☐ Weddings

What strikes you about this serene little spa, a typical Desert Hot Springs design with its motel units surrounding the pool, are its lovely palm trees (40 of them), its sweet cacti and rock gardens and its squeaky clean facilities. If meticulous care of the pool areas and the rooms is particularly important to you, Lido Palms surely must get the town's award.

Also important to know is that it is one of the hillside spas—1,500 feet above the valley floor—where the weather is more moderate and soft natural breezes more likely.

Still sporting the gaudy neon sign from the '30s when it was owned by the Rachanellis (Capone and his boys from Two Bunch Palms hung out here), the spa is now in the able hands of a single mom and her daughter—"the Lido ladies."

Like other spas in the desert, Lido Palms has its own natural mineral water that springs crystal clear and odorless (as many Desert Hot Springs spa owners like to boast) from its 160-foot-deep well. The well feeds its three pools: The large outside pool is a comfortable temperature and inner tubes are available if you want to float your cares away. (Wear a straw or cotton hat to protect your head against the hot sun.) A small outside Jacuzzi pool is a hotter 105 degrees, and a good-sized hot soaking pool inside is great for those days when you'd rather not be in the sun. A large dry (cedar) sauna is next to the indoor pool. As with all Desert Hot Springs spas, massage appointments can be made at the desk ahead of time, and the massage practitioner will come to the spa.

All the rooms are at ground level and range from standard doubles to extra spacious units with fully equipped kitchens (some with microwaves) and cable TV. Lido Palms invites extended stays, and to that end, the owners have redecorated all the rooms in Southwest decor and provided all amenities needed to create the "home-away-from-home" atmosphere most guests appreciate.

They also want to attend to the small details that mean so much to your stay—courtesies such as turning on the air conditioner before your scheduled arrival and providing classy Euro-Bath gel soaps and soft, over-sized towels, delivering a daily newspaper to your room and serving chilled champagne, compliments of "the Lido ladies." Recently introduced are on-site massage (unusual in Desert Hot Springs), body wraps, facials and nutrition counseling. Finally, in the lobby you will find a generous selection of novels and a stash of games and puzzles. At the moment, this is my favorite Desert Hot Springs spa.

Lido Palms Spa

HOURS
•Open all year.

INCIDENTALS
•No day-use-only.
•No guests under 18.
•Weekly and monthly rates available.
•Off-season rates from May through September. Holiday rates are higher.
•Credit cards accepted: MasterCard and Visa (subject to surcharge).
•20% deposit for lengthy stay in season.

Linda Vista Lodge

67-200 Hacienda Drive
Desert Hot Springs, CA 92240
(619) 329-6401
(800) 334-7200
(619) 251-2873 fax

The nicest thing, still, about this unassuming little spa is its proprietor, Jay, who has owned and operated Linda Vista with his family for years. Jay is relentlessly cheerful and unusually attentive to the moods, tastes and demands of his guests, most of whom are old faithfuls. Jay and Bharti emigrated from India in 1981, and in the years that followed, he brought over various family members to help him in his spa operations. (Jay used to own the Sandpiper as well.)

Linda Vista (which has the AAA seal of approval) has 42 units, 28 with kitchens; one is a two-bedroom suite and two are one-bedroom suites. (Rooms without kitchens all have refrigerators.) As throughout the town, the rooms face the central swimming pool (90 degrees) and outside hot pool (104 degrees), which are fed by his natural hot mineral water well (300 feet deep) where the water comes in at 136 degrees. Linda Vista also has two enclosed therapeutic pools and a new cedar sauna with a temperature control you can set yourself. (Ever

Spa #5
map page 364

$$ Cost
■ Overnight
☐ Program
☐ Day Use
■ Hot Springs
■ Hot Tubs
■ Sauna
■ Massage
☐ Skin Care/Salon
☐ Exercise
☐ Meals
☐ Spa Products
☐ Workshops
■ Children
☐ Pets
☐ Weddings

health and safety conscious, I asked Jay about guests adhering to the 10-minute suggested time limit. He told me that a light comes on in his reception area to alert him that someone has been in the sauna for the prescribed time.)

Besides the family feeling Jay gives to Linda Vista Lodge (they have two adorable girls themselves), families are especially fond of this little spa because of its shuffleboard courts, ping-pong and billiard room, and nine-hole miniature golf course.

Talking with Jay makes it quite clear that he is as smart in business as he is warm and easygoing with his guests. He is here to stay, and I suspect that if the tempo of Desert Hot Springs changes (the promise still lingers) Jay will shift into its new rhythm without missing a beat.

HOURS
•Open year round.

INCIDENTALS
•Massage by appointment.
•Weekly and monthly rates available.
•Children allowed; wee ones (under 3) cannot be in pools and all children must be strictly supervised.
•Cable TV.
•Direct-dial telephones in room.
•Complimentary coffee.
•Airport pickup and delivery on request.
•Credit cards accepted: MasterCard, Visa and American Express.

Sunset Inn

67585 Hacienda Avenue
Desert Hot Springs, CA 92240
(619) 329-4488

Sunset Inn had just changed hands at the time this book was going to press. Under Japanese ownership, Sunset will see yet another evolution from its grand opening in 1987 when it was done up in lavish Southwestern decor by the Stoyko family. The new owners plan to retain that theme, but, in the near future, to add 40 rooms and a Japanese-style garden. In fact, the vision is to offer guests both worlds, side by side. Here are the highlights of Sunset that you will still be able to enjoy:

Out of his love of the desert, Walter Stoyko wanted to re-create its astonishing sunset colors inside the facility to create an indoor-outdoor panorama. He commissioned a local muralist, Luisi, to create desert scenes on three walls of the palatial dining area that opens in front of you as you enter the comfortable lobby. Luisi used desert purples, mauves and sage greens in his murals, and Stoyko carried out the color combination in the conference room (the largest in Desert Hot Springs) and in each of Sunset Inn's 20 rooms.

Spa #6
map page 364

$$ Cost
■ Overnight
☐ Program
☐ Day Use
■ Hot Springs
☐ Hot Tubs
■ Sauna
■ Massage
☐ Skin Care/Salon
☐ Exercise
■ Meals
☐ Spa Products
☐ Workshops
■ Children
☐ Pets
☐ Weddings

Sunset Inn

In addition to the formal dining room overlooking the pool area and out to the desert beyond, the Sunset still has a simple coffee shop just inside the lobby area for breakfast and on-the-run snacks and lunches.

All of the present rooms look out to the desert and into the courtyard pools—one large body-temperature pool and two hotter whirlpools that can go as high as 107 degrees. (Put your big toe in first and whenever possible move gradually from warm to hot to hotter.) As it is everywhere where natural mineral waters spring from deep in the ground, the feel of the water is divine. Sunset is one of the spas in the prized hillside area of Desert Hot Springs, and the view of the desert from poolside is quite special.

Spa services—sauna, steam and massage—are given downstairs. As in most Desert Hot Springs spas, advance appointments for massage are made at the desk and the massage practitioner comes in from outside at the scheduled time. If you want a particular massage form, or if you prefer a man to a woman or vice versa, simply make your requests at the time you reserve.

I remember Sunset Inn as being a place I would recommend to anyone who wanted the comforts and amenities of a major hotel but on a smaller scale and in a more beautiful setting. There is ample parking, a newspaper rack in the entryway and telephones in every room. All of that, I understand, remains untouched.

I will look forward to seeing Sunset once this expansion and East-West integration has been completed. Sounds wonderful. If you get there first, do write and let me know.

HOURS
•Open year round.

INCIDENTALS
•All rooms have telephones, refrigerators and balconies. Two have full kitchens and two have mini-kitchens.
•Weekly and monthly rates available.
•With six nights, the seventh is free.
•Conference and banquet facilities (100 persons) and group discounts available.
•Credit cards accepted: MasterCard, Visa and American Express.

Two Bunch Palms
Resort and Spa

67425 Two Bunch Palms Trail
Desert Hot Springs, CA 92240
(619) 329-8791
(800) 472-4334

Spa #7
map page 364

$$$ Cost
■ Overnight
☐ Program
☐ Day Use
■ Hot Springs
■ Hot Tubs
■ Sauna
■ Massage
■ Skin Care/Salon
☐ Exercise
■ Meals
■ Spa Products
☐ Workshops
☐ Children
☐ Pets
☐ Weddings

As I said in the last edition of my guidebook, the only reason Two Bunch Palms is in this section on Desert Hot Springs spas is because it is geographically located in Desert Hot Springs. Psychologically and sociologically, it occupies its own world—something everyone will agree to from the head of the town's Chamber of Commerce to any guest who ever stayed here.

Now, Robert Altman's satirical film, *The Player*, has put Two Bunch on a much larger map than the local Chamber of Commerce provides (and, actually, Two Bunch is not a Chamber member so you won't find them there). The latest brochure material from this maverick spa bills Two Bunch as perhaps "the most romantic spot on this planet." Hot stuff.

Like many other spas, here and elsewhere throughout the state, Two Bunch has its Native American origins (and they have recently added a "Native American treatment" to their expanded list of spa services; see below), but the tale everyone wants to tell is the Al Capone legend. The story goes that Miami police had given him 24 hours to get out of town. And since the walls of his winter castle at Biscayne Bay had been breached, Capone insisted on a hideaway where any "enemy" could be seen from miles around. Two Bunch was the ideal place. He had a bungalow of solid rock constructed at the site, complete with elegant (stained glass) and grim (a sentry turret) medieval touches to soothe his mounting paranoia.

The legend permeates the place still, even though all of its luxury condominiums and villas, its man-made lakes, its tennis and racquet ball courts almost overshadow the notorious old casino, bath house, massive safe, and still-standing (how could it fall?) Rock House that welcomed Capone's gangster buddies and Hollywood greats in the '30s.

In 1978, you could amble down a dirt road leading to the namesake two bunches of palm trees without being greeted or stopped by anyone. Now, however, this glitzy spot has a security gate and guard. The one I faced down in 1988 didn't have a scrap of charm or humor. I chalked it up to management's desire to keep the gangster image alive. Although on return visits, I have found the security guards to be accommodating, I mention this first experience again because others have confirmed it. Actually, this security system testifies to the spa's zealous attention to your privacy when staying at Two Bunch Palms. Anyway, this place is not for the timid.

I am still enamored of the countless details that make Two Bunch a singular spa, not just in this desert region but in the state. I love the casino-turned-dining room/sitting room, the catacomb-like spa down below, and the original bungalows where Victorian antiques, Edwardian lighting and Art Deco accessories all manage to live harmoniously despite their generation gaps.

One of the previous brochures from Two Bunch ended by saying: "Two Bunch Palms is a small body of precious water completely surrounded by an aura of esoteric pleasure." I still like that description because, for all its new reputation as a "playground for the rich and famous," there's no denying that their water, and the stunning way it is "contained," continues to be a main feature distinguishing this spa from all others. At Two Bunch, the water is wildly embraced by big, muscular rocks in a rambling free-form grotto, the larger 99-degree section narrowing into a smaller area where the temperature rises dramatically. Move in slowly.

Their well is located on what is called "Miracle Hill" and water comes out of the ground at a very high temperature—I've been told everything from 148 degrees to 200 degrees. Presumably, the higher the temperature the more impurities are flushed out and, because the water is constantly flowing—you'll see it coursing down across your path as you walk through the property—fewer chemicals are required to keep the rock pools free of contaminants.

It was in 1987 that Two Bunch Palms developed the back of the property and gave the spa a whole new ambience: Spacious villas and casitas with elegant shared courtyards, an enormous carp-filled pond, and a large rectangular swimming pool share space with the beautiful tamarisk trees that whisper fiercely in the desert wind. This area provides a secluded, almost self-contained village on the property. The same beautiful antique furnishings that are the trademark of this spa also adorn these units.

Whether you are drawn here by the miracle of its water, by the Al Capone Suite and charming older bungalows near the grottos, or by the more recently constructed villas and casitas, you need to know a surprising truth: Two Bunch has no structured exercise programs and you can leave your calorie finder in your Gucci bag.

Spa services have been expanded, as I mentioned before, and I am very impressed with its present menu of services. First of all, you know that it's the only place in Desert Hot Springs where you can get a mud bath, but, beyond that, feast your eyes on its present menu of services designed to meet the spa director's new theme of "well-being."

Most exciting to me is that the spa offers Watsu massage. As far as I know, the only other facility offering this incredible underwater therapy is Harbin Hot Springs in Northern California (although I did come across a massage therapist in Point Reyes Station who runs a bed and breakfast and offers Watsu). Two Bunch describes Watsu as "yoga that stretches,

Two Bunch Palms Resort and Spa

nurtures and massages your body while you float and dream in the private Watsu pool."

Another item on the list that makes me yearn to vacation here again is the "Native American" treatment. It starts with a camphor sauna and a body brush with fresh eucalyptus followed by a massage that uses healing herbs blended with warm oil. You are then wrapped in a hot, herb-infused sheet while your therapist (and I can't believe this one) "re-creates sounds of long ago with rattles or drums." (No irreverence intended, but if I collapse in peels of laughter, will it be understood as a breakthrough experience?) To restore you to the world of the here and now (and not a moment too soon, I say), you are placed in a cool mineral water shower. The entire treatment lasts an hour and a half. I love it. I want it.

Those are at the top of my list, but you can also indulge yourself in "Esoteric Massage" (again one-and-one-half hours) to "integrate and harmonize the physical, mental, emotional and spiritual bodies" according to individual needs, and t'ai chi, the Chinese art of harmonizing the mind, breath and body through slow, gentle, dance-like movement, which is offered as instruction, privately or for two or more.

The massage modalities offered at Two Bunch are equally elaborate: Swedish and shiatsu, of course, but also Trager® (my favorite), deep tissue, jin shin do (not in this book's massage glossary, it is described as "a meditative acupressure technique designed to balance energy flow through the acupuncture meridians" and effect deep relaxation), lymphatic massage, reflexology, sports massage, aromatherapy and—another surprise—cranio-sacral massage, which, as far as what is covered in this guidebook, is offered only here and at the Berkeley Massage and Self-Healing Center in the San Francisco Bay Area.

For body care, you can have a "Salt Glo and Herbal Steam" treatment (topped off with a liniment rubdown and light reflexology), a "Roman Celtic Brush" (derived from a Baden Baden specialty treatment), a scalp massage, a sea algae body wrap (a mud wrap) and something quite exotic called an "Egyptian Clay Body" treatment that is an effort to re-create an ancient Egyptian rite. First you are dry-brushed to cleanse your body of toxicity, then massaged with the mineral water green clay that is special to Two Bunch, and "sheaths your body in a crystalline structure." Then you are wrapped in a blanket. The final touch is an anointment with the essential oil of your choice. Cleopatra, move over. (I laugh but I am tempted to board a plane for Desert Hot Springs as I write.)

Facials include a mineral water clay cleansing facial, a rehydrating paraffin facial, an aromatherapy facial (which includes acupressure massage and foot massage), a mineral water clay back facial and a therapeutic paraffin treatment for hands and feet that is given in association with any of the above facials.

Finally, for mud baths, Two Bunch Palms' enriched green clay is warmed with hot mineral water from their well. They offer different

Two Bunch Palms Resort and Spa

variations of mud treatments, a "Mudbath Body Wrap" with and without massage, an "Herbal Body Wrap" with and without massage, "Mud n' Sun" where, after luxuriating in a mud bath for 10 to 15 minutes, you are escorted to the sundeck to bask in the desert sun before showering off in mineral water, and "Mud n' Steam" where, after luxuriating in a mud bath for 10 to 15 minutes, you shower in mineral water and then steam off for another 15 to 20 minutes.

A host of other special touches and recreations await you here, from an occasional bunny rabbit crossing your path to the lighted tennis courts at the ready for night owls. Two Bunch is unmistakably a place for romance as much as for reading scripts and cutting deals. The spa strives to accommodate couples (side-by-side mud baths are popular) and provides a clothing-optional sundeck and outdoor "sun bins" that assure serene privacy.

When you call for your reservation, be prepared to have a discussion about which ambience you want for your sleeping quarters—the upper and older or the lower and newer; they'll help you figure it all out. Two Bunch has a mailing list of over 10,000 names and, like most celebrity spas, has been written up over and over again. Who was it who said that once is never the beginning of enough?

HOURS
•Open year round except for the month of August.

INCIDENTALS

Two Bunch Palms
Resort and Spa

•No children under 18; no pets.

•Not a day-use spa; however, if you call in the morning you might be able to schedule same-day appointments at the spa or reserve a place at the restaurant, depending on that day's availability.

•Complimentary sauna and mineral water showers, 9 a.m. to 6 p.m.

•Casino Restaurant: Selection of entrées served from 6:30 p.m. to 9 p.m., with seating every half hour by reservation. Private dining room for eight can be reserved at no extra fee.

•Two Bunch Palms spa clothing and products are for sale in the front office.

•Credit cards accepted: MasterCard, Visa and American Express.

Appendices

Too Late to Visit!

All entries that follow are derived from brochures sent to me too late for my research deadline. They have been elaborated on, in some cases, through conversations I had with spa owners or managers.
—Laurel Cook

Grover Hot Springs State Park
Markleeville, CA 96120
(916) 525-7232
(916) 694-2248

Grover Hot Springs is a 700-acre park located in the Hot Springs Valley of the Sierra Nevada Mountains at an elevation of 6,000 feet. It has a campground, a picnic area, a swimming pool and a developed hot spring. Water comes out of the ground at 142 degrees Fahrenheit and is cooled to about 103 degrees. Pool waters are sanitized with bromine for public safety. The swimming pool next to the hot pool is kept at 70 to 80 degrees Fahrenheit (and makes a great "cold" plunge for those who like to alternate between hot and cold). Although there are no other spa services here, taking a winter soak in this scenic alpine spot south of Lake Tahoe appears to be popular among skiers and other mountain-loving folk.

Pools are closed for annual maintenance for two weeks in September. Twenty sites for tents and RVs. Nominal park admission fees for adults and children. Write for schedule of winter programs.

Paraiso Hot Springs
Soledad, CA 93960
(408) 678-2882

Too Late to Visit!

From under its 230 acres in the unlikely town of Soledad, Paraiso Hot Springs' mineral water, which comes out of the ground at about 117 degrees Fahrenheit, flows downhill into Paraiso's three pools at an unbelievable 40,000 gallons of hot water, per pool, per day. On five or six sheets of colored paper, Paraiso lays out everything it has to offer, and it appears to be a lot: In addition to the pools, there is a lodge, coffee room, snack bar, recreation and game room, picnic tables and barbecues. Accommodations range from camping sites with bathhouse, RV hookup facilities for monthly stays, mobile homes, hillside cabins, tent cabins, yurts and housekeeping cottages, some with complete kitchens. There are restaurants and grocery stores nearby and the historic Soledad Mission. Paraiso charges everyone the same daily entrance fee (adults and children) and it gives you access to the mineral pools, the picnic area, the snack bar, the rec room and the hiking trails. Even dogs don't get in free, but, hey, they get in! (A $5 fee per dog per day is charged.)

For the enclosed adults-only hot bath, there is a nominal extra charge, and bathing suits are required. Children are permitted at Paraiso and are expected to be well supervised at all times. No credit cards accepted. Prices are in the $$ to $$$ range, depending on which accommodations you choose. Write or call for more information.

Post Ranch Inn
Highway 1, Post Office Box 219
Big Sur, CA 93920
(408) 667-2200
(800) 527-2200 reservations

At the opposite extreme from Paraiso is the new Post Ranch Inn. A stunning example of organic architecture designed by G. K. Mickey Muennig, who has lived in Big Sur since 1971, the new, posher-than-posh Post Ranch Inn is getting a lot of media attention. (The name owes itself to William Brainard Post, we are told—the first to stake a claim to this Big Sur wilderness in 1860.) Among its many distinctive features, the Inn's accommodations—the Coast House, the Mountain House, the Ocean House and the Tree House—have been lauded and applauded by Zahid Sardar writing for the *San Francisco Chronicle* as well as by a writer from the *Orange County Register* whose words were deemed descriptive enough for the Inn to include in its own brochure: "...squirreled away on an unseen ridge is a 30-room, 98-acre testament to the enduring magic of Big Sur." Post Ranch Inn offers no TV, no tennis, no golf. Its spa, as you might imagine, is elegant. Hour-long massages (Esalen or sports massage) or an herbal wrap or herbal facial can be taken in your suite—and yes, of course, aromatherapy is offered as an enhancement to your massage. The Inn also offers its guests private yoga instruction, guided nature hikes and guided wilderness hikes (in the Ventana Range) as well as aerobic speed walking. Each suite has either an

ocean or mountain view, a private tub and a
massage table, a wood-burning fireplace and a
stereo system. (Nightly room rates and spa ser-
vices in the $$$ range.) Send for a brochure.

Too Late to Visit!

Burbank Spa
2115 West Magnolia Boulevard
Burbank, CA 91506
(818) 845-1251

A Finnish-owned and operated spa offering
therapeutic massage and sauna, with separate
facilities for men and women. Shower and sauna
are encouraged before your massage as well as
after. You are permitted extended use of the fa-
cilities before and after your treatment. De-
scribed by others as a modest place that has
seen a celebrity or two, Burbank Spa is described
by its owner as unpretentious, authentic and
"squeaky clean." According to Jouni Passi,
"[We] strive to be an island of peace and health
in a mad world." They also recommend Fin-
land Baths in Sherman Oaks, Finlandia in
Granada Hills, and Nice To Be Kneaded in
Burbank. Juice and sauna accessories available
at desk.

Open Monday through Friday, 9 a.m. to 9
p.m.; Saturday 9 a.m. to 6 p.m.; Sunday 10
a.m. to 6 p.m. Gift certificates available. Checks,
MasterCard and VISA accepted.

Caring Hands Massage
555 West 19th Street
Costa Mesa, CA 92627
(714) 631-5831

Members of Associated Bodyworkers and Massage Professionals, Caring Hands specializes in Swedish massage, sports massage, and deep tissue therapy. Their facility, simple and clean with dimmed lighting and soothing music for reducing anxiety, is located inside a major health facility. Eight certified massage therapists are there to work on whatever problems you bring to them. They like to know their clients personally and follow their progress.

Open Monday through Friday, 7:30 a.m. to 9 p.m.; weekends 10:30 a.m. to 4:30 p.m. Walk-ins are welcome. 15-minute sessions, half-hour sessions, one-hour sessions, and six one-hour series sessions (discounted) are available. Call for appointment.

Futureshape Spa of El Paseo
72695 Highway 111, Suite A-1
Palm Desert, CA 92260
(619) 773-0032

Billed as a "total fitness center and salon," Futureshape offers memberships as well as walk-in services. Full gym (Nautilus, free weights, treadmill, Stairclimber, aerobics and stretching classes, private training). Services include: skin care (aromatherapy facials), massage (done indoors and outdoors) including Swedish, acupressure, and deep tissue; body treatments including salt glow, reflexology, steam box, and body wraps, as well as hair care, nail care, pedicures, makeup application (Joe Blasco line), waxing and tanning services.

Too Late to Visit!

Open Monday through Friday 7 a.m. to 8 p.m.; Saturday, 9 a.m. to 4 p.m.

Aida Grey Institut de Beauté
Edith Morre Galleries
73-690 El Paseo
Palm Desert, CA 92260
(619) 773-2480 *and*
Westin Mission Hills Resort
Dinah Shore and Bob Hope Drive
Rancho Mirage, CA 92270
(619) 770-5901

Lana Brunella, aestheticican, owns both of these "prestigious, full-service salons" which specialize in haircutting and styling, weaves and coloring; manicures and European pedicure baths and paraffin treatment for hands and feet; a variety of facials, including glycolic acid peels; makeup application and instruction; massage, reflexology, body polishing and full-body treatments with black mud and seaweed. Her services are offered to men as well as women.

New Beginning
Salon of Personal Care & Hair
138 North Lake Avenue
Pasadena, CA 91101
(818) 449-1231

"Treat yourself to a new beginning" is the appeal made by New Beginnings' owner-manager Baarbra (not a typo!) Elleck since 1971. New Beginnings offers: facial toning (nonsurgical face-lift); a variety of facials including back facials and Parisian body polish; massage, including paraffin wax body facials and cellulite massage; and use of a steam cabinet. All treatments are described in informative handout brochures. In addition, you can enjoy such ancillary services as electrolysis, lash and brow tint, makeup application and instruction, hand and foot conditioning, hair care (including braiding and weaving), nail care and extensive waxing services (for men and women.) Gift certificates available. Boutique on site.

Open Monday, 9 a.m. to 4 p.m.; Tuesday through Thursday, 9 a.m. to 8:30 p.m.; Friday, 9 a.m. to 6 p.m.; Saturday, 9 a.m. to 5 p.m. MasterCard and Visa accepted.

Sanwa Health Spa
120 South Los Angeles
Los Angeles, CA 90012
(213) 687-4597

In the shadow of Los Angeles City Hall, located on the fourth floor of The New Otani Hotel, Sanwa provides shiatsu and Amma massage as well as Swedish massage, facial massage and a Jacuzzi. Managed by Haruko Hosokawa and staffed by seven skilled massage therapists. Advance appointments are necessary.

Open Monday through Saturday, 10 a.m. to 11 p.m. (last appointment at 10 p.m.); Sunday noon to 9 p.m. (last appointment at 8 p.m.). Validated parking. MasterCard, VISA and American Express accepted.

Spa Finder

For those of you who want some direction in finding a spa that suits you, here are some suggestions to assist you. Keep in mind that what follows is highly subjective, based on my personal experience at various spas. Always call ahead to confirm that what you are hoping for is indeed what the spa can provide. That said, here are some considerations you might have and the places that might respond to them.

•*I want to do my own thing with minimal fuss.*
Harbin Hot Springs—p. 65
Isis Oasis—p. 74
Dancing Springs Spa at Konocti—p. 78
Stewart's Mineral Springs—p. 116
Vichy Springs Resort—p. 122
White Sulphur Springs—p. 126
Wilbur Hot Springs—p. 131
Willow—p. 138
Calistoga spas—pp. 149-194
Albany Sauna and Hot Tubs—p. 197
Berkeley Sauna—p. 204
F. Joseph Smith's—p. 227
Grand Central Sauna & Hot Tub Co.—p. 229
Kabuki Hot Spring—p. 234
The Physical Therapy Center—p. 254
Piedmont Springs—p. 258
Shibui Gardens—p. 261
Sycamore Mineral Springs—p. 286
Glen Ivy Hot Springs—p. 306
Wheeler Hot Springs—p. 356
All Desert Hot Springs spas except Two Bunch
  Palms—pp. 376-391

•I want a complete program offering fitness regimes, healthy diet and take-home materials.
Skylonda (30 max. participants)—p. 264
The Ashram (10 max. participants)—p. 295
Cal-a-Vie (24 max. participants)—p. 300
The Golden Door (39 max. participants)
  —p. 311
The Oaks (91 max. participants)—p. 333
The Palms (91 max. participants)—p. 333

•I want a spa program that leaves me more personal choice and offers recreational activities on site or nearby.
Konocti/Dancing Springs (251 rooms)—p. 78
Sonoma Mission Inn (170 rooms)—p. 108
La Costa Resort (400 rooms)—p. 317
L'Auberge Del Mar (123 rooms)—p. 323
Marriott's Desert Springs (780 rooms)—p. 327
Rancho La Puerta (140 rooms)—p. 340
Spa Hotel and Mineral Springs (230 rooms)
  —p. 349

•I want a self-contained spa, far from the maddening crowd.
Harbin Hot Springs—p. 65
Pocket Ranch Institute—p. 97
Stewart's Mineral Springs—p. 116
Vichy Springs Resort—p. 122
White Sulphur Springs—p. 126
Wilbur Hot Springs—p. 131
Willow—p. 138
Skylonda—p. 264
The Ashram—p. 295
Cal-a-Vie—p. 300
Wheeler Hot Springs—p. 356
Two Bunch Palms—p. 392

•*I want to do my own cooking.*
Harbin Hot Springs*—p. 65
Isis Oasis Retreat Center*—p. 74
Orr Hot Springs*—p. 84
White Sulphur Springs—p. 126
Wilbur Hot Springs*—p. 131
Willow*—p. 138
Calistoga Spa Hot Springs—p. 152
Dr. Wilkinson's—p. 159
Golden Haven—p. 164
Nance's Hot Springs—p. 186
Pine Street Inn and Eurospa—p. 189
Roman Spa—p. 193
Emerald Springs—p. 379
Flamingo Resort—p. 382
Lido Palms—p. 384
Linda Vista—p. 387
Sunset Inn—p. 391
　　　　(* = community kitchen)

•*I want a full-service hotel and spa with conference facilities.*
Konocti Harbor/Dancing Springs—p. 78
Sonoma Mission Inn—p. 108
Claremont Resort and Spa—p. 214
La Costa Resort and Spa—p. 317
L'Auberge Del Mar—p. 323
Marriott's Desert Springs—p. 327
Spa Hotel and Mineral Springs—p. 349
Desert Hot Springs Spa Hotel—p. 376
Sunset Inn—p. 389

•*I want my children to be entertained.*
Konocti Harbor/Dancing Springs—p. 78
Vichy Springs Resort—p. 122
Calistoga Spa Hot Springs—p. 152
Calistoga Village Inn and Spa—p. 155
Indian Springs Resort—p. 167
Glen Ivy (weekends)—p. 306
La Costa (children's camp)—p. 317

•*I want to be comfortable as a woman alone.*
Isis Oasis—p. 74
Pocket Ranch—p. 97
A Simple Touch—p. 104
Sonoma Mission Inn—p. 108
White Sulphur Springs—p. 126
Willow—p. 138
Calistoga spas—p. 149-194
Claremont Resort and Spa—p. 214
Kabuki Hot Spring—p. 234
Skylonda—p. 264
Heartwood Spa—p. 281
Kiva Retreat (women's mornings)—p. 283
Sycamore Mineral Springs—p. 286
The Ashram—p. 295
Cal-a-Vie—p. 300
Glen Ivy Hot Springs—p. 306
The Oaks and The Palms—p. 333
Rancho La Puerta—p. 340
Lido Palms—p. 384
All day spas and urban retreats

•I want a spa with romantic appeal.
Isis Oasis—p. 74
Sonoma Mission Inn—p. 108
Willow—p. 138
Lavender Hill Spa—p. 174
Lincoln Avenue Spa—p. 178
Sycamore Mineral Springs—p. 286
Glen Ivy Hot Springs—p. 306
L'Auberge Del Mar—p. 323
Rancho La Puerta—p. 340
Wheeler Hot Springs—p. 356
Two Bunch Palms—p. 392

•I want a spa where clothing is optional (in designated areas).
Harbin Hot Springs—p. 65
Orr Hot Springs—p. 84
Wilbur Hot Springs—p. 131
Heartwood—p. 281
Kiva Retreat—p. 283
Two Bunch Palms—p. 392

•Among day-use spas, I want a bit of elegance.
A Simple Touch—p. 104
Sonoma Mission Inn and Spa—p. 108
Sonoma Spa—p. 113
Mount View Spa—p. 182
Cheek t' Cheek—p. 211
Claremont Resort and Spa—p. 214
Mister Lee's—p. 243
Spa Nordstrom—p. 273
Glen Ivy Hot Springs—p. 306
La Costa Resort and Spa—p. 317
L'Auberge Del Mar—p. 323
Spa de Jour—p. 346
Spa Hotel and Mineral Springs—p. 349

Tipping Policies

Tipping policies vary somewhat from one spa to another—or, actually, from one type of spa to another. Although you can always ask the staff person at the desk what the spa's tipping policy is, here is some general information to go by:

At day spas and urban retreats, you will almost always find a "tip basket" in the treatment room with a little "thank you" sign to clue you in. If you are paying by credit card or personal check, you can always include a tip there.

In day spas and particularly at urban retreats where you might have had two or more people working on you—one for massage, one for a makeup application, another for a facial—you may want to tip each person in a different amount. I would first ask whether tips are pooled; if not, you can certainly designate the amounts you would like to go to each. Apportioning your own tips is made simpler when the spa provides small, manila tip envelopes at the counter, as many do. Then you can write the practitioner's name on the envelope and feel more comfortable that your tip is going exactly where you want it to go. A number of Calistoga spas provide envelopes at the counter. Some provide both tip baskets and counter envelopes.

At major spas and hotel resorts, where you are more likely to be on a program or where your valuables are in a storage locker rather than in the room with you, a gratuity (or "service charge") is usually included in the final bill written up for you when you leave. The amount varies from about 14% to 20%. In most places, no one will stop you from adding to that amount if you want to. The staff should point out to you when the gratuity is included and you may want to check to see what percentage you are paying.

In some major spas I found that the gratuity charged is not turned over in full to the massage practitioner or facialist; the percentage is apportioned according to systems devised by the individual spa—the practitioner's experience or seniority, for example. In most places, however, all tips are simply passed on.

In one major facility where the service charge is relatively low (14%) I was told that most employees refuse any additional tips. Certainly that's the most comfortable; for myself, I am aware, generally, of how easily an "extra" amount becomes something I feel obligated to do rather than something I want to do because I found the person or service truly special.

Finally, there are places, small and large but usually small, where the person working on you is the owner or principal in the business. In that case, you need not tip, although no one is likely to throw it back at you if you do.

Questions and Answers about Glycolic Acid

The following text was derived from material prepared by Cell Renewal Systems, Inc., a company located in Ojai, California that manufactures and distributes botanically formulated glycolic products. The most comprehensive information I was able to find, it is used here with their permission. Thanks to Gail Schwartz of Cheek t' Cheek in Mill Valley for the original handout and for directing me to its source. For more information about Cell Renewal Systems or their products, call (800) 285-8553.

What is glycolic acid?

Glycolic acid, a member of the alpha hydroxy family, is derived from fruit sugar acids. Some of the more well-known alpha hydroxy acids (AHAs) are citric acid from citrus fruit, lactic acid from milk and tartaric acid from wine.

How long have AHAs been used in recent times to improve the quality of the skin?

For the past decade, skin researchers and physicians have been studying AHAs' effects and used them to alleviate a variety of skin conditions.

Is glycolic acid safe to use?

Yes. It is a 100% nontoxic substance that does not enter the bloodstream. Because it is not considered a drug, no prescription is needed. Although approved by the FDA for home use in small concentrations, in higher concentrations it should be used only in salons by licensed, trained professionals.

What are the side effects of glycolic creams sold in stores?

As long as you use them appropriately—letting your skin get used to it gradually over time—you should experience no negative side effects aside from mild stinging or minimal flaking in the beginning.

Is it safe to be in the sun when I have used glycolic acid on my skin?

Yes. It is not considered a photo-sensitive substance. However, everyone should use a sun block to protect skin from skin cancers and premature aging. If you use glycolic acid products and are in the sun a lot—and do *not* use a sunscreen—you will probably burn faster.

Exactly how does glycolic acid work?

Glycolic acid works by dissolving a glue-like substance in the stratum corneum (the upper layer of the skin) and this causes already dead skin cells to be sloughed more quickly from the surface of the skin. The increase in cell turnover stimulates the skin to increase collagen production and improve the strength and integrity of the tissue. In other words, the skin becomes tighter, tone is improved, and fine lines and wrinkles are less visible. This sloughing also improves the general texture of the skin—dramatically. When the stratum corneum becomes thick, the skin can appear to be dry and scaly. With the release of old, dried cells, pore size appears smaller, the overall color and health of the skin improves because of the increased circulation, and the skin looks and feels soft and silky. At the moment (as with numerous physiological processes), the exact mechanisms and chain of events involved have not been established.

Additional effects seen with appropriate use of glycolic acid are: (1) aging skin is stimulated to push up fresh cells that have a greater ability to hold water, that function more efficiently and, as a result, impart a translucent quality to the skin; (2) acne buildup is reduced and acne scarring appears to fade because glycolic acid reduces hyperkeratosis (the buildup of dead cells) and penetrates the follicular orifice, thus opening up and draining pustular acne; (3) hyperpigmentation is lightened by the action of glycolic acid in accelerating the release of pigmented surface cells. (A sun block is essential to prevent re-pigmentation.) In this regard, "age spots" that appear on face and hands are often benign keratoses; glycolic acid can reduce some of these superficial lesions, and even act preventively to avert future skin problems; (4) "cross-linking," a major contributor to the aging of the skin, appears to be slowed down. Cross-linking also occurs in response to ultraviolet light (which we are exposed to daily and more so when we work or lie in the sun) as well as to stress, pollution, excessive toxins and even normal metabolic processes.

Will I run out of skin cells if I routinely use glycolic acid to stimulate production of new cells?

No. Some researchers believe that the cells of the human body have the ability to reproduce effectively up to the age of 140!

What happens if I start and stop using glycolic acid products?

Users of Retin-A once feared that the skin would instantly age when or if they discontinued its use. This does not happen with glycolic acid. When you stop using a glycolic acid product, your skin will gradually revert to its original condition and normal aging will begin again.

When I first started using glycolic creams, my skin flaked. Is this normal?

Yes. Within the first few weeks while your skin is getting used to glycolic acid, it might go through this flaking stage. It can occur because of the accelerated release of accumulated dead cells on the skin's surface. Simply using a gentle face scrub and a good moisturizer will eliminate the flaking.

Sometimes when I use glycolic creams my skin stings. Why?

If your skin stings, it is usually because there is still too much water in the tissue. To avoid stinging, pat dry after washing and wait a few minutes before applying the cream. As with all skin products, avoid any areas where you might have a cut or scrape, or where you abraded your skin by scrubbing too hard.

How often should I use glycolic products on my skin?

Everyone's tolerance is different but, in general, you will want to gradually work up to applying it every morning and night, using the strongest concentration you can without causing irritation to the skin. High-strength products are sold only in salons and should be used with the guidance and advice of your esthetician.

Do I need to change the rest of my skin-care program?

No, not really. But remember that with fewer layers of dead cells on the skin's surface, all skin products will penetrate more easily. So be more aware of using only products with safe ingredients and shift to a gentle, liquid, pH-balanced cleanser. As you probably know, most bar soaps tend to be harsh and drying. Daily use of scrubs would irritate the skin, and are unnecessary.

What other products might I use on my skin to regenerate it and keep it healthy?

Facial oils with vitamins A, D, C and E nourish and protect the skin. Anything with wheat germ (high in vitamin E) is good, or carrot oil (high in vitamin A, the "skin vitamin"), and aloe vera, which, throughout the ages, has been known to stimulate healthy skin renewal. Some new substances that are being used in products to help the skin to regenerate are Beta Glucan, derived from a yeast cell wall extract, and Epidermal Growth Factor, a naturally occurring chemical found within the skin that seems to assist in dermal repair. Many essential oil blends are also purported to be rejuvenating. Essential oils are very potent essences; they are extracted from specific herbal plants which are then diluted with "carrier" oils. Consult an aromatherapist for a blend that will best benefit your skin type.

If I had only one glycolic peel, would it do anything?

Yes! A "freshening peel" will help to loosen the buildup of dead skin cells and debris in the pores, lighten pigmentation or discoloration, make your skin feel smoother to the touch, and help it to look healthy. (The skin does not actually "peel" as it does when done by dermatologists and other physicians.) Freshening peels are done in salons and consist of the application of a stronger concentration of glycolic acid than what is available to you for home use. It is applied with a brush, left on for only a few minutes, then carefully cleansed off and neutralized. Often, the esthetician will finish by applying a "rejuvenating" substance.

*How many peels would it take to have a
visible effect on pigmentation? On wrinkles?*

It depends, of course, on the severity of your skin problems, but you should see a nice improvement after three to six peels. Essential to good results is your continued use of a home-care product and a good sunscreen. Softening of light wrinkle lines will be noticeable after about 8 to 12 professional peel treatments. Deep lines (where elastin fibers are too far gone) might be softened but will not vanish. Home care creams increase the effectiveness of the peel.

INDEX

Other Outdoor/Recreation Guides
Published by Foghorn Press

California Hiking: The Complete Guide
by Tom Stienstra & Michael Hodgson
$17.95, 800 pp, 5 3/8 x 8 3/8"

Southwest Camping: The Complete Guide
by Dave Ganci
$14.95, 500 pp, 5 3/8 x 8 3/8"

California Camping: The Complete Guide
by Tom Stienstra
$17.95, 832 pp, 5 3/8 x 8 3/8"

Pacific Northwest Camping: The Complete Guide
by Tom Stienstra
$16.95, 700 pp, 5 3/8 x 8 3/8"

Rocky Mountain Camping: The Complete Guide
by Tom Stienstra
$14.95, 512 pp, 5 3/8 x 8 3/8"

The California Dog Lover's Companion:
The Inside Scoop on Where to Take Your Dog in California
by Maria Goodavage, illustrated by Phil Frank
$14.95, 600 pp, 5 3/8 x 8 3/8"

The Dog Lover's Companion:
The Inside Scoop on Where to Take Your Dog in the Bay Area & Beyond
by Lyle York & Maria Goodavage, illustrated by Phil Frank
$12.95, 320 pp, 5 3/8 x 8 3/8

Southwest Golf: The Complete Guide
by John Marvel
$14.95, 432 pp, color insert, 5 3/8 x 8 3/8"

California Golf: The Complete Guide
Ray March, Editor
$17.95, 800 pp, color insert, 5 3/8 x 8 3/8"

Hawaii Golf: The Complete Guide
by George Fuller
$16.95, 408 pp, color insert, 5 3/8 x 8 3/8"

California Fishing: The Complete Guide
by Tom Stienstra
$19.95, 768 pp, 5 3/8 x 8 3/8"

CALL (800) FOGHORN (364-4676) TO ORDER

Great Outdoor Getaways to the Bay Area and Beyond
by Tom Stienstra
$14.95, 348 pp, 5 3/8 x 8/38"

Epic Trips of the West: Tom Stienstra's 10 Best
by Tom Stienstra
$9.95, 232 pp, 5 3/8 x 8 3/8"

California Thrill Sports
by Erik Fair
$14.95, 360 pp, color insert, 5 3/8 x 8 3/8"

Great Outdoor Adventures of Hawaii
by Rick Carroll
$12.95, 304 pp, color insert, 5 3/8 x 8 3/8"

Reclaiming Our National Parks: Your Guide to Making a Difference
National Parks and Conservation Association
$10.95, 320 pp, 5 3/8 x 8 3/8"

Special Olympics: The First 25 Years
California Special Olympics
$19.95, 232 pp, color insert, 8 1/2 x 11"

The Camper's Companion: The Pack-Along Guide for Better Outdoor Trips
by Rick Greenspan and Hal Kahn
$12.95, 464 pp, illustrated, 5 3/8 x 8 3/8"

America's Secret Recreation Areas:
Your Guide to the Forgotten Wild Lands of the Bureau of Land Management
by Michael Hodgson
$15.95, 512 pp, color insert, 5 3/8 x 8 3/8"

Careers in the Outdoors
by Tom Stienstra
$12.95, 416 pp, 62 b/w photos, 5 3/8 x 8/3/8"

Best Places to Go: A Family Destination Guide
by Nan Jeffrey
$14.95, 328 pp, illustrated, 5 3/8 x 8 3/8"

The Complete Buyer's Guide to the Best Outdoor & Recreation Equipment
by Kevin Jeffrey
$14.95, 412 pp, illustrated, 5 3/8 x 8 3/8"

Adventuring with Children: The Family Pack-Along Guide
by Nan & Kevin Jeffrey
$14.95, 328 pp, 50 b/w photos, 8 3/8 x 5 3/8"

CALL (800) FOGHORN (364-4676) TO ORDER